CITIZEN TELEVISION
A Local Dimension to Public Service Broadcasting

CITIZEN TELEVISION
A Local Dimension to Public Service Broadcasting

Edited by
Dave Rushton

Institute of Local Television

Research Monograph 1989-1993

John Libbey

JL

LONDON • PARIS • ROME

British Library Cataloguing in Publication Data

Citizen Television: a local dimension to
public service broadcasting
(Institute of Local Television Research Monograph,
ISSN: 0969-9872)

    I. Rushton, Dave II. Series

    384.55

ISBN: 0-86196-433-0

Cover design: Jane McKay

Published by

John Libbey & Company Ltd, 13 Smiths Yard, Summerley Street,
London SW18 4HR, England
Telephone: 081-947 2777 – Fax: 081-947 2664
John Libbey Eurotext Ltd, 6 rue Blanche, 92120 Montrouge, France
John Libbey - C.I.C.s.r.l., via Lazzaro Spallanzani 11, 00161 Rome Italy

Typeset by the Desktop Publishing Centre, Edinburgh and printed by
Whitstable Litho Printers Ltd, Whitstable, Kent.

Contents

APPENDICES

Acknowledgements

This study has grown over four years largely from voluntary contributions, spurred on by finding local television thwarted at every twist and turn of the broadcasting debate. Galvanised by deadlines imposed by regulatory changes and supported by impossible budgets squeezed from desktop publishing or television conferences there has surprisingly been no lack of contributors wishing to donate their time and expertise researching and developing the local broadcasting arguments. To mention one contributor whose name is not already here will surely mean missing ten. To concentrate solely on academic contributions will diminish the emotional support and administrative assistance which has helped work on local television progress with growing confidence and good humour. My thanks to all who have been involved.

A persistent feature of local broadcasting; of the campaign for broadcasting freedom; for greater freedom of information and for amplification in broadcasting of the voices of listeners and viewers has been a network of academics, campaigners and TV users whose interests and concerns have grown closer together. With the removal of the brake of organised labour upon the commercialisation of value and public representation in broadcasting the unity of this new lobby and its growing cohesion is to be welcomed for the social balance and new values it is able to introduce.

In future our broadcasting will increasingly be determined at a European level. The Meeting of Local Television held at the Palais de l'Europe in Strasbourg in October 1991 was particularly important for defining priorities for local television in the '90s. Here the renewed interest in democratic and accountable broadcasting from countries breaking with the Soviet Bloc mingled with expressions of anxiety in western Europe about the continued plurality in broadcasting. How to halt commercialism reducing still further the significance of local cultural values, reducing the diversity of social relations throughout Europe? For how long would there be anything different left to say to each other and how could we know of those differences if our broadcasting organisations spoke only in a commercial monotone?

So my acknowledgement and thanks are due to everyone involved with developing the arguments for local and community broadcasting – for radio and television; to Queen Margaret College for establishing a course in local television and providing assistance to research Channel 5 as well as the television programme *TV Soapbox*; to everyone at John Libbey Ltd for their courtesy and patience in ensuring that this book finally happened. Lastly, my thanks to you the reader for taking time to consider this new approach to public service broadcasting. Without your contribution there is no discourse and without the debate your reading will support television's future will surely otherwise fulfil the dumb promise of its immediate past.

Institute of Local Television

The Institute of Local Television was set up in 1989 following detailed research in Edinburgh on the demand for a local television service. Since then the Institute has published several reports and hand-books on the development and introduction of local television and has monitored the introduction of cable in Britain. Representations have been made to government and regulators and increasingly ILT has drawn upon examples of European local television while undertaking research for public bodies to assess demand for local participation in British broadcasting.

The Institute has provided a research base for students on placement from European colleges and universities and has strong links with Queen Margaret College in Edinburgh where Local Television has been introduced as an option on the Communication Studies B A Hons course. From the start of Academic Year 93/94 ILT's post-graduate research course will be validated by the college.

Introduction

The 1988 White Paper *Broadcasting in the '90s: Competition, Choice and Quality* attempted to catch-up and to regulate the arrival of new television channels being delivered by satellite and cable. The White Paper introduced sealed competitive bids for the new round of commercial ITV regional television licenses. It proposed a new Channel 5 to cover 70% of the country to appease demands for competition in television advertising. The White Paper announced a possible Channel 6, for no other reason than it seemed possible and that its service might reach a third of the population. It proposed using microwave (MVDS) to challenge cable in the local delivery of television services and measures to regulate satellite services.

With Channels 5 and 6 the White Paper departed from the central commitment of public service broadcasting to provide services which would reach everyone in Britain. Through competition and choice a new and more varied and perhaps uneven television landscape was beckoning beyond the four terrestrial BBC 1, 2, ITV and Channel 4 services that together comprised public service television in Britain. The new television agenda would be determined by commercial advantage rather than by an equality of access to programming and the broadcasting maxims to inform, educate and entertain would be less evident as the public service broadcasters' duties became less onerous in order to enable them to compete. The old rules of the game were being suspended to allow new players onto the pitch. In appearance at least the White Paper suggested it was to be the spectators – the viewers – who would decide from now on which form the game would take. Four years after the White Paper had sketched out the future for commercial television the BBC responded to the 1992 Green Paper on its own future with a glossy document titled *Extending Choice*.

In four years all of British broadcasting has grown used to characterising the television viewers as consumers and reconciling their mission statements to deliver choice if not as a major objective certainly as an inevitable influence upon the way the service is structured. With the quiet removal of the principle of universal access to programmes for all the choice that can be made is reduced for some as much as it is extended for others depending on where the viewer lives but also increasingly on whether the viewer wishes to pay for specific services. Television as a service free at the point of reception is being converted to pay-per-view and subscription.

The Broadcasting Act of 1990 set out to disturb the balance of shared objectives that united commercial television and the BBC as public service broadcasters by loosening the reins on the commercial ambitions within the would-be broadcasting companies and by reducing the public service obligations of Channel 3. Publicly sensitive forms of regulation gave way to lighter more commercially attuned forms of regulation which in turn proved powerless to intervene in a wider public interest when commercial ambitions broke out of the stockade. The Independent Television Commission did not intervene to prevent Rupert Murdoch's News International from increasing its influence by expanding control of broadcast and press media as Sky absorbed the 'public service' BSB satellite service. With barely a rumble of resistance the satellite market had become a virtual monopoly in which Sky controlled many of the new channels and the most widely used decoders for unscrambling subscription channels. The rapid implementation of de-regulation in commercial broadcasting, the tolerance of maverick satellite television monopolisation has left the BBC isolated. Public service television broadcasting had been a result of the virtual monopoly of supply for forty years, could such a hot house bloom survive in a rapacious television jungle?

Does the increasing emphasis on immediate and paid for gratification from television jeopardise services which are dependent upon secure frameworks in which to work and upon which to rely for distribution? With the increased characterisation of the viewer as a consumer where do the longer term expectations of continuity of service, of quality and of expectation associated with the viewer as citizen fit in? Social benefits that might arise from the new forms of television distribution allowing new public service structures to be formed cannot be contemplated by the BBC when it faces a battle to retain audiences in the face of entertainment led competition and a threat to the licence fee if it does not swim successfully in the muddier commercial waters.

By extending choice, broadcasters have recognised that each viewer has the will to decide what to watch and increasingly the technical means to exercise that will and reach out and take down a programme or game of their choice from the cable and satellite shelf. In this greater self-determination the viewer becomes more isolated from the shared identity of a national public service broadcasting service. If the viewer is enabled by 'choice' to become individually more powerful by selecting from amongst an extended range of programmes on offer they have less use of broadcasting in a form which the licence fee supports and in proportion have reduced the power of the broadcasters' collective influence. With greater individual choice, the traditional broadcasting process becomes fragmented and more market-led in search of that diminishing club of viewers content for their programming to be nationally structured and spoon fed by the schedulers.

But how can the market ensure that a plurality of views are reflected that are essential to the interaction and flow of democratic accountability and even to making a democratic *choice* ? If television is already too metropolitan and centralised to reflect adequately the local and regional diversities how will larger scale satellite delivered programming enable the more locally focused views to be expressed?

As more and more of the television audience turns to programming supported by advertising and subscription it is inevitable that the BBC has to address the issue of its own future and that the rest of us assess the future of public service broadcasting in relation to the BBC's sense of its role. The BBC's need to defend itself as an institution and to retain the licence fee cannot be equated with a defence of public service broadcasting. Within itself the BBC has never been a representative slice of British life, nor below the government appointment of the Governors is its organisation of account-ability anything more than a peculiar spiral of self-appointing back-slapping commit-tees. In fact, the BBC remains well protected from the outside world it so badly needs to involve in its survival. The loss of influence of trade unionism in broadcasting and the increased government influence upon the BBC Governors has reduced the BBC's independence over the last decade, leaving it with less and less internal plurality upon which to gauge its priorities.

In market terms, the difficulties the BBC faces lie in balancing its future audience ratings against the commercial competition of multi-channel television simply in order to justify to government and public its requirement for the licence fee. Falling upon the BBC as the 'cornerstone of public service broadcasting' is an increasing public service and social role left behind in the retreat from public obligation and heightened entertainment priorities among its former and new competitors. However, to focus upon *extending choice* is perhaps to place a great store by the present circumstances of change – which are actually more precarious for the advertising dependent services than they are for the BBC. What is missing at the BBC is a demand to develop a broadcasting policy that strides across this transitional introduction of multi-channel television and which identifies unfulfilled demands and aspirations among the audi-ence for new forms of television that commercial services cannot, for a while at least, deliver. What has the BBC still got to offer by way of a new broadcasting vision?

According to John Birt, it has no grand plan at all. In fact, the BBC has overlooked in its continuing public review that its services are based upon trust between the broadcaster and the viewer. This relationship has much of the character of a contract renewed annually in advance for the supply of services. On more commercial terms, the licence fee is an advance instalment in a lifetime's investment in the future of public service broadcasting – and while forced by law to continue to invest while using a television set – few of us actually grumble; yet. A good medium and long term vision from the BBC is not only important; it is required by its shareholders. Without a new future for public service broadcasting that skilfully puts aside the consumer's immediate needs and articulates a new objective sooner or later the viewer will clamour to invest elsewhere. Rupert Murdoch has a vision; John Birt has a lame defence of services that on their own are not enough and in organisation for the future are simply inadequate.

In paying the licence fee the viewer is entering an agreement that is quite different to paying off a loan for a second hand car or purchasing a Sky satellite dish. In this contract the viewers are entrusting the BBC with a duty to provide services of continuing value, for themselves and the rest of those in the household for which the licence applies. The viewer is not a consumer, so much as he or she is a citizen within the 'state' of public service broadcasting. Whether described as a contract, a tax or a shareholding the relationship between the viewer and the BBC far exceeds the shallow transitory bond of supply and demand. With the BBC we have long term expectations tied to the value and continuity of our licence fees.

I believe that broadcasters in their defence of public service broadcasting have been addressing increasingly shallow and short term issues. Put on the back foot by Mrs Thatcher they have resorted to protecting their institutions and ignoring the relationships of service these were set up to provide, ignoring ways of involving the viewers in the process of broadcasting and change. There has been a tendency to turn away from demonstrating the social value and distinctiveness of public service broadcasting in a world filled nationally and internationally by alternative commercial TV stations.

This retreat along an ever narrower ledge of debate can be illustrated in the following way. If I am asked as a *customer* about my use for the local hospital, on my evidence of use it should surely be closed. I have had no cause to use it in twenty years. If a choice is presented between closing the swimming pool or the hospital, I would be obliged to keep the swimming pool, if I am asked purely as a service user or customer. It would not affect me directly if the hospital were to shut, but it would if the swimming pool were to close.

Yet, if I am asked as a *citizen* whether it is a good thing to keep open the local hospital I would answer believing that I might need hospital care in future, or by imagining the convenience to its current users, if not to other members of my own family. As a citizen I can value a service other than through my own immediate experience of its use. As a citizen I exist in a socially interactive form through time and space: as a consumer I exist only at the moment of my consumption.

I suggest that if broadcasters narrow viewers' horizons to 'choice', then viewers can only address their immediate concerns. Broadcasting has been redefined to exclude exploration of the future need to secure and enrich the wider social relationships that have till now been represented over time through public service broadcasting.

Internally public service broadcasting questions have been answered in all seriousness which have suggested that current affairs programmes should sink or swim on the basis of audience ratings. The argument for maintaining a healthy and vigorous investigative element in broadcasting is surely similar to the argument which was made to keep open the hospital: even if I don't watch the programme this week it does not mean that the investigative job of the programme should not be done.

If large numbers of people do not want to watch each current affairs programme it cannot be inferred from this that those that don't watch would want it to be closed down. Many citizens recognise that the role of the Fourth Estate is necessary to maintain a watchful public eye over areas we have no other collective way of scrutinising. Good public service television cannot be justified by the number of viewers for particular programmes but by the breadth of its portfolio as a comprehensive public service fulfilling that wider sense of duty. Having listened to John Birt, the BBC seems to have lost that wider role, and if not happy behind the drawbridge it has drawn up at least reconciled to its decision.

The BBC has failed to acknowledge that the special nature of the relationship it has with its viewers represented through the licence fee as a contract links us all in this collective enterprise and requires that the BBC continues to develop and not simply to protect its own reduced public service broadcasting in the light of new opportunities offered by technology to both public and commercial television. Standing still is falling back. Without a future the BBC will lose the present.

By turning itself inwards for its review and without involving the viewers in a realistic way in the processes of change – and a broadcasting organisation could hardly be better placed to involve the public in its affairs than the BBC – the BBC has treated its listeners and viewers as the beneficiaries of its services rather than as its true benefactors. The trust upon which the social and economic contract is founded is jeopardised by being overlooked at this time of crisis.

As citizens and shareholders the viewers have long term interests in the well being and structure of the BBC enterprise. If treated only as customers for services the viewers will probably, like all customers, shop around and become increasingly fickle. The relationship of trust, of aspiration and intellectual investment is lost in the BBC's reaction and defensiveness and without a unique long-term goal public service broadcasting will cease to have any special significance as other shops open up offering similar day-to-day products on a casual basis.

The BBC's future lies in re-invigorating its social and democratic role and undertaking to provide services that cannot be expected from commercial suppliers – and to put those services in place until all viewers have reasonable access to them for future commercial influence not to undo their social value.

Citizen Television explores the public's demands for new television services. It finds that the public wants local forms of television: citizen television. If citizens are encouraged to participate in the expansion of broadcasting they can make a contribution to a shared understanding of the social and cultural processes which affect us all in our immediate lives. Participation in broadcasting extends the viewer's choice by a significant magnitude and puts a more appropriate social stride into the gait of our seventy year old public broadcasting service.

The Institute of Local Television began its studies in 1989 following publication of the White Paper *Broadcasting in the '90s : Competition, Choice and Quality.* The White Paper announced new television technologies that would offer local options in television. This major departure from the focus on national and regional arenas in television, together with the high level of interest for local television found among people living in Edinburgh, prompted the production company TU/TV, which had carried out the early studies, to set up the Institute of Local Television to continue studies in this area.

Whether the new local television services that the White Paper made possible would be delivered by microwave or by cable or via terrestrial transmitters allocated to Channels 5 & 6, or by all of these means, in the end proved to be irrelevant. By the time the White Paper had been redrafted as a Bill to put before parliament and then had passed into law as the 1990 Broadcasting Act, and had fully come into force in 1993, each of the 'local' options had been forgotten or withdrawn without public comment or consultation. ILT have continued to research local television throughout this period, and in the course of five years the debate on the future of broadcasting has skirted serious discussion of what the public actually wants from the new television services. Choice lay in what was being offered, not in what was being asked for.

In reality the choice in broadcast television remains as stark as it ever was; to watch or not to watch. There is no choice which enables the citizen to participate and to become involved in the processes of broadcasting or to use television to communicate with the neighbours. As television services expand, while offering more and more to choose between, each of the viewers receives proportionately less and less about where they live. The local issues that affect us most are passed by unless magnified to regional or national proportions or treated as flecks of example across a national canvas.

Five years of continuous debate and numerous articles and conferences on the future of broadcasting have convinced us not to accept a growth in television from around the globe and to be content to live in our own television deserts.

The ambition of public service broadcasting to provide every citizen with access to radio and television regardless of where they lived or whether they could pay has given virtually all the population the four terrestrial television channels. The focus on the viewer as consumer has come about because the majority of homes are able to afford to extend themselves beyond broadcasting by using VCRs to gather other programmes to view and by using time-shifting to determine when to watch particular programmes. In spite of the explosion of television channels and the diverse means by which programmes are being delivered to the TV sets in our sitting rooms, bedrooms and kitchens we are still unable to speak to each other through television.

Public service broadcasting remains attached to a mass broadcasting model because it was originally conceived for the delivery of mostly the same programmes using large transmitters to reach largely undifferentiated audiences. It is hills not cultures that determine the siting of transmitters. The shape of regional broadcasting especially is the product of geographical accident rather than social design.

Yet the case for providing a universally available local television service – now that the national objectives have been achieved – is as strong as that once made for the national public broadcasting service. Public service broadcasting owes its existence to resisting commercial pressures in order to ensure equal availability of service while commercial services elsewhere sought out the most lucrative options. The resistance to the commercial imperative has collapsed at the centre and is unrecognised coming from the edge.

Seventy years of public service broadcasting will be rolled back if the BBC remains unwilling to extend the principle of public service broadcasting from national into locally accountable broadcasting services. The BBC is currently responding to the competitive agenda and to the protection of the institution rather than, as it was set up to do, elaborate, fulfil and sustain a dynamic social objective.

Unless efforts are made over the next two years to move public service broadcasting into new areas which commercial television services neglect public service broadcasting itself will cease to be relevant.

Local television is a public service issue not so much because it has not been established commercially but because the involvement of the community in the service is the democratic demand that the service can achieve. Citizen can speak unto citizen.

Local forms of television distribution through cable have been franchised by the Cable and Broadcasting Act since 1984. That legislation is now nine years old and still there is very little local television. And very little cable. Local terrestrial transmitters have been identified to provide local services on Channel 5. But Channel 5 has been withdrawn for an extended period of closed review by the Independent Television Commission.

Research by the Institute of Local Television and the Independent Television Commission has shown that when the public want news, they want local, national and international news. The large transmitters serving regional commercial television do not provide sufficiently local television. There is less demand for regional news than for local and national news. The building blocks comprising regional services remain largely because the bidders for Channel 3 needed to know what they were bidding for. Evidence that this regional transmitter configuration does not provide television the public particularly wants is entirely irrelevant. The motor for change was set by competition to find new owners and provide the Treasury with additional income. Viewer choice and the quality of service came a poor second in the invention of Channel 3 just as it does throughout the Broadcasting Act 1990.

In the city studies that ILT has undertaken since 1989 we have found a high level of public interest in forms of television which have local relevance. The ITC's national studies show that the majority of people in Britain want to relate some part of the programming they watch to their own experiences. ILT has shown that many people seem to want to go further and to actually represent themselves on their local television service.

Yet without the small scale of city sized services public participation and accountability are unrealisable ambitions. This may well have been a factor – rather than a consequence – in removing the local options from the proposals that led up to the Broadcasting Act of 1990. There is a national paranoia evident among broadcasters and politicians. After so long without a voice, giving people a local say now might lead to views of Britain that are entirely different from those promoted centrally.

In a diverse country such as Britain, local views represent powerful cultural, economic and social differences across the country. Television successfully suppresses these differences. Television regions have no cultural integrity. The BBC is not sure whether Scotland is a country or a region. Scottish Television thinks it serves a country but only reaches a region. Experience related television will inevitably be mostly local and real: the rest of television even when relevant is still vicarious and distant.

Without a range of localised forms of television citizens will continue to be denied what has been a basic right of free expression enjoyed by many European and North America citizens for decades. Outside Britain it is not controversial to be able to broadcast and express your views and to share those views with people living in the area where they most count. The right not to watch of course complements the right to have your say. And in this its simplest form local TV as open access has democratic objectives and is neither a competitor nor substitute to programme broadcasting. In this country the high quality of television programmes has confused us as to the wider uses to which television broadcasting can be put, especially with the arrival of multi-channel options.

In Britain the social or cultural opinions of the majority are prohibited from free circulation and are conveniently assumed by broadcasters and politicians alike to be uniform or compartmentalised in their diversity or even incapable of being represented by the national broadcasting services.

Without extending public service broadcasting from universal access to universal involvement the BBC has lost significant moral grounds for exclusive access to the licence fee and the role of public service broadcaster. In Europe and North America either a percentage of the licence fee or a local tax on cable company profits supports at its simplest the open and access public television services. Why not here?

Yet the struggle in Britain to develop television to include local forms of communication, as a focus for cultural and social exchange and to enable local voices to be taken up nationally or shared with other local services has at every turn been undermined. As new delivery technologies have made localised services possible their absence without just or even indifferent government and regulatory argument has become farcical.

I invited the Director General of the BBC John Birt to explain why the BBC had no policy towards providing local television at the Glasgow meeting on *Extending Choice* on the 6th April 1993. The question remained overlooked for the full two hours of the meeting and in the end the author politely held up ever larger placards scribbled on bits of BBC publicity to remind the host Kirsty Wark of her assurance that all questions however difficult would be answered and that none would be ducked.

Hostility towards local television is not confined to the BBC. One of the studies undertaken in *Citizen Television* details the twists and turns of the Cable Authority and then its successor the ITC to protect cable operators from their legal responsibilities by interpreting the legislation in a most irrational manner. Most cable companies have avoided the clear obligations laid down to provide community services on cable and a culture of benevolence has been adopted whose gains are unequal to the benefits the cable operators receive in accessing the city streets as if they are providing the services of a public utility or statutory authority.

The central organisation of public service broadcasting may have been in the public good while the principle objective was to deliver to all the same service and fend off commercial fragmentation. But it is surely no longer consistent with the public good to retain a centralised regulation of broadcasting which dominates and patronises the public. Nor is it consistent with the universal objectives of public service broadcasting to allow its regulators and guardians to turn their bureaucracies over to commercial operators; to reorganise broadcasting on the basis of discredited market philosophies; to dispense with seventy years of public accountability and to refuse to extend equality of access into the processes of broadcasting that lie behind its products. The new television technologies cut two ways: they can be used to enable a more democratic and localised restructuring of public service broadcasting or they can be regulated so as to ensure that a market dictatorship in broadcasting and television distribution remains.

Television regulation in Britain was never more ridiculous than when placing the onus for choice on the free market with one hand while arm wrestling with Red Hot Television and its 30,000 subscribers on grounds of moral corruption. The market may not always give us what we want. When it does, for some at least who make this choice, this may not be what the government had in mind by allowing choice to prevail.

In the last five years the public service element in broadcasting has not been clearly developed to secure long term benefits for the public. It is necessary now to rebuild public service television, to extend its services, to ensure local accountability in the structuring of local broadcasting; to include the public in the broadcasting process through use of the licence form as voting slip and questionnaire. The devolution of broadcasting and the introduction of local accountability; the provision for local investment; for local licences or public shareholdings are now essential elements in the revival of a genuine public service element in British broadcasting.

Part One of *Citizen Television* is a compilation of local television research studies undertaken in the UK between 1989 and 1992. The research reveals a demand for local and community television channels. Part Two draws upon this research to provide a commentary on the television debate begun by the government's 1988 White Paper *Broadcasting in the '90s: Competition, Choice and Quality*. Both parts explore the public's demand for localised forms of television and the regulation of broadcasting which has resisted, if not entirely excluded, the local choice the public has made.

Part One: Research and Analysis

Chapter One is a detailed market survey of one city's priorities for cable services and specifically for local television. The research was undertaken by Peter Kitchenman in 1989 in Edinburgh and in its detail offers a useful model for local television studies in other cities as cable begins.

Chapter Two is Adrian Friedli's analysis of the written commitments made by the cable companies in their franchise applications to the Cable Authority. The companies were encouraged by the 1984 Cable and Broadcasting Act to make provision for community and voluntary agencies to use the local network.

In Chapter Three Inken Schindler documents the meeting of Highways Authorities with the cable companies and provides examples of the confusion that has arisen from light-touch cable regulation and the lack of adequate investment which cable companies have committed to their franchises.

Lyndsey Bowditch's research in Chapter Four explores how education and local economic activity can be enhanced by using cable for television and telecommunications. Cable undertakings have helped create pockets of activity and fields of emptiness. Most local authority departments are simply unable to look beyond their own immediate responsibilities.

Chapter Five is Dave Rushton's analysis of the ITC's study *Mapping Regional Views* which surveyed public interest in regional television services. This 1990 ITC study confirmed public interest throughout the UK in receiving more localised rather than regionalised forms of television. Despite the evidence , the presentation of the original research confuses local requirements with the present regional service. The ITC appear transfixed by a regional television culture that survives on the lie of being more local than it can possibly be.

In Chapter Six Julie White follows up Peter Kitchenman's 1989 study of local cable channels and examines the Cable Authority and ITC's reasons for not introducing the local television proposals made by the cable companies in their franchise applications.

Section Seven is Dave Rushton's summary of the current development of cable. This suggests that the regulation of cable is in a state of crisis. Dormant cable franchises serve only to protect territory until investors are willing to commit themselves. This denies the supply of local services by other means.

Part Two: Local Public Service Television

Chapter Eight, *Making Local Work*, was written for publication in *Television*, the journal of the Royal Television Society in December 1990 and suggests that local television should not depend on one form of delivery and that commercial and licence fee supported programming can co-exist on a local channel.

Chapter Nine includes the Amendments put forward to the Independent Television Commission drafted by Amanda Gibbs and Dave Rushton following the publication of the ITC's *Draft Invitation to Apply for Channel 5*. This Chapter proposes that local television should be recognised as a distinctive third tier of public service broadcasting with its own form of local accountability and that the ITC should develop a consistent approach to regulating local television services regardless of the means by which they are delivered to the home.

Chapter Ten looks at the frequencies allocated to Channel 5 and considers those most suitable for local television services across the UK.

Chapter Eleven examines the scale of local television and compares the demand for local services with the advertising proposals put forward by the Institute of Practitioners in Advertising.

Chapter Twelve is a review of a meeting of the Organisation of Local Televisions held at the Palais de l'Europe in Strasbourg in October 1991.

PART ONE

Research & Analysis
Citizens and the Local Choice

1   Edinburgh Television Study

Peter Kitchenman, University of Edinburgh, 1989

1.   Summary

Research was carried out [in 1989] to forecast the market for cable television and for a local television channel for the City of Edinburgh. Eight cable stations in the UK were visited to determine the interest in local television within the industry. Local television was found to have a low profile with only four out of the eleven operating broadband stations actually providing local programmes.

240 households were surveyed in Edinburgh. CACI, a large market analysis company supplied a random sample of addresses stratified by ACORN. Their sampling frame was the postal address file. The final selection of respondents was carried out in the field using quota sampling.

A coded questionnaire provided by AGB of London was redesigned to suit the Edinburgh study. 101 interviews, each lasting approximately 45 minutes, were carried out by the author. The remaining 139 interviews were carried out by five others carefully selected and trained by the author. The questionnaire was laid out using PageMaker on an AppleMac. The raw data was analysed using StatView. The research findings suggest that:

- the forecast penetration for a typical cable TV package consisting of a basic service plus a number of premium channels is between 7% and 51% depending on the number of premium channels selected. If only the basic service is purchased at £7 then penetration will be 51%. However, if the all-in package is purchased at £22 then penetration drops to 7%. These are upper bound solutions which will only be achieved if extensive marketing is carried out to persuade the 'fairly likely's' to subscribe.

- there is a high demand for most types of channels, the exceptions being the Sports and Childrens' channels.

- interest in cable TV is most evident among:

    the 25-34 age group
    the ACORN Groups E, F and G (council housing)
    C1, C2 social grades
    VCR users

- over 50% of the city's population would be interested in participating in local television on subjects in which they have a particular interest.

- there is a high percentage of people (around 90%) interested in watching a diversity of local television programmes. This interest is fairly uniform over all age groups, social grades and ACORN groups.

- satellite TV does not present an immediate threat to cable TV in Edinburgh (as 78% of respondents were unlikely to buy satellite TV in the next 3 years).

2. Introduction

This chapter forms part of a feasibility study being carried out by TU/TV Ltd [the production company which established the Institute of Local Television] of Edinburgh. The initial brief focused on market research for a local TV station/channel for Edinburgh. It was assumed that local television in Edinburgh would become available under provisions anticipated in the 1988 White Paper *Broadcasting in the '90s: Competition, Choice and Quality*,[1] and that it would be distributed by a Multipoint [Microwave] Video Distribution System (MVDS). Cable TV, which is another way of distributing local television, was not considered at first because another company, Cablevision (Scotland) possessed the franchise and licence for providing cable television services in Edinburgh. A comparative study of cable, satellite and MVDS is provided in Table 1 (opposite). Cablevision (Scotland) has held the franchise since February 1986 when the Cable Authority first approved its application. Since then construction of the network has been in abeyance while the company looks for finance for their £40m operation.

Cablevision (Scotland)'s hold over the franchise loosened in July 1989 when the Cable Authority threatened to cancel franchises which did not show enough progress:

> The Cable Authority has told 14 'laggard' cable operators to let it know by July 3 whether they have made any 'substantial and concrete progress towards the early start of operations'. The authority will consider withdrawing the offer of a franchise from those who have not made enough progress.

> In January, [Jon] Davey [Director General of the Cable Authority] told the 14 operators that the authority 'expects the award of a franchise to involve a presumption that the construction of the system will follow in a timely manner. Franchisees cannot expect to continue to hold rights to a franchise if they do not implement it within a reasonable time.[2]

TU/TV Ltd felt a change of emphasis was appropriate in the wake of the Cable Authority's announcement on 'laggards'. Its revised strategy included preparing contingency plans for a cable operation with a significant focus on local programming should Cablevision not retain the franchise.

	Cable	Satellite Dish	MVDS
Number of Channels	Virtually unlimited	Depends on satellite: 16 on Astra; 5 on BSB	10
External aerials needed	No	Yes	Yes
Hardware required	Single connection supplied by operator, with any necessary set-top box	New dish for each satellite (or steerable dish). New receiver (or combined receiver) for each transmission standard (PAL, DMAC, D2MAC, SECAM). New decoder for each scrambling method (Eurocrypt, Eurocypher, Videocrypt).	Microwave aerial. Set top converter/ decoder.
Viewing one satellite channel while recording another	Connection supplied by cable operator	Second satellite receiver, possibly second dish and decoder.	Separate converter/ decoder.
Non-satellite channels?	Yes	No	Possibly
Local channels?	Yes	No	Possibly
Interactive services?	Yes	No	No
Telephone services?	Yes	No	No
Data transmission	2 way	1 way only	No
Planning permission?	No	Sometimes	Probably not
Availability	Comprehensive in cable areas	Only to those with sight of the satellite(s)	Only to those with line of sight to microwave transitter
Maintenance	Included as part service	Maintenance contract may be available	Arrangements not yet clear
Cost	Small conection fee Monthly subscrioption depending on programme channels received.	Substantial capital cost (sometimes plus equipment rental). Monthly subscription depending on programme channels received.	Substantial capital cost (could be supplied by local operator). Monthly subscription depending on programme channels received.

TABLE 1: From 1988-1989 Cable Authority Annual Report

It was to these ends that a field survey was conducted by the author to evaluate the market for cable television services and especially for high quality local programming whether or not for delivery by cable.

3.   Background

This market research for cable and local television in Edinburgh is part of a Feasibility Study being carried out by the production company and consultancy TU/TV Ltd. The study has been partly financed by Edinburgh District Council. In the short term, the market research has commercial value for a local cable operation.

The Feasibility Study involves two major linked activities:

> Developing the meaning and understanding of local television in Edinburgh while exploring a multitude of reactions to this increasingly concrete and manifest idea.

The first part of the activity involves publicity and marketing of the idea of local television to the people and organisations in Edinburgh, and exploring some of the implementations of local television further afield. The second activity is analysis and market research on cable and local television.

During the course of this study TU/TV Ltd has taken on a wider role which has led to the formation of the Institute of Local Television in order to carry out local television study, monitor demand for services and undertake research in this area across the UK.

In the course of the study it has been necessary to construct a general profile of local television and to raise the level of expectations from local television services not least among media writers and broadcasters. The *Really* New Television Conference has been organised to coincide with the Edinburgh International Television Festival of 1989. This has provided opportunities for co-operation between local television operations and helped to introduce ideas specific to local television to the broader television industry.

During the course of this study, Dave Rushton, a director of TU/TV Ltd, has participated in a television programme made for Channel Four, titled *Remote Control*, which has presented a variety of arguments in support of greater broadcasting autonomy and community input to television over the next decade.

A presentation to an Edinburgh audience on the objectives behind the study was held for community and business groups, councillors and local associations titled *Television in the 90's*. This brought forward features that would be distinctive to local television broadcasting and a charity, Edinburgh Television Trust, was set up to encourage greater public participation in the development of local television broadcasting.

Because Edinburgh is the first city in the UK to look at local television in the light of the White Paper *Broadcasting in the '90s* , a national role as well as international interest for this work has quickly arisen. The Institute of Local Television anticipates that Edinburgh will benefit directly from the pioneering work on demand identified here for a local television station. The Institute hopes to contribute towards local programming by increasing attention paid to the local requirements of the Cable and Broadcasting Act 1984. (The relevant section of the 1984 Act is reproduced in Appendix One.) As a result of this study and during the course of the debate on broadcasting raised by the White Paper the Institute intends to give shape to what it perceives as an unfulfilled demand for local involvement in television and especially in future localised broadcasting operations.

Why choose Edinburgh for a study of demand for local television? My notes in preparing this study indicate that TU/TV believed that the present broadcasting service in the area was inadequate for local needs and that the new broadcasting proposals in the White Paper on Broadcasting while raising issues of public choice did not seek to resolve choice with demand and might possibly even make matters worse. In the conference papers following a debate on local television at Edinburgh's Filmhouse held in April 1989 the following outline appears:

> Do we need local TV? Perhaps the tide is turning; in a diverse city like Edinburgh, there is a market for good quality local programming – including drama, music, entertainment and educational programmes as well as current affairs, news – a rich and varied local channel … The 'local' in local broadcasting raises questions about the control and representation of television … De-regulation of television, some argue, may kill the local production industry in Edinburgh, in Scotland and elsewhere [outside London] … So local television is an economic strategy issue as well as an expression of the vitality of our local entertainment, education and culture. Edinburgh – a high profile internationally oriented Capital City without a television station, enters an era of multi-channel viewing with no voice of its own!! Is that possible? Ask people if they believe STV favours Edinburgh or Glasgow or neither as a *local* station. 'Glasgow' will be the reply. That is where the main audience is; the market for mass advertising. If Grampian Television folds and STV takes over as the Scottish station, STV will be jumping around like a frog trying to be local 'everywhere' *and* the national station while competing with satellite [for the general audience]. [3]

4.   Research Objectives

The research objectives for the field survey are:

   1.   a forecast of cable TV penetration in Edinburgh

   2.   a forecast of the interest in local television with regard to:

         a) participation in local television
         b) watching local television
         c) interest in different types of local programming

   3.   an indication of the prices consumers are prepared to pay for:

         a) a basic package
         b) a combined basic plus optional package

   4.   the forecast demand for a range of channels (film, sport, news, etc)

5.   a forecast analysis of the cable TV market in Edinburgh by:

   a) age
   b) ACORN
   c) social grade
   d) VCR owners

6.   a forecast of satellite TV penetration in Edinburgh

5.   Expected Use of Market Research Findings

The findings of the market research will:

1.   Provide penetration and pricing data for input into a business plan.

2.   Highlight the demand for different types of channels and therefore assist with channel purchase decisions.

3.   Provide market intelligence data with regards to whom and where marketing efforts should be directed (and where the build should start) and proceed to maximize short-term penetration.

4.   Assist with investment decisions regarding local television facilities and production personnel.

5.   Comment on the extent satellite TV and VCRs are a threat to cable and local TV in Edinburgh.

6.   Methodology

6.1   Research Design

6.1.1 Exploratory Research

The initial brief was to determine if there was a market in Edinburgh for a local Multipoint Video Distribution System (MVDS) or combined MVDS/Cable Channel/ Station.

An exploratory questionnaire focusing on local programming and to be administered by mail was developed by the author. However, during the piloting phase it became evident that more information would be elicited if the author visited as many of the eleven cable stations operating in the UK as was possible considering time and financial constraints. Consequently eight of the eleven cable stations were visited and interviews conducted with either the managing directors or marketing managers. The interviews averaged one and a half hours including a visit around the facilities. The eight stations visited were:

   Aberdeen Cable Services Ltd
   Clyde Cablevision Ltd, Glasgow
   Cabletel Communications Ltd, Ealing

Westminster Cable Company Ltd, London
East London Telecommunications Ltd, London
Swindon Cable Ltd
United Cable Television (plc), Croydon
Coventry Cable Ltd

A qualitative summary of responses to each one of the questions asked during these exploratory interviews is provided in Appendix Two.

The author also had extensive interviews with personnel from AGB Research in London as they have wide experience in the UK in the field of television audience research.

At this stage in the exploratory phase of the market research the emphasis shifted from a qualitative study of the feasibility of local television to a quantitative study of cable television encompassing, inter alia, local channels. This shift arose from a change in strategy adopted by TU/TV Ltd. Cablevision (Scotland) who has held the franchise for Edinburgh since February 1986 had been described as 'laggards' by the Cable Authority in the early July 1989 edition of *New Media Markets*. The Cable Authority had also written to Cablevision (Scotland) asking them to provide an assurance that they had serious intentions to start building in the near future. TU/TV Ltd's revised strategy included putting pressure on Cablevision (Scotland) to provide high quality local programming while preparing contingency plans for a cable operation should Cablevision fail to retain – or indeed relinquish – their franchise. The author therefore sought advice from AGB Research as to how to go about conducting an extensive field survey to determine the likelihood of a market for cable television in Edinburgh. AGB provided a copy of a questionnaire used some years before to study the propensity for cable television in the UK. The exploratory phase of the research was now complete.

6.1.2 Descriptive Research

The exploratory research had indicated that the initial brief needed to be revised. The revised brief was to research the market for cable television in Edinburgh and to find out to what extent residents were interested in participating in and watching a local television channel. A number of variables needed to be measured and these have been summarised in the section on 'Research Objectives'. The geographical boundary for the research was chosen to be the area under the jurisdiction of the Edinburgh District Council (EDC): Cablevision (Scotland)'s franchise area is the area defined by the old EDC boundary. This area did not include Balerno which was brought under the jurisdiction of EDC in 1982. Table 2 (over leaf) shows the number of households and population within the EDC catchment in 1989 and compares this with the number of households and population of Cablevision (Scotland)'s franchise in Edinburgh in 1986.

The question remained as to how this research was to be carried out. Qualitative research in the form of focus groups and in-depth interviews with various segments of the population was contemplated. However, the thrust for something more tangible in the form of quantitative research came with the changing strategies of TU/TV. A cross-

	Edinburgh City (1989)	Cablevision (Scotland) (1986)
Number of households	191,584 [1]	183.376 [3]
Population	438,721 [2]	- [3]

Sources:
1. Edinburgh District Council, Councillor's Research Unit (this figure includes 49,054 local authority housing units).
2. Registrar General's 1988 Annual Update of the 1981 Census of Population.
3. Public document accompanying Cablevision (Scotland)'s franchise application to the Cable Authority lodged with Estates and Economic Development Department of Edinburgh District Council.

TABLE 2: Number of households and population in Edinburgh.

sectional propensity study of cable television in Edinburgh would provide the information (should the results prove favourable) to put pressure on the existing franchisee to provide high quality local programming for Edinburgh. Alternatively this information would help in making a decision as to whether or not an offer should be made to buy the franchise from the incumbent. At all events, the objective was that if a demand for local services was found then this would maximise the bargaining position with an Edinburgh cable operation.

The author reviewed the two main methods of selecting respondents from a population – probability and non-probability sampling. Probability samples are distinguished by the fact that each respondent has a known, non-zero chance of being included in the sample. With non-probability samples there is no precise way of estimating the probability that any respondent will be included in the sample, thus there is no way of rigorously ensuring that the sample is representative of the population. Many market research surveys, however, use a non-probability method of sampling households or individuals at the final selection stage within the sampling areas, though the areas themselves are normally selected by probability methods. The most commonly used non-probability method is quota sampling.

Interviewers are supplied with 'quotas' or set specifications regarding the number of people of various kinds that they must interview. Provided that the specification is fulfilled, they are free to interview whom they wish within the designated area. This contrasts with probability samples where the interviewer must interview everyone on their address list. Non-responses are noted and interviewers call back up to four times (industry accepted norm) if the respondent is not at home. Because of time and financial constraints the author followed market research practice and adopted 'quota' sampling at the final stage of the sampling process. In order to randomise the process as much as was feasible it was decided to randomly select the areas to be surveyed. The three most common sampling frames were investigated – the electoral list, the postal address file and the telephone directory. CACI in Edinburgh was approached for a quote for randomly selecting addresses from their computerised sample frame (postal address file in this case). It was also decided to review the manual methods of sampling. It would

8

have been feasible to use information generated by the Councillor's Research Unit (CRU) of Edinburgh District Council. The CRU has identified through the 1981 Census of Population the proportional split of employment categories in all 62 political wards in Edinburgh. It would have been feasible to randomly select on a stratified basis a sample from the electoral list. This would have been an interesting exercise from an academic point of view. However, it was finally decided that CACI's method of random stratified sampling using ACORN as a discriminator (rather than employment category or social grades) would yield information that would be more commercially valuable in the future. This decision to go with CACI was fortunate because at the time the author was unaware of the extent to which Cablevision (Scotland) had carried out market research in Edinburgh. Later on in the study it was discovered that Cablevision (Scotland) had also employed CACI in 1983 through AGB to develop a random stratified sample according to ACORN. So some parity, by coincidence, had been established with previous market research.

6.2   Previous Relevant Research

6.2.1 Quantitative Research

Two research surveys were carried out in 1983, each by one of the two cable consortia that merged to apply for the Edinburgh franchise. These were both quantitative surveys utilising pre-coded questionnaires and were accompanied by a leaflet illustrating the programme choice likely to be available through cable TV. Both were based upon a randomly selected sample. The survey conducted by Research Surveys of Great Britain (RSGB) on behalf of Cablevision (Scotland) Ltd covered 400 interviews in Edinburgh, whilst that of Audits of Great Britain (AGB) Cable and Viewdata, on behalf of Capital City Cablevision, provided 500 interviews.

The two surveys indicated that those most likely to subscribe were in the C1,C2 socio-economic groups and larger (with children) and younger (under 35) households. The propensity to subscribe was found to be proportional to the existence of key precursors:

> Medium to heavy TV viewing
> Multi-set ownership/rental
> VCR ownership/rental, especially the latter

A third quantitative survey was carried out by AGB Cable and Viewdata in 1985, again using a pre-coded questionnaire.

The 1985 study was designed to facilitate the 'projection' of the results on to the base population of Edinburgh to produce estimated likely connection rates for different areas of the city.

This was achieved by allocating an ACORN code to each respondent's address and by collecting demographic information relating to each household in which the interview took place. ACORN is a classification of the small areas used in the interrogation of the Population Census by a UK market analysis company called CACI. These areas are classified into distinctive types according to the characteristics of the households measured by demographics, economic activity, car ownership and housing type. The central idea of ACORN is that a set of areas with similar demographic and social characteristics will share common lifestyle features and thus present similar potential for the sales of any product.

6.2.2 Qualitative Research

In addition to the quantitative research studies, Cablevision (Scotland) engaged in some qualitative research conducted by System Three Scotland and used groups located within the participants' own homes. The objective was to provide a broader based view of the market place, to identify the reasons for cable's appeal or lack of it and to emulate to some extent the sales situation by showing groups extracts of the various programme channels and monitoring any changes in attitude on the part of the group members using one group as the 'control' group.

During the course of the field survey, respondents were also asked about their attitudes to a range of non-entertainment cable services. The service that elicited the main interest across the various social/age and ACORN groups was home security.

Brief studies were also carried out on business and institutional use of a cable system as Edinburgh was thought to be particularly well placed to take advantage of the development of a business and institutional cable network at the appropriate time. It would appear that large organisations then did not have a communications strategy with a clear decision-making structure.

The source for the above information is an unpublished 1986 MBA dissertation by A R Wilson from the University of Edinburgh. [4]

At the end of a two hour meeting in September 1989 between Cablevision (Scotland), TU/TV Ltd, Edinburgh District Council and Lothian Regional Council at the Edinburgh offices of the British Linen Bank, the author approached the Managing Director of Cablevision (Scotland) and requested access to the above mentioned 1983 and 1985 market research studies. Cablevision (Scotland) said that they would furnish this information so long as they had equal access to the current market research being carried out by the author. They were advised that this was not acceptable as it was an unequal exchange of commercial information and that Cablevision (Scotland)'s research was so dated as to be of little value other than from an academic perspective. Negotiations for access to this information continued over a period of weeks. It was obvious that Cablevision (Scotland) did not wish to be seen as uncooperative towards the TU/TV feasibility study as TU/TV was being partially funded by Edinburgh District Council and Cablevision (Scotland) had a vested interest in maintaining good relationships with EDC, their local authority. In the end Cablevision (Scotland) provided two pieces of information from their 1985 study:

> the cumulative percentage likely to subscribe to an all-in package priced at various levels and VCR penetration

6.3   Primary Data Collection

6.3.1 Questionnaire Design

A questionnaire designed to measure the propensity for cable television was provided by AGB during the exploratory phase of the research. The questionnaire was manually transported into an AppleMac desktop publishing software file and edited to meet the requirements of the 1989 Edinburgh Study. Major changes were introduced in the areas of scale definition and measuring the response to the likelihood of paying a quoted figure for various cable services. The adopted propensity scales were of the five point type ranging in the main from 'very interested' to 'very uninterested' or from 'very likely' to 'very unlikely'. These are not interval scales and it would be incorrect to reach any conclusion about the meaning of the distances between scale positions. Respondents are merely ranked along a continuum relating to the study of a particular attitude. Moreover, it cannot be assumed that the mid-point on the scale is necessarily the precise middle between the two extreme scores. The scale for measuring the response to the likelihood of paying a quoted figure for various cable services was changed from a harsh 'yes/no' response to a more gradual 'very likely' to 'very unlikely' response. This gave the research analyst a better measure of the sensitivity to price changes.

The 'local' dimension was built into the questionnaire by the author. During the exploratory phase of this study a lack of any detailed market research in the area of local television anywhere in the UK had been identified. It appears that in the past, most research companies have only been requested to provide a simple measure of the demand for local television in their propensity studies. The local dimension was explored in more depth in this study. Questions concerning participation in local television and the level of interest in different categories of local programming were included. The author also attempted to measure the breadth and depth of interest in the local dimension by measuring the respondent's current interest in local radio and newspapers.

The AGB questionnaire provided little scope for gathering demographic data concerning the respondent and other people living in the household. They had left it to the interviewer to subjectively assess the social grade of the principal wage earner. Apparently this is standard industry practice when experienced market researchers are employed. However, as the author was inexperienced in this area and it was likely that other inexperienced people would assist with the interviewing it was decided to gather comprehensive demographic data. The process requires a judgement to be made about which social grade the principal wage earner falls into (if social grade is to be adopted as a discriminator in the study). The subjectivity can be minimised by gathering data on salary, job title, required skills for the job and level of responsibility held. The other major discriminator in the field survey was ACORN. However, more about this in the section on sample design.

The questionnaire begins with a quick series of simple inventory-type questions which lead on to a question concerning the respondent's use of television. The author believes this approach is preferable to launching immediately into interesting and thought-provoking questions. The hypothesis here is that the respondent is still gauging how safe it is to answer the questions, particularly, if the interviewer has been invited into the respondent's house. The initial questions are non-threatening. The demographic questions were placed at the end because they were the last to be designed.

6.3.2 Coded Sheets, Show Cards and Illustrated Boards

Associated with the questionnaire are coded sheets, show cards and illustrated boards. The use of coded sheets was an attempt to reduce the amount of photocopying by getting the interviewers to mark the answers directly onto a single coded sheet at the time of the interview rather than providing 240 eighteen page questionnaires. It was appreciated that concentration and diligence would be required by the interviewer to ensure the information was placed in the correct box on the coded sheet during the interview.

Showcards were used to assist the respondent in answering the questions.

The illustrated boards were made up from material gathered during the exploratory research. The basic and optional packages were designed with reference to what was offered by existing cable companies and what was thought to be reasonable with respect to what channel providers charge to cable companies. The graphic layout was developed by cutting and pasting hard and soft copies using scissors, paste and an AppleMac desk top publishing package. The finished product was colour copied and laminated in plastic to preserve it during the interviews.

6.3.3 Pilot Questionnaire

The questionnaire was piloted through ten interviews. Errors in question design, coding and routing were identified and corrected. One interesting piece of feedback that came out of the pilot study was the response to the question that sought to identify the respondent's race. In the first draft the wording was: 'Could you tell me which of the groups on this card best describes you ......' [*Show Card ...*]

A.	BANGLADESHI	B.	BLACK - CARIBBEAN
C.	BLACK - AFRICAN	D.	BLACK - OTHER
E.	CHINESE	F.	INDIAN
G.	PAKISTANI	H.	EUROPEAN
I.	OTHER		

The feedback suggested that this was offensive to non-white people. The advice of the Multi Cultural Education Centre in Edinburgh was sought. They said that there was no universal solution to the sensitive issue of recording race or cultural grouping on questionnaires. Their solution was a listing that included:

White	Other
Black Afro - Caribbean	Black Asian/Chinese
Chinese	Black African

This was rejected on the basis that it was too colour orientated. The colour dimension was removed by asking which cultural group the interviewee most closely identified with and offering a list of global regions to choose from.

6.3.4 Sample Design

The constraints placed on the research in terms of time and finance dictated that sampling points would be selected by a random stratified process and selection within a sample point would be by quota according to age and sex. What was needed was a suitable discriminator on which to base the results. Sex, age and social grading are common market research discriminators. However another discriminator called ACORN developed in the early 1970's by CACI has penetrated the research market. ACORN identifies areas with similar demographics and social characteristics where households share common lifestyle features and thus present similar potential for the sales of any product.

CACI and their ACORN classification was chosen as the process for selecting a random stratified sample. CACI's sampling frame is the postal address file.

The sample size was initially estimated to be 300. This figure was not calculated by any precise mathematical formula. Although there is a formula for calculating sample size when the sample is stratified [5,6] there is little point in doing this and adhering to it if the final selection of respondents is carried out by quota. There are similarities between pure stratified samples and stratified quota samples. Both involve the divisions of the population into segments and the selection of elements from each segment. There is one key difference, though. Sample elements are selected probabilistically with stratified samples, whereas they are selected judgementally in quota samples. This has important implications. Because the sample elements are selected probabilistically, stratified samples allow the establishment of the sampling distribution of the statistic in question, which in turn allows confidence interval judgements. Quota samples allow no objective assessment of the degree of sampling error and thus preclude confidence interval estimates and statistical tests of significance.

Some researchers [7,8] argue that quota sampling methods have so improved that it is in order to calculate the standard error on the same lines as for random sampling. This view, however, is not widely shared [9] and most survey organisations, particularly official ones, accept the statistical limitations of quota sampling.

During the exploratory research the author was advised on a number of occasions that the industry norm for quota sampling was 30 samples per variable of those studied. As there are 10 ACORN groups in Edinburgh this would suggest a sample size of 300. Churchill [10] suggests that for an analysis with few variables a typical sample size for a region would be 200-500. For an analysis with an average number of variables the typical sample size for a region would be 500-1000. The figure of 240 was chosen due to limitations of time and finance and because two of the ACORN groups in Edinburgh are significantly smaller than the others so 8 groups by 30 gives a sample size of 240.

Initially however the sample size was estimated at 300. CACI advised using enumerator districts (ED's typically contain 150 households) as the way to segment the household population and estimated that the industry norm for successful interviews within an ED was 10. On that basis 30 ED's were randomly chosen and stratified according to ACORN from all the ED's within the Edinburgh District Council boundary. CACI therefore provided the author with a list of all the addresses within each one of the 30 ED's selected at random. The author specifically asked CACI to include the delivery point designation on the address file – in other words how many letter boxes existed at each address. However, either the postal address file maintained by the Post Office does not identify delivery points or CACI's system omits to provide them.

Which ever is the case many addresses with no delivery points shown had in the field more than one delivery point. This disrupted the process of the final selection of households because it was hoped to randomly select households from the office before going out into the field. This was not to be.

The final selection of households was left to the interviewer with a quota according to age and sex as a guide.

6.3.5 Field Survey

The field survey of 240 interviews was carried out between August and September 1989. The author conducted 101 interviews and the remaining 139 were carried out by five other interviewers who were all university graduates. One of the five interviewers had previous market research experience (6 months of telephone surveys) and the others were trained by the author. The training consisted of going through the interview pack with the new recruit. The interview pack consisted of a ring folder containing the: questionnaire; showcards; illustrated boards; blank coded sheets; handout on local television; sample point address list with quotas; copy from street map with highlighted addresses; letter of authenticity from Director of MBA Course, University of Edinburgh; interviewer's manual; [11] Guide on Social Grading.

The new recruits were then asked to study the pack in their own time and return the next day to clarify unresolved issues. Most would go away and interview an acquaintance as a trial run. After the second meeting the new recruits were ready to start interviewing. The author would meet up with each interviewer after their first day to go through the completed coded sheets and spend some time talking over the interviewer's Guide on Social Grading. The interviewers were asked to use the quotas provided by CACI as a guide in the final selection of respondents. They were also asked to skip three delivery points after each successful interview before knocking on the next door (this is another unwritten industry norm among market researchers).

The sample points chosen at random were at the most eight miles apart.

7.   Analysis and Presentation of Data

The data on the coding sheets was typed into a file on EMAS-3, a main frame University of Edinburgh computer. This was done to permit the data to be analysed by the statistical package SPSSX. The author in the meantime was introduced to another statistical package called StatView which could handle all the study's statistical requirements; is designed for AppleMacs; has superior graphics, and is interactive.

A small computer programme was therefore written to rearrange the three records per case into one long record ready for transfer down to an AppleMac micro computer and analysis by StatView. The output file of raw data from SPSSX also needed some manual editing to remove carriage returns before sending it down to the microcomputer. A piece of software called Kermit was needed to allow the two systems to communicate with one another.

StatView was used for:

- frequency distributions
- calculating means, standard deviations etc
- graphing
- recording data
- cross-tabulations

PageMaker and CricketGraph, two pieces of software designed for desk top publishing and graphics respectively, were used extensively throughout the project.

8. Research Findings

8.1 ACORN Groups and Types Sampled

The survey sample of 240 respondents was selected from 30 enumerator districts (ED's) chosen at random from all ED's in Edinburgh and stratified according to the ACORN classification.

There are 38 Acorn types and 11 Acorn groups in the UK. Edinburgh is represented by 18 ACORN types and 10 ACORN groups as shown in Table 3 (overleaf). It can also be seen from Table 3 that in some cases there are up to four sampling points in enumerator districts with the same ACORN type. 8 interviews were carried out in each ED, so some ACORN types are represented by eight interviews while others are represented by 21 interviews. On the other hand looking at ACORN groups, 4 ACORN groups are represented by thirty two or more interviews, while 3 ACORN groups are represented by 8 interviews. The stratification process has slightly over-represented the J & K ACORN groups.

8.2 Demographic Data Analysis

The other main discriminators apart from ACORN are:

Sex	Refer Table 4
Age	Refer Table 5
Social Grade	Refer Table 6

Sex compares favourably with data online at *The Scotsman* newspaper office in Edinburgh and sourced from RSGB. The social grade distribution is of the same order of magnitude as the other classifications of Social Class shown in Tables 7 and 8.

Other minor discriminators are:

Employment Categories	Refer Table 9	
Household Type	Refer Table 10	Tables 9-14
Principal Wage Earner	Refer Table 11	appear in
Household Income Groups	Refer Table 12	Appendix Three
Innovators/Laggards	Refer Table 13	
Number of Children in Household	Refer Table 14	

Groups	Types	Sample Point No.		ACORN Type	% ACORN Group in Sample	% ACORN Group in Population
B	B04	SPl	-	B04	10	9.1
	B05	SP2	-	B0S		
	B07	SP3	-	B07		
C	C09	SP4	-	C09	3.3	4.0
D	D14	SP5	-	D14	3.3	4.6
E	E17	SP6	-	E17	13.3	14.1
	E18	SP7	-	E18		
		SP8	-	E18		
		SP9	-	E18		
F	F20	SP10	-	F20	10.0	10.0
		SP11	-	F20		
	F21	SP12	-	F21		
G	G22	SP13	-	G22	13.3	13.6
		SP14	-	G22		
	G24	SP15	-	G24		
		SP16	-	G24		
H	H29	DP17	-	H29	3.3	0.1
I	I30	SP18	-	I30	10.0	11.9
		SP19	-	I30		
	I31	SP20	-	I31		
J	J33	SP21	-	J33	16.7	17.7
		SP22	-	J33		
		SP23	-	J33		
	J34	SP24	-	J34		
		SP25	-	J34		
K	K37	SP26	-	K37	16.7	14.7
	K38	SP27	-	K38		
		SP28	-	K38		
		SP29	-	K38		
		SP30	-	K38		

TABLE 3: ACORN Groups and Types represented in Edinburgh

	Edinburgh Television Study (1989)	RSGB (1989)
Male	42	44
Female	58	56
		Note: RSGB's projection is described as relatively unstable.

TABLE 4: Demographic Data - Sex

	Edinburgh Television Study (1989) %	Edinburgh District 1981 Census %
Aged 16-24	15	19
Aged 25-34	23	18
Aged 35-55	38	27
Aged 55+	24	36
		Note: RSGB's projection is described as relatively unstable.

TABLE 5: Demographic Data - Age

	Edinburgh Television Study (1989) %	RSGB (1989) %
A	5	2
B	23	18
CI	32	25
C2	23	23
D	11	14
E	6	18

Notes:
1. RSGB 's projection is described as highly unstable
2. The philosophy and mechanics of social grading can be found in JICNARS publication 'Social Grading in the National Readership Survey'.

TABLE 6: Demographic Data - Social Grade

	% Edinburgh (taken from 1981 Census of Population)	Where
A	16	A - Professionals, Employers and Managers
B	15	B - Intermediate Non-manual
C	24	C - Junior Non-manual
D	16	D - Skilled Manual
E	15	E - Semi-skilled Manual and Personal Service
F	8	F - Unskilled Manual
G	6	G - Others (eg. armed forces, or inadequately described occupations)

TABLE 7: Demographic Data - Social Class (Edinburgh District Council)

Social Class of Household Head	% Edinburgh	Index (100 = British Average)
1	9	162
2	26	103
3N	18	132
3M	26	81
4	13	82
5	6	118
Armed Forces/Other	2	74

Where
  1 - Professional Occupations
  2 - Intermediate Occupations
  3N- Skilled Occupations - Non-manual
  3M-Skilled Occupations - Manual
  4 - Partly Skilled Occupations
  5 - Unskilled Occupations

Note here that the previous occupation is used to categorise pensioners, unemployed, the sick etc. (Whereas in the author's study these are categorised as 'E' unless they have access to private means other than state pensions or disability benefits etc.)

TABLE 8: Demographic Data - Social Class (according to CACI)

8.3   Penetration

8.3.1 Likelihood of Buying Basic Cable Package

The figures in Table 15 show the cumulative percentage of all households likely to subscribe to the basic package at successively lower prices. The propensity shown as a two part scale is a sub group of the five part scale offered to the respondent.

Figures 1, 2 and 3 (opposite and overleaf) show the likelihood of subscribing to the Basic Package in relation to the discriminators Age, Social Grade and ACORN group respectively at various price levels. The two part scale has been combined into a one part scale for ease of interpretation. That is, those who responded 'very likely' or 'fairly likely' to subscribe have been recoded as 'likely' to subscribe. (This information is presented in tabular form in Table 16 in Appendix Three.)

	Very Likely to Subscribe	Very and Fairly Likely to Subscribe
£10	16%	42%
£ 8	26%	44%
£ 6	38%	52%

TABLE 15: Cumulative Percentage of All Households Likely to Subscribe to a Basic Package Priced at Various Levels (n = 240)

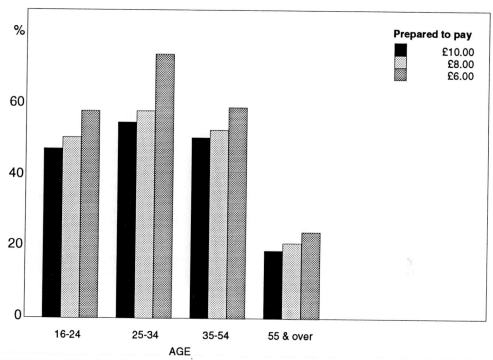

FIGURE 1: Cumulative percentage likely to subscribe to **basic** cable package according to **Age**.

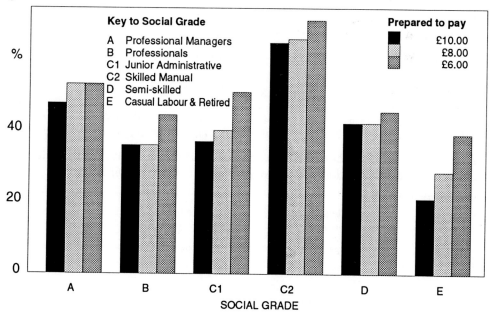

FIGURE 2: Cumulative percentage likely to subscribe to **basic** cable package according to **Social Grade**.

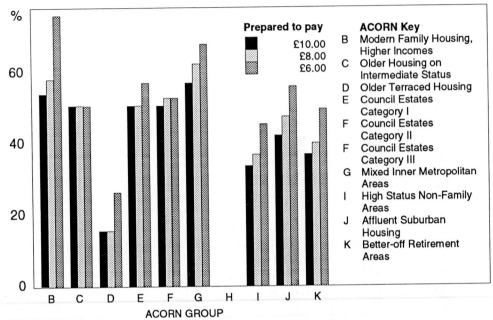

FIGURE 3: Cumulative percentage likely to subscribe to **basic** cable package according to ACORN Group.

Summarising Figures 1, 2 and 3 suggests there is a greater market for a basic package among:

- 25-34 years old
- Cl, C2 social grades
- in the B, C, E, F and G ACORN Groups.

8.3.2 Likelihood of Buying All-in Package

The figures in Table 17 show the cumulative percentage of all households likely to subscribe to the combined basic plus optional packages at successively lower prices.

The figures in Table 17 can be contrasted with the results from Cablevision (Scotland)'s research of April 1985 conducted by CACI/AGB and shown in Table 18.

	Very Likely to Subscribe	Very and Fairly Likely to Subscribe
£20	8%	19%
£15	15%	27%
£10	32%	47%

TABLE 17: Cumulative Percentage of All Households Likely to Subscribe to an All-in Package Priced at Various Levels (n = 240)

	Likely to Subscribe
£17.95	7%
£15.95	10%
£13.95	14%
£11.95	17%
£9.95	27%

TABLE 18: Cumulative Percentage of All Households Likely to Subscribe to an All-in Package Priced at Various Levels (AGB, 1985) (n = 440)

Figures 4, 5 and 6 (overleaf) show the likelihood of subscribing to the combined Basic plus Optional Packages in relation to the discriminators, Age, Social Grade and ACORN Group respectively at various price levels. The two part scale has been combined into a one part scale for ease of interpretation. That is, those who responded 'very likely' or 'fairly likely' to subscribe have been recoded as 'likely to subscribe'. (This information is presented in tabular form in Table 19 of Appendix Three.) Summarising Figures 4, 5 and 6:

- The market for an all-in package generally decreases as the age group increases.

- C1, C2 and D are prepared to pay more for the all-in package than are the other social grades.

- ACORN groups E, F and G are prepared to pay more for the all-in package than the others.

8.3.3 Interest in Subscribing to Cable TV

The figures in Table 20 show the interest in subscribing to cable TV assuming the price is affordable.

Key to Interest	Sample Count	%
Very interested	25	10
Fairly interested	100	42
Neither interested nor uninterested	13	5
Fairly uninterested	14	6
Very uninterested	88	37

TABLE 20: Interest in subscribing to cable TV (n = 240)

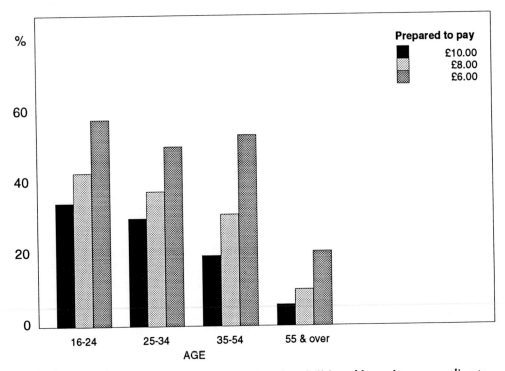

FIGURE 4: *Cumulative Percentage likely to subscribe to **all-in** cable package according to Age.*

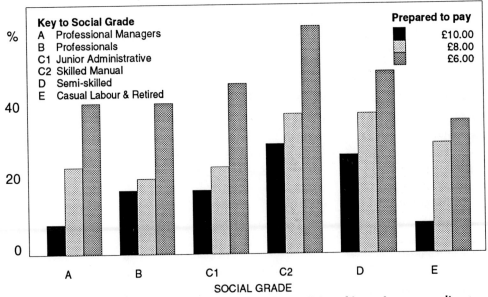

FIGURE 5: *Cumulative Percentage likely to subscribe to **all-in** cable package according to Social Grade*

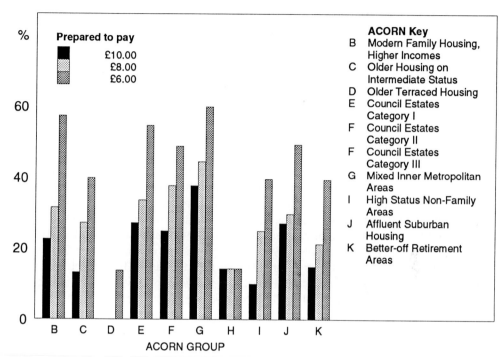

FIGURE 6: *Cumulative percentage likely to subscribe to **all-in** cable package according to ACORN Group.*

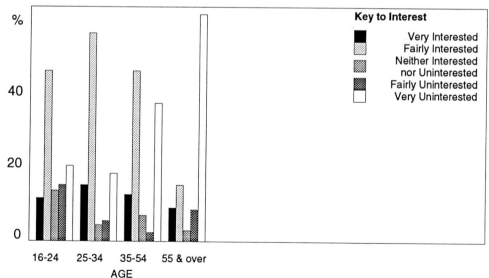

FIGURE 7: *Interest in subscribing to cable assuming it is affordable according to **Age**.*

Figures 7, 8 and 9 (overleaf) show the interest in subscribing to cable TV in relation to the discriminators Age, Social Grade and ACORN Group respectively. This information is presented in tabular form in Table 21 of Appendix Three.

Summarising Figures 7, 8 and 9 suggests that there is a greater interest in subscribing to cable TV among:

- 25-34 year olds
- C1, C2 Social Grades
- ACORN Groups B, E, F and G than among the other elements of these groups.

8.3.4 Estimate of Penetration

Penetration figures need to relate to the selling price of the product. It is estimated that the Basic Package would sell for around £7 per month and the Optional Package at around £15 per month. This would mean an all-in Package would cost around £22 per month. Upper and lower bound estimates of the penetration for an all-in package of £22 can be found by extrapolating or calculating from a line of simple regression. This is done by referring to Table 15 and plotting a simple regression of 8%, 15% and 32% 'very likely' to subscribe against subscription rates of £20, £15 and £10 respectively and extrapolating or calculating for £22. This would result in 2% 'very likely' to subscribe to cable TV at £22 monthly subscription. The exercise is repeated for the 'very likely' and 'fairly likely' to subscribe at £22 monthly subscription. 2% and 11% penetrations are therefore the lower and upper bounds respectively for a £22 per month subscription for an all-in package. The upper bound penetration will only be realised if an extensive marketing effort is made to convert the 'fairly likely' to 'very likely'.

Simple regression lines drawn from Table 15 provide lower and upper bound values of 32% and 48% respectively for a £7 per month subscription for the basic package. It is not possible without further data to estimate the penetration range for a less comprehensive package, say the basic package plus a number of channels at a per channel rate (which is what the average UK cable subscriber purchases).

The 11% penetration for a £22 per month all-in package is the upper bound limit for the sample as noted above. Confidence limits can be estimated for the population of Edinburgh if the sample is assumed to be a probabilistic sample. It has been argued in a previous section that if the sample was selected by quota, statistical inference, although not statistically rigorous, may be made. With reference to estimating population proportions in Harper [12], for the 11% sample penetration it can be stated that the population penetration at the 95% confidence level

$$= 0.11 \pm \left(\frac{0.11(1-0.11)}{240}\right)^{\frac{1}{2}} = \text{between 7\% and 15\%}$$

8.4 Local Television

Figures 10 to 16 (following pages) show the levels of interest among respondents towards local television with regard to:

- participation in local television
- watching local television
- interest in different types of local programming

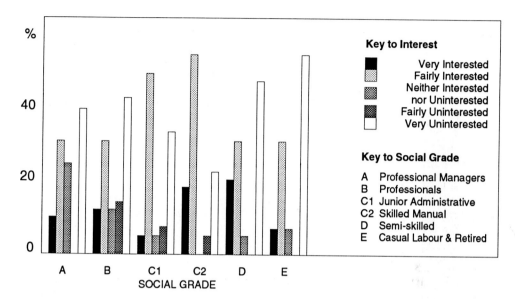

FIGURE 8: *Interest in subscribing to cable assuming it is affordable according to **Social Grade**.*

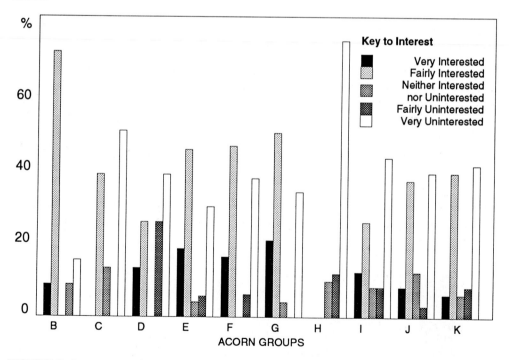

FIGURE 9: *Interest in subscribing to Cable assuming it is affordable according to **ACORN** Groups.*

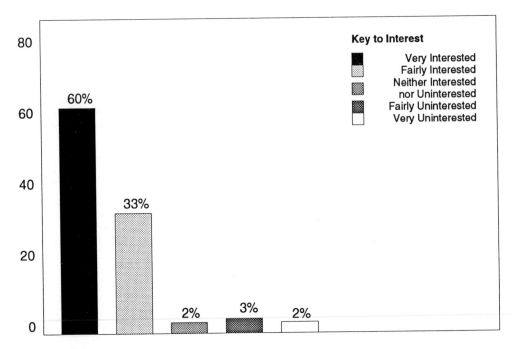

FIGURE 10: *How interested are you in watching a locally made programme about one of your hobbies/leisure interests or other activities of particular interest to you? (n = 240)*

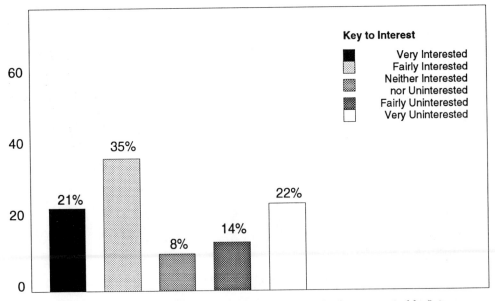

FIGURE 11: *If a local television programme were being made about your hobby/leisure interest or other activity of particular interest to you how interested would you be in helping with or appearing in this programme? (n = 240)*

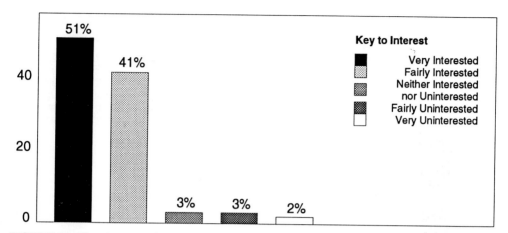

FIGURE 12: How interested would you be in watching a local television channel that screens Local News? (n = 240)

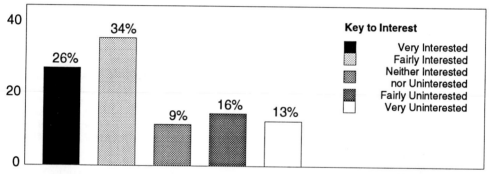

FIGURE 13: How interested would you be in watching a local television channel that screens Local Amateur and Professional Sporting Events and Meetings? (n = 240)

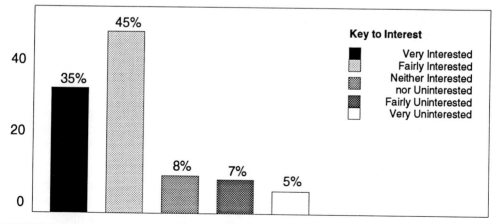

FIGURE 14: How interested would you be in watching a local television channel that screens Local Current Affairs? (n = 240)

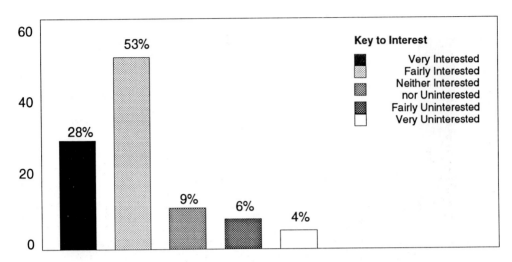

FIGURE 15: How interested would you be in watching a local television channel that screens Local Special Interest Programmes? (n = 240)

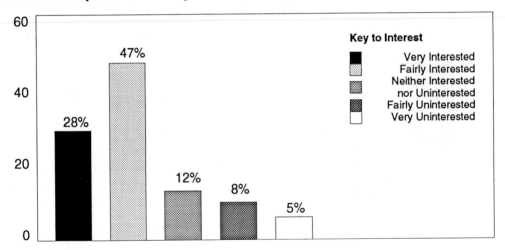

FIGURE 16: How interested would you be in watching a local television channel that screens Local Entertainers and Local Neighbourhood and City Festivals? (n = 240)

With the exception of watching local sport there is overwhelming support for local television. Attention is drawn to the observation that whereas 93% of respondents are interested in watching local TV, only 52% are interested in subscribing to cable television assuming it is affordable.

It would seem from this that there may be a case for investing in good quality local television as a means of increasing cable penetration. Figures 17 to 19 show the levels of interest in local television with regard to Age Groups, Social Grades and ACORN Groups.

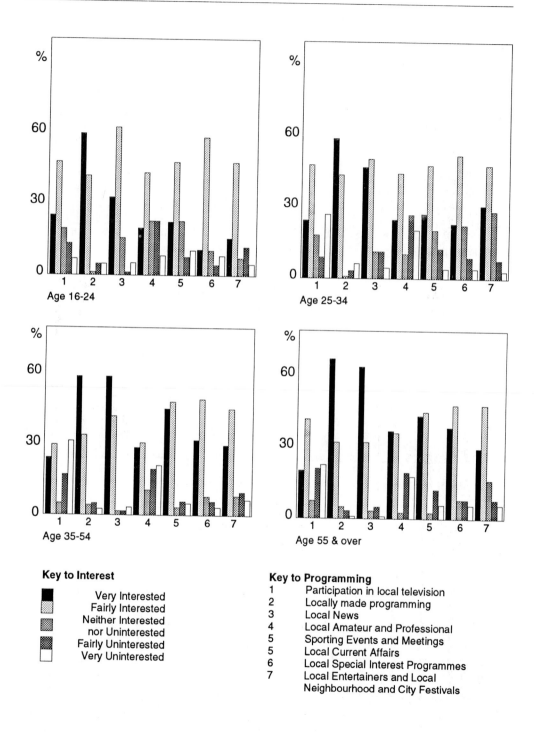

Key to Interest

- ■ Very Interested
- ▨ Fairly Interested
- ▨ Neither Interested nor Uninterested
- ▨ Fairly Uninterested
- ☐ Very Uninterested

Key to Programming

1 Participation in local television
2 Locally made programming
3 Local News
4 Local Amateur and Professional Sporting Events and Meetings
5 Local Current Affairs
6 Local Special Interest Programmes
7 Local Entertainers and Local Neighbourhood and City Festivals

*FIGURE 17: Interest in local television by **Age** (n = 240)*

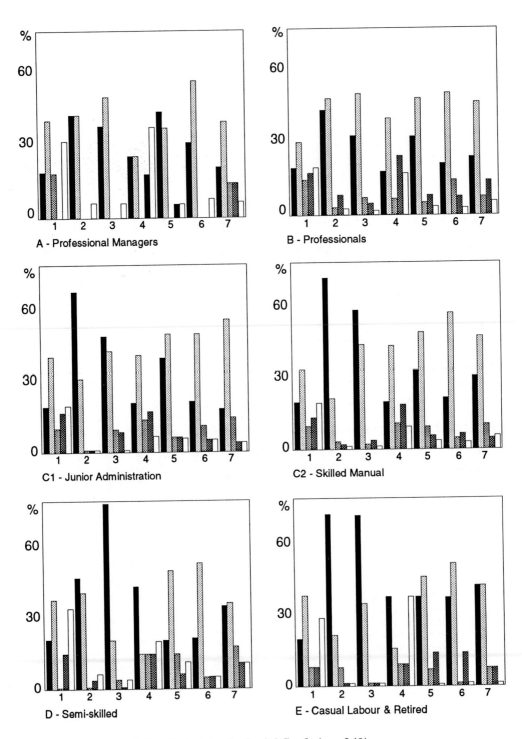

FIGURE 18: Interest in local television by **Social Grade** (n = 240)

8.5 Generic Channels

Figure 20 (see page 34) shows the levels of interest in different types of cable television channels.

8.6 Forecast of Satellite Television Penetration in Edinburgh

Figure 21 (see page 34) shows the likelihood of buying or renting equipment necessary to receive satellite TV in the next 3 years. From this figure one can infer that satellite television is not an immediate threat to cable television.

8.7 Interest in Cable TV among VCR Owners

Video Cassette Recorders (VCRs) have been of central interest to studies relating to cable TV, because VCR owners have already actively taken steps to extend the facilities afforded by standard TV. They can do this either by time-shift viewing, by storing TV programmes for multiple use, or by renting or buying pre-recorded films and other programmes. The VCR is a TV-related commodity which has an identifiable significant extra cost – either through monthly rentals or the funding of an outright purchase.

Figure 22 (see page 35) compares the interest in subscribing to cable TV among those who own/rent VCRs with those who don't. It can be seen that VCRs don't present a threat to the interest in cable TV. Table 22 cross-tabulates those who own or rent VCRs with the discriminators Age, Social Grade and ACORN Group and notes overall possession of VCRs. Table 22 also contrasts this information with the research carried out by CACI/AGB who were commissioned by Cablevision (Scotland) in 1983. [13]

		Edinburgh Television Study (1989) %	Cablevision (Scotland) Study (1985) %
AGE	16-34	74	44
	35-54	90	40
	55+	45	12
SOCIAL GRADE	AB	72	23
	C1	70	30
	C2	84	51
	D	78	29
	E	43	8
ACORN GROUP	B	92	44
	C	75	49
	D	50	20
	E	91	36
	F	63	26
	G	84	39
	H	75	-
	I	54	16
	J	68	26
	K	65	32

TABLE 22: Cross-tabulation of those who own a VCR with the discriminators Age, Social Grade and ACORN Group (n=240)

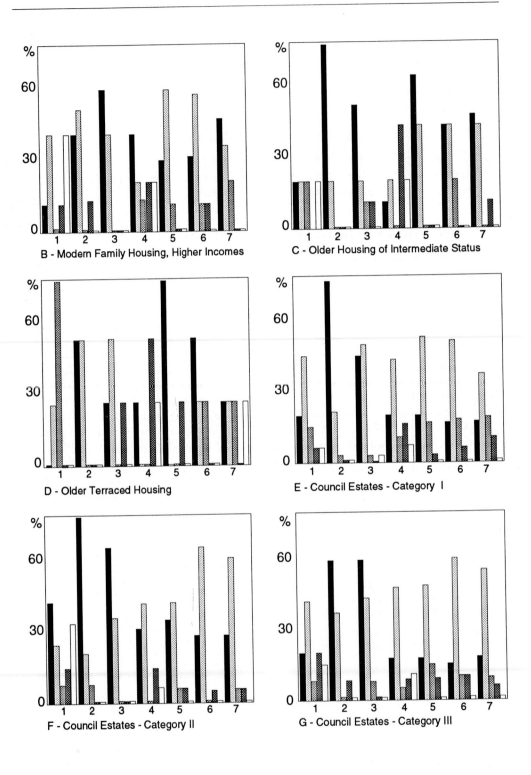

B - Modern Family Housing, Higher Incomes

C - Older Housing of Intermediate Status

D - Older Terraced Housing

E - Council Estates - Category I

F - Council Estates - Category II

G - Council Estates - Category III

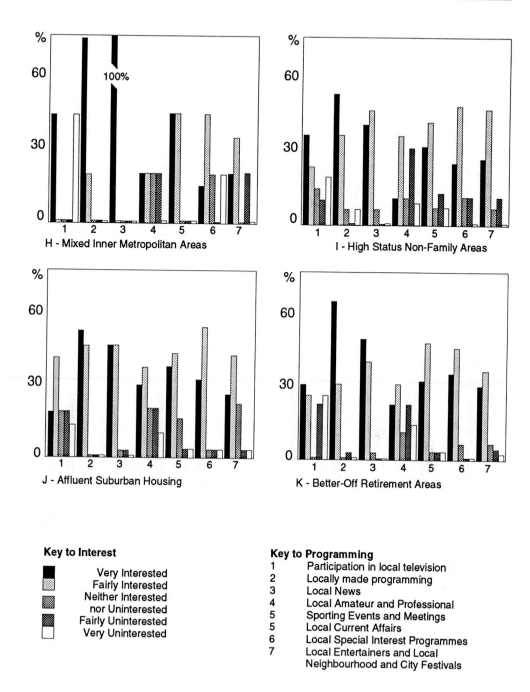

Key to Interest

■ Very Interested
▨ Fairly Interested
▦ Neither Interested
nor Uninterested
▩ Fairly Uninterested
☐ Very Uninterested

Key to Programming

1   Participation in local television
2   Locally made programming
3   Local News
4   Local Amateur and Professional
5   Sporting Events and Meetings
5   Local Current Affairs
6   Local Special Interest Programmes
7   Local Entertainers and Local
Neighbourhood and City Festivals

*FIGURE 19: Interest in local television by **ACORN** Group (n = 240)*

9. Limitations

9.1 Sampling Errors

Although the sample chosen was not strictly a probability sample for reasons explained elsewhere the author is going to side for the purposes of this section with those researchers who argue that quota sampling methods have so improved that it is in order to calculate the standard error on the same lines as for random sampling. The author defends this position from knowledge of how the sample was arrived at and the intelligent manner in which the interviewers carried out the surveys.

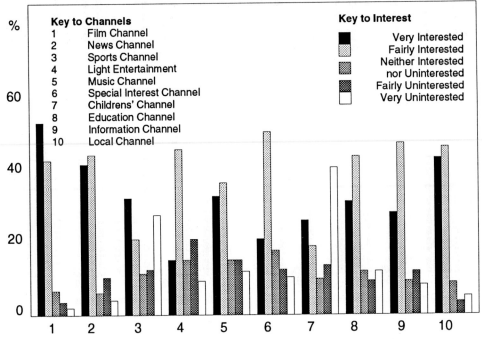

FIGURE 20: Interest in different types of Cable Television Channels (n=152)

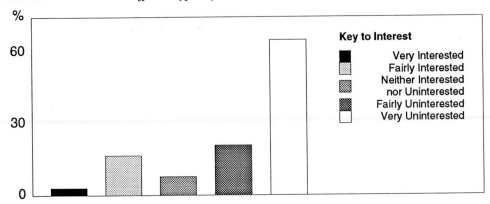

FIGURE 21: Likelihood of buying satellite television in the next three years (n=240)

Sampling error depends on three factors. First, the variability of the characteristic under study in the population – and in this case because the entire population of a city is being surveyed one can assume that there is a high variability in many of the variables under study. Second the size of the sample selected: the larger the sample the smaller the sampling error. In the case of this study it has been shown that the sample size is near the minimum accepted by the industry. The third factor influencing the amount of the sampling error is the sample design. The author has tried to minimise this by commissioning a reputable market analysis company to provide the address list for each sample point. The author however did experience some problems with the ACORN method of segmentation. In one area surveyed the area was quite definitely two distinct types of housing with different types of occupants. This was a severe example. In other areas there were large spacious detached houses, at the beginning of a street leading off a major road. In former times this would have been a cul de sac leading into pastureland. Now the areas have been typically built up with local authority housing.

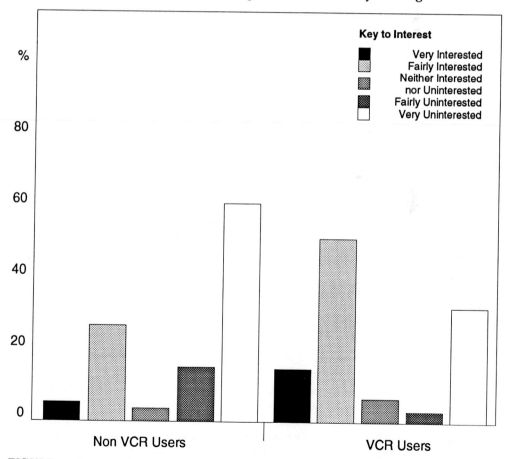

FIGURE 22: Interest in cable TV by those not using and those using VCRs.

9.2 Bias

Although it has been argued that the sample chosen could be described as a probability sample, it is worthwhile to comment on the bias that could have been introduced into the selection process. The first bias arises from the observation that as most interviewing took place during the day between Monday and Friday there would be a bias towards men who work shifts. For example the author interviewed at least three off-duty policemen out of 100 respondents. Another bias is the non-response factor. A strict check on non-response was not kept by any of the interviewers (this was an oversight on the author's part). However, the interviewers estimate that the non-response rate was around 10%. This is quite low by market research standards (20% is the industry norm). However, this can be explained by the manner in which the interviewers introduced themselves to the respondents. The University of Edinburgh was included in all introductions as were statements about doing market research for local television. The author identified a certain degree of anger and jealousy among some respondents over the fact that BBC Scotland's headquarters and main studio and production facilities are located in Glasgow and the ITV regional station STV is also based in Glasgow. It is estimated that a reasonable proportion of the 10% non-response was due to calling at an inconvenient time.

The most common method of assessing bias in the sample is to compare known population characteristics with those of the achieved sample. This has been done and is included in the section on research findings.

9.3 Specific Problems of Quota Sampling

Research by Moser and Stuart [14] on the representativeness of quota sampling methods has shown them in the past to be unrepresentative in two major factors, occupation and education. There was a definite tendency for interviewers to interview too high a proportion of better educated people. In addition, there was some bias evident in the occupations of respondents obtained by quota methods, a smaller proportion of respondents in manufacturing were interviewed when compared to known population figures. In both these cases if there was a similar bias in the Edinburgh study it would indicate that the percentage interested in cable is likely to be larger than the lowest estimate provided by this study because traditionally AB social grades are not heavy TV users and manufacturing is a relatively small business sector in Edinburgh.

Another problem of quota sampling lies in the marked tendency for interviewers, even when experienced, to select distinctly different samples. This variability is not present in random sampling. It would seem that interviewers may, consciously or otherwise, avoid certain districts or types of people because of personal dislikes. However this problem will be small in this study because ACORN has been used to segment the population. Quota sampling is easily frustrated by the interviewers' pattern of work; at different times of the day samples of the same size may be quite dissimilar. It may also suffer from the bad spacing of calls, when interviewers fill up their quotas as quickly as possible by calling at the nearest house in a street or targeting only those households where there are toys lying on the ground outside. These dangers have been minimised in this study by careful recruitment of alert, intelligent and trustworthy individuals.

10.   Presentation to Economic Development Officers in Local Government

An oral presentation of the results of this market research will be given to a gathering of Officers from a number of Local Authorities throughout the UK in order to promote what may become known as the 'Edinburgh Model' for developing local television.

11.   Conclusions

11.1   Forecast of Cable TV Penetration in Edinburgh

It has been shown in section 8.3.4 that the forecast population penetration for the all-in package selling at £22 is between 7% and 15% at 95% confidence limits. This upper bound penetration, however, will only be realised if the 'fairly likelys' are converted to 'very likelys' by extensive marketing of the product. The lower bound penetration of the population could, by inspection, be zero at this price level.

Similarly the forecast population penetration for the basic package selling at £7 per month is between 45% and 51% at 95% confidence limits. Again this upper bound penetration, however, will only be realised if the 'fairly likelys' are converted to 'very likelys' by extensive marketing of the product. The lower bound penetration of the population would be between 29% and 35% at 95% confidence limits.

The 'typical' package bought from cable stations is a basic package (although excluding the five 'must carry' BSB Channels, for they are not commencing broadcast services until the Spring of 1990) plus a number of premium channels at a per channel rate. This 'typical' package currently sells for an average of £17 to UK cable subscribers. The forecast population penetration for this type of package is therefore, by inspection, between 7% and 51% depending on the choice of premium channels offered and their cost. This is an upper bound estimate which again will only be realised if the 'fairly likelys' are converted to 'very likelys' by extensive marketing of the product.

Table 23 shows Cablevision (Scotland)'s penetration rate and basic service charge for the first decade of operations 4. This basic service includes a film channel (carried by some operators as a premium service).

Comparing the information in Table 23 (overleaf) with the forecast population penetration figures from this market research study it can be postulated that Cablevision (Scotland)'s estimated penetration is high for the purposes of a Business Plan and conservative financial planning.

11.2   Forecast of Interest in Local Television

11.2.1 Participating in Local Television

From Figure 11, 56% of respondents were interested in helping with the making or

	Year									
	1	2	3	4	5	6	7	8	9	10
Basic Service Penetration (%)	25	30	35	37	39	40	40	41	41	41
Charge for Basic Service, ex VAT, in money of the day	£15.50	15.50	17.09	17.95	18.84	19.78	20.77	21.81	22.90	24.05

TABLE 23: *Cablevision (Scotland)'s Estimated Penetration Rate and Basic Service Charge*

appearing in a programme where its content was associated with an interest of theirs.

11.2.3 Watching Local Television

From Figure 10, 93% of respondents were interested in watching a locally made programme about one of their interests.

11.2.3 Interest in Different Types of Programming

Local News

From Figure 12, 92% of respondents were interested in watching Local News on a local television channel.

Local Amateur and Professional Sporting Events and Meetings

From Figure 13, 60% of respondents were interested in watching Local Amateur and Professional Sporting Events and Meetings on a local television channel.

Local Current Affairs

From Figure 14, 80% of respondents were interested in watching Local Current Affairs on a local television channel.

Local Special Interest Programmes

From Figure 15, 81% of respondents were interested in watching Local Special Interest Programmes on a local television channel.

Local Entertainers

From Figure 16, 75% of respondents were interested in watching local entertainers and Local Neighbourhood and City Festivals on a local television channel

11.3 Demand Prices

11.3.1 Basic Package

From Table 13, 44% of respondents said they would be very likely or fairly likely to pay £8 for a basic package. This is about the market rate for a basic package.

11.3.2 All-in Package

From Table 17, 19% of respondents said they would be very likely or fairly likely to pay £20 for an all-in package. The Market price for an all-in package is around £25.

11.4 Forecast of Demand for a Range of Channels

From Figure 22, it can be seen that in Edinburgh in general there is a high demand for most types of channels available on the market. There is less interest, however, in a Sports Channel and a Children's Channel.

11.5 Interest in Cable TV According to Various Discriminators

11.5.1 Age

From Figure 7, the highest interest for cable TV lies in the 25-34 age group.

11.5.2 ACORN

From Figure 9, the highest interest for cable TV lies in ACORN groups Higher Income, Modern Family Housing and in categories I, II and III of Council Estates.

11.5.3 Social Grade

From Figure 8, the highest interest for cable TV is among the Cl, C2 social grades.

11.5.4 VCR Owners

From Figure 22, there is a significantly higher level of interest in cable TV among users of VCRs than among non-users.

11.6 Satellite TV Penetration

From Figure 21, 78% of respondents were unlikely to buy satellite television in the next 3 years.

References

1. *Broadcasting in the '90s: Competition, Choice and Quality*, HMSO, London, 1988.

2. *New Media Markets*, Financial Times Newsletters, 21st June, 1989.

3. *What is local television?*, Edinburgh Television No 1, TU/TV Ltd, Edinburgh, 1989.

4. A R Wilson, *Cable Television in Edinburgh: an appraisal*, unpublished MBA Dissertation, University of Edinburgh, 1986.

5. *Social Grading in the National Readership Survey*, JICNARS, 1985.

6. G A Churchill, *Marketing Research*, Dryden Press, Chicago, 1987.

7. P M Chisnall, *Marketing Research*, McGraw-Hill, London, 1986.

8. G Hoinville & R Jowell, *Survey Research Practise*, Gower, Aldershot, 1985.

9. C A Moser & G Katton, *Survey Methods in Social Investigation*, Gower, Aldershot, 1985.

10. Ibid, 6.

11. *Interviewers' Manual*, Social Community Planning Research, London, 1984.

12. W M Harper, *Statistics*, Pitman, London, 1988.

13. Two page extract from *Research Report on Cable TV in Edinburgh* carried out by CACI/AGB in 1985 on behalf of Cablevision (Scotland).

14. C A Moser & A Stuart, *An experimental study of quota sampling*, Journal of the Royal Statistical Society, Vol 116 Pt V, 1953.

2   Cable Company Franchise Commitments

Adrian Friedli, Institute of Local Television, January 1991

1.   Introduction

In the first Annual 'Worldview Address' at the Edinburgh International Television Festival in 1990, Steven J Ross, the Chairman of Time-Warner Inc the world's largest media and entertainment conglomerate, chose to highlight the potential which advances in media technologies offer for increasing the global reach of communications systems. He concluded by suggesting that:

> We are fast approaching that era envisioned at the dawn of the cable
> industry, some twenty years ago, when television – indeed, all video
> information – would be characterised by abundance, rather than scarcity.

One of the opportunities which this increased capacity has opened up is the potential for cable systems to cater to both global and local demand. Indeed, Ross specifically identified cable operators as being well placed to grasp consumer demand, as a result of being in 'such close touch' with the community served. But are they in close touch?

An emphasis on the importance of a close relationship with local communities forms a significant part of all the successful applications for cable franchises in Britain. The point is well made in North Estuary Cable's application for the Thames Estuary North area:

> While local programming is perceived to be of value by a relatively small
> segment of the cable system's subscribers, those who watch and partici-
> pate consider local programming highly valuable and a strong motivation
> for continuing as subscribers.

This experience draws on North Estuary Cable's parent company United Cable in America. It highlights a dilemma which faces cable operators with local programming.

If such programmes do only attract a relatively small audience then advertisers are unlikely to be keen to underwrite their production. However, in the absence of local programming production there is no unique service to attract the audience, and the distinctive relationship between the cable operator and the local community becomes lost.

Perhaps mindful of the detailed requirements made on behalf of local programming under Section 7 of the 1984 Cable and Broadcasting Act (see Appendix One) – that operators include 'programmes calculated to appeal specifically to the taste and outlook of persons living in the area' – none of the successful franchise applicants has avoided altogether local commitments. However, there are a wide variety of approaches made by the applicants to this commitment.

Without scrutinising the public documents provided by all the successful applicants it is not possible for individual local authorities or their communities to understand the range of options provided for local television in different areas.

There is a very real danger that if the local responsibilities of the 1984 Act are left solely to the interpretation of the cable operator they will provide an inconsistent and uneven service to different communities across the country. Should the cable operators – largely US telecoms and cable operators often with US managers – decide what will appeal to the people of each city? If national rather than local regulation is to be favoured then its benefit must be a consistent standard of service locally available.

Yet very different interpretations of the legislation have arisen among the cable companies. The Cable Authority supervising the Cable and Broadcasting Act 1984 has not offered clear guidelines. In this situation, local authorities and other interested local organisations are left to turn to the cable company franchise applications as a guide to local services they should expect to see from each cable company.

The Independent Television Commission has replaced the Cable Authority and continues not to ensure the provision of local services. Many of the US companies cabling Britain provide local services under statutes favouring the community throughout North America. In Canada a local service appears to be generally accepted as a central plank of cable development. In Europe cabled communities often receive a range of independently produced and edited local services distributed by their local cable operators. [1]

2.   How 'local' is local?

The purpose of this study is to provide a guide to those written commitments to local services made by the successful franchise applicants. It is based on a survey of the 119 public documents lodged by successful cable operators with the Cable Authority/ITC, otherwise only available individually at central libraries in every cabled town or city. (There are 18 franchises for which no public documents are provided. The missing paperwork mostly relates to the early franchises where both the public and confidential parts of the application were bundled together and not published for reasons of business confidentiality.) The list of cities for which cable franchises have been awarded appears as Appendix Four.

While all cable operators claim to be committed to the community they serve, and to providing programming by and about that community, some seem more willing than others to resource their commitments and to provide a timetable for implementing those services.

The first thing which is immediately apparent when looking at successful applications is that there are a significant number of identical public submissions forming part of franchise applications for a number of different areas.

Nearly 10% of all franchises have been awarded to companies which have submitted *virtually the same application*. In such circumstances, should we be wary of cable company commitments to their local communities? The acceptance by the Cable Authority of applicants who adopt this strategy, changing the town map and name, suggests an indifferent if not entirely cynical value attached to local involvement anticipated by the legislation as a precondition and influence upon awarding a franchise.

Stafford Communications Ltd claim in their application for the Stafford area that:

> Stafford Communications has been set up specifically to operate a cable network within the Stafford/Stone area and it is imperative that the company becomes integrated with all aspects of the local community.

However, an identical application was made for the Harlow/Bishop's Stortford/Stanstead area by Stort Valley Cable. There are identical applications by Maclean Hunter for the Cheshire North, Colchester & Ipswich, Devon South, Lancashire East and Stoke areas, despite each being made under a different name. There are numerous other examples.

What will appear in the public library of each cable town, has been presented to the community as a unique and locally relevant set of options and solutions to the local delivery of television. Clearly, this is largely a false impression, but not one that the Cable Authority or the Independent Television Commission has sought to discourage. Has cable arrived on each city's doorsteps on false pretences? Only the Cable Authority, now the ITC, and each applicant know the full extent of the financial commitments attached to the statements made about local training and community programme support. If the only original feature in many applications is the area's name and map then repeated references to 'community' should be regarded with some suspicion.

2.1   Community

It is worth noting that 'community' is rich in associations but is also notoriously elusive of attempts at a more precise definition.

It is helpful, therefore, that the most frequently repeated use of 'community' in cable applications should be highlighted in an attempt to guide our understanding of the term. For example from Cablevision Bedfordshire's application for the Luton and Dunstable area:

> The term community is used in the following senses:
>
>> Communities of Interest
>> Cultural and Ethnic Communities
>> Neighbourhood Communities

As will be clear from this definition, each geographical area is likely to have a number of different 'communities', each with legitimate demands to be represented on a community channel. Indeed, it may be necessary for the cable operator to provide a number of community channels to adequately service the particular demands of its locality. For example, Cable London in the Camden area has made special provision for the business community based in the City of London, while also supplying programming for the significant Greek community in its franchise.

2.1.2 Individual Access

Another term which is open to wide interpretation is 'access'. The different responses to 'access' among franchise applicants suggest that without some central guidance different interpretations are likely to lead to an inequality of service in different parts of the country. The motivation for attention to this feature of cable provision is also to be found in the demands of Section 7 of the 1984 Cable and Broadcasting Act, namely that the cable operator include programmes in which persons living in the area 'are given an opportunity to participate'.

One response to participation is the provision of a videobox [2] along the lines of the Channel Four model, and used in a programme format made up of a combination of Channel Four's *Right to Reply* and the BBC's *Points of View*. About 15% of applications surveyed offered such a service. In three areas, Southampton, Stafford and Harlow, the videobox represented the sole form of 'access', and in the case of Stafford and Harlow, which do not produce their own programming, this amounted to a significant proportion of their expected local output. Obviously, 'participation' under such a restricted interpretation is limited to the person contributing their ideas in a format and at a location decided by the cable operator. Although the Southampton application suggests the videobox will be used to 'generate a wealth of ideas for community programmes' there is no clear sense of any further participation by the local person in the resulting community programme which might be derived from his or her contribution.

2.1.3 Participation

A more extended view of participation is evident in proposals for areas where the videobox is supplemented by some training in a studio environment, with training as the key to access to production facilities for the making of programming about and from the community. However, this more ambitious approach in such areas as Peterborough, Norwich and Harpenden has to be set against an indication by the companies in these areas that such a policy requires 'a co-operative venture with other local media operators' in order to introduce the service in the short term. No precise time scales are supplied, but it is acknowledged that local programming will, at least initially, have to be in the form of a text information channel.

2.1.4 Programme Access

Another common use of the term 'access' is to provide air-time for programming already generated by accredited local organisations. This is an option among 20% of the applicants examined. Clearly, this would preclude individuals and organisations without the necessary finance or skills to produce their own programming. This 'access' would seem to privilege the existing local production community, an inference borne out by Sheffield Cable Media's opinion that while it is 'willing to help local people with developing television production skills', it is nonetheless 'expected to be appropriate to use and build on the considerable skills already available in Sheffield'.

While the existing independent production community is one perfectly legitimate community of interest for which to cater, one might argue that this is also a limited interpretation of how to enable local people to participate in the programming on their local cable network.

Perhaps the vaguest commitment to access is provided in Mid Downs Cable's application for the Crawley area, where it states that:

> Historically, Public Access has been a difficult service to develop in a meaningful fashion, particularly in small systems; thus at this stage the company can only allocate the channel space whilst discussing the best use of this facility with interested parties.

Yet N-Com Cablevision seems to take the opposite line in its application for the Burton-on-Trent area. It argues that its experience of promoting local channels in communities with as few as 1,600 subscribers has confirmed that a local channel 'can be an effective tool and resource for the community.' Accordingly, it will make at least one channel available for locally produced material, and supply 'suitable equipment' with which to realise this, such as cameras and editing equipment and initially a 'portable studio'. This will be supplemented by a text generator in order to provide a community notice board. Finally, the commitment will be backed-up by staff specifically trained to actively encourage local 'involvement and participation' in the Community Channel.

All of which appears considerably more ambitious than Mid Downs Cable's willingness to offer some channel space and hold out the possibility of a chat in future. Both companies have the same access to their communities and the same opportunities to exploit their monopoly over the local delivery of television and their public utility advantages!

The most eloquent advocates of the potential for community access are from the Canadian companies Videotron, in their application for the Wandsworth area, and Maclean Hunter in their five applications.

Both companies highlight the possibility of converting passive viewers into active participants in the production of programmes. Videotron makes an important observation in relation to training, based on its study of the first community television station, Swindon Viewpoint. It argues:

Several important factors have emerged – members of the public who express an interest but are unfamiliar with television equipment need to be motivated, trained and assisted to produce their own programmes on a regular basis.

To this end Videotron established a community television scheme with the intention of generating a 'comprehensive local service of three to four hours of original programming each week'.

Maclean Hunter in its application for the Exeter area lays stress on the provision of training workshops and user-friendly equipment to enable as wide a participation as possible. Maclean Hunter also give an undertaking that the three major towns in the Exeter area will each have their own 'studio, outside broadcast vehicle and production equipment', together with the necessary technically trained staff. The clear implication from both these examples is that Community Channels require a significant long term commitment of both time and resources, and these will not come about simply because a slot is allocated in the schedule for access programming. Access is something which entails more than just talking.

That said, there are a couple of qualifications that raise doubts as to the quality of local programming provision by both Videotron and Maclean Hunter. Firstly, it is very difficult to discover a time scale for implementing these developments in the Maclean Hunter application. 'Community television facilities will be built' and 'training workshops will be offered', but there is no indication of when, nor whether these facilities are intended to come on stream at the same time, or whether there will be a gradual phasing-in process, and if so, what will be on the screens in the meantime.

2.2   Quality and Editorial Controls

An important general doubt about all the applications, including the Videotron proposal, concerns the questions of quality and editorial control. Videotron, is saying that it wants the comprehensive local service to realise three to four hours programming a week, and the application goes on to say that this should be achieved 'utilising comparatively limited technical, financial and staff resources'. It is difficult not to conclude that community is being equated with 'cheap television'. This view is given greater weight as the application continues:

> We are, however, aware that production standards may be to a certain extent lower than that of normal broadcasting but feel that its local relevance and consequent high local interest value will compensate for this.

The opposite conclusion is reached in Cable London's application for the Haringey area, which states that:

> Television presentation has come to mean a certain standard of professionalism, and few viewers will accept amateur productions, even with a community bias.

This point was endorsed on Channel Four's *The Media Show* of 28th October 1990 which looked at the impact of new technologies on various aspects of the media. Part of the programme was devoted to the highly successful *TV Viva* community television station in Brazil, which attributed a large part of its popularity to the high production standards it adhered to. Without these, a spokesman argued, *TV Viva* would never have retained its audience in the face of competition from the national networks.

The point is not to create a fetish out of professionalism, which is already sufficiently mythologised, rather it is simply that local television will take for granted the same production standards as broadcast television: why would it do anything else? This, presumes that there will be a sufficient level of resourcing as part of the local bargain for access to e ach city, without good resourcing production standards will be 'to a certain extent lower than that of normal broadcasting'. This becomes something of a self-fulfilling prophecy.

The question of who should control local and community television programming is raised by Videotron. Videotron states that the conditions of the 1984 Cable and Broadcasting Act require it to assume editorial control over community produced programming. Indeed, a little over 10% of the applications assume a similar position, with a number of others signalling the presence of a local advisory board before which such matters would be resolved.

Retaining editorial responsibility by the cable operator for local programming is taken a stage further in Southdown Cablevision's application for the Brighton area. Southdown emphasises that it will 'maintain the right to impose restrictions upon programming, to ensure that the Company's quality standards will be upheld'. This last statement makes explicit what is elsewhere more often implied by way of control arising from misguided evocations of the Cable and Broadcasting Act. Cable company control of local television could arguably be the very reason quality is so often poor and most often programming is non-existent.

The cable operators are no more liable under the Cable and Broadcasting Act for local channels than – in practice – they are for any of the other cable channels they carry. Nowhere do we see a suggestion that cable operators are seeking to retain editorial control over Bravo's material, over Indra Dhnush or Sky or MTV's output. Could this be because the cable operators presume that only the community programming is going to be editorially sub-standard or even critical or irresponsible? What possible justification is there for such a position? Is it not in the cable operator's hands to provide a quality service which embraces a fuller social dynamic than regional or national television? Or is it simply too expensive to do so when the obligations are not controlled as a condition of the franchise? [The new Licensable Programme Services Licence which comes into effect with the 1990 Broadcasting Act places the legal responsibility for programming on the channel provider rather than on the cable operator. This removes the last vestiges of the requirement for cable operators to retain editorial privilege on the basis of legal obligation.]

It is worth repeating that there is nothing in the Cable and Broadcasting Act of 1984 which suggests or implies that locally produced television should be anything other than of the same production and editorial standards as national network television. Access is not meant to be an inferior form of communication but an exchange between community and cable operator for which the cable company benefits by accessing the city streets and buildings and the community given rights to make their own programming. The equality of this exchange when implemented entirely on a voluntary basis by the cable companies is cause for grave public and political concern. The provision of a broadcasting space for programming for and from the local community is expected of the cable company in law. Attempts to marginalise this service by assuming that poorer quality will arise or can only be provided undermines the intention of the legislation and make local television the victim of cable company parsimony and regulator collusion. The Cable Authority and since 1990 the ITC has preferred not to establish a standard for community programming consistent with the intention and detail of the Act. It was expected as a matter of course that cable delivery over small areas would give the cable communities their own distinctive service but when this has not happened this failure has been overlooked rather than resolved to the satisfaction of the communities.

3.   On a scale from 1 to 10?

One of the problems in assessing the local provisions made in applications for cable franchises is that they are tremendously vague. Vague about the number of local channels offered; vague about the facilities to be made available and particularly vague about the time-scale for bringing them about. Many applications indicate that local programming will be introduced when 'subscription increases' or 'as the system grows'. These expectations are the norm.

In a business where investments of £50m upwards are being put on the line in competition with DTH satellite and terrestrial television only a few companies are prepared to talk with any seriousness about the unique television service which cable has to offer: the local television service and its accountability to the local communities it is intended to serve.

Possibly the most detailed example appears in the application from Cambridge Cable for the Cambridge franchise.

The Cambridge Example

The application gives a detailed breakdown of the funding to be allocated to local programming. From a basic £150,000 per annum promotional budget, £100,000 is earmarked as a subsidy for local programming:

> ...on the grounds that this would be both an extension of the network's promotional activities and a pump-primer for what should eventually become a larger and more sophisticated service.

To this figure is added a revenue component of £1 per subscription per month, such that the local channel income in year one, as the network passes 12,000 homes with a projected 18% take-up, is £57,684. By the end of year two this figure has risen to £142,462 with the network passing an additional 18,000 homes, and achieving an additional 18% take-up.

Cambridge Cable does not envisage providing its own studio facilities in the immediate future. Instead it is seeking a time-share arrangement with a local AV training studio. In order to undertake and oversee the locally-based production work Cambridge Cable has enlisted the cooperation of Cambridge Video Unit.

Within the first few years Cambridge Cable believes it unlikely that full-time, fully-professional local programming will be feasible, so an infrastructure will be built up slowly through an access TV service run by local people and groups to ensure that potential is later realised. Cambridge Cable undertakes, in conjunction with a local AV training studio, to run training programmes for the community. They intend to train 200 people, to a level at which they can run a three-camera studio and production suite, in the 12 months prior to launch.

Cambridge Cable will rely to some extent on local AV studios for production facilities, but it is undertaking to spend £35,000 on a small portable TV studio, and a further £7,000 on a van to house it, thereby providing a remote edit suite and a semi-permanent studio at the company's head-end.

Fortunately, this is not an isolated application. There are a few other companies committed to offer a good range of facilities, both for production and training. However, Cambridge Cable has the merit of giving definite figures in respect of both funding and subscriber levels. This raises the obvious question: why not the rest and why were concrete local commitments not made obligatory when they failed to materialise voluntarily?

The Hackney Example

This outline (see Figure 1 overleaf) formed part of Cable London's application for the Hackney area and sets out in schematic form the progressive introduction of services. Such time-tabling is rarely disclosed in other applications. But a similar approach is also indicated in City Centre Cable's attitude towards local and community programming in the Hammersmith area:

> We see this starting with text services, evolving into interactive text, and later developing into fully-fledged productions made with the help of community groups.

The logic behind this approach is more clearly evident in Britannia Cable Systems' application for the Portsmouth area:

> Community programming will be a modest element of the Portsmouth area cable television system at the beginning. The development of an audience for community programming will, as a matter of necessity, have to await the construction and marketing of the cable system.

In order to allow for this course of events Britannia Cable Systems describe a two-phase local service.

Condition	Service	Requirements
10,000 + homes passed	Rolling text	Low investment
		Manpower requirements small
50% + build with	Some programmes	Some camera equipment and
growing sales and good		availability of editing. Established
research from programmes		training scheme
already shown		
80-100% build and clear	A pattern of programmes	Infrastructure in place.
proof of retention of		Trained pool of effort.
trained skills within area	Regular programmes	Studio and associated
Full build and		overhead established
penetration with	Daily schedule	Expansion of facilities
evidence of static or		
reducing churn		
	Special events	OB capability
As and when		
opportunities arise		
	Programmes sales/exchange	Sales/marketing
		structure
At a future time		
should the right mix		
of opportunity and	Technically complex	Innovation skills and
requisite skills arise	programminginvestment	

FIGURE 1: The Hackney Example

The first, operational from the outset, is predominantly text-based, with occasional video commissions 'to draw attention to the potential of the cable television media and to encourage future sponsorships.' (It will be noted that this is precisely the rationale which convinced N-Com Cablevision to commit itself to a community channel (apparently) straight away.)

The second phase for the Portsmouth franchise will commence after 16 months when Britannia Cable Systems feels it will have attracted the 11,400 subscribers thought to constitute a sufficient subscriber base for 'community television with fuller support'.

The ratio of 11,400 subscribers to a potential audience of 150,000 (less than 10%) is fairly typical of other (available) figures at which local services are expected to start. The figure of 5,000 subscribers passed out of a potential of 465,000 households in the case of the Birmingham Cable application for the Birmingham area is a major exception. Hackney's 10,000 is out of a potential of 150,000 subscribers, while Cambridge's first year figure of 12,000 is in relation to a total of 140,000 homes in the franchise.

An example of a three-phase local programme development appears in Cable Communications' application for the Wigan and St. Helens areas.

The St. Helens and Wigan Example

The first stage in both areas is activated as the system is turned on with the appearance of a text channel generated by the computer, supplying photo quality pictures combined with messages. Monitors are installed in public places to ensure wide exposure.

The second stage is launched in both cases once 10,000 subscribers are connected to the system – for St. Helens from a franchise of 100,000 homes, for Wigan from a franchise of 110,000 homes. In each case this stage marks the launch of a channel comprising video programmes made and supplied by community groups. Training courses are offered, with the appointment of a coordinator to oversee programme production. Indeed, Cable Communications has appointed a Group Community Producer to preside over community programming throughout all of Cable Communications' franchises.

The third stage sees the establishment of a 'fully fledged professionally produced local channel, developed in conjunction with established TV and video production companies' in each location. It is estimated that this third stage would come on line in the case of St. Helens in the fifth year of the franchise.

Wigan and St. Helens are also part of another trend evident in cable applications, namely the creation of groups of franchises owned by the same operator, most often in close proximity to each other. In the case of Wigan and St. Helens this is Cable Communications, 17% owned by Owen Oyston and 80% by Southwestern Bell. The logic behind this approach is set out by Cable London in declaring their aim to set up a 'North London Channel' by combining its areas – see notes on 47. Haringey and 82. Hackney, below.

4.   Conclusion

All successful franchise applicants offer to provide some form of text service, and at the very least the capability of developing interactive services once they are more widely available. From there, approaches to local programming diverge markedly, with three broad groups becoming apparent.

Group One

Those applications for which there was virtually no evidence to substantiate their pledges of commitment to local provision. Therefore, while Andover Cablevision claims it is 'highly committed to the development of the Local Channel' in its application for the Andover area, all that can be found to support this is a vague offer to 'make available some audio-visual equipment to assist local residents in producing their own programmes' but no mention of training. Equally discouraging is Southdown Cablevision's intention to charge for facilities described under the public access section, and then to insist on the right to impose restrictions if they feel the material produced is beneath their 'pre-defined standard'. Whatever else such an approach achieves, it would seem difficult to understand it to be encouraging participation. Under 5% of the applications surveyed required some form of payment for the use of facilities to make community programmes.

Group Two

The second group divides into two, but broadly follows a phased development approach. This either takes the form of waiting for subscriber numbers to reach sufficient mass to sustain an expansion from the original text channel, or finds cable operators seeking to collaborate with existing media concerns – frequently local radio or newspapers – to accelerate that process. An example of the former approach is taken by Cable Communications and Britannia Cable, and the latter approach by Leicester Communications' successful collaboration with Q Studios, Leicester Sound and the City Council for the Leicester area.

Group Three

Finally, there are those operators prepared to make a substantial commitment to resourcing the local channel in advance so that it is in a position to provide access and local programming almost immediately. The obvious example here is Maclean Hunter.

While it is true that Maclean Hunter's applications do not give any clear indications as to timetable for the phasing-in of facilities, the important point is that there is a firm undertaking to provide a certain level of resources. If an operator says in their application that they are going to supply something, and specific reference is made to facilities and levels of resourcing, the operator should be encouraged for being willing to provide a hostage to fortune on behalf of the community by remaining open to being called to uphold this undertaking. If, however, all the operator does is make vague allusions to being committed to the 'idea' of local programming, and the possibility of 'some audio-visual equipment' it is going to be much more difficult as the cabling begins to hold this franchise to such promises.

A false belief circulates and is nourished by the Independent Television Commission's attitude that cable companies offer local services out of the goodness of their hearts. They do not. Despite national centralised regulation which ensures that cable companies have rights of access to the streets and footpaths within each regional Highway's Authority area – and this applies regardless of local demand for cable or concerns for its effects – the expectation of community access to the cable channels to provide local services independently from the cable operator is not enforced. This asymmetry of this form of regulation favouring cable company over community undermines the intention of the 1984 to provide communities with their own television services.

5.   Synopses of Local Commitments

This is an analysis of local programming and local channel intentions from publicly available documents to be found in the successful applications for cable franchises awarded by the Cable Authority between 1985-1990.

Each main town or city library will have on file the public documents for that area's cable franchise. However, the papers can only be found together at the Independent Television Commission who took over cable responsibility from the Cable Authority in 1991. Together they enable a comparison that locally cannot be made.

Franchise applications are detailed here in the order in which they appear in the Cable Authority's listing which was published in their Annual Report for 1989/90 (see Appendix Four). Each franchise will be designated by the number given to the area by the Cable Authority. Several franchise application papers were missing at the ITC when this study was conducted –*missing franchises are evident in the interrupted sequence below.*

The name of each franchise will be followed by a number in brackets **(1)**, **(2) or (3)**, indicating the three classification groups to which we believe the particular application seems to belong. The following summarises the three groups:

> **Group 1** There is virtually no evidence to substantiate the applicant's pledges of commitment to local provision on the local channel/s; there are few, if any, provisions for training and only the vaguest offers are made to provide equipment.

> **Group 2** Generally takes the form of a phased development approach: where the applicant either waits for subscriber numbers to reach sufficient mass to sustain an expansion from the original text channel, or where cable operators seek to collaborate with existing media concerns to accelerate the process.

> **Group 3** There is a firm, substantial commitment to resourcing the local channel in advance, so that it is in a position to generate both access and local programming almost immediately.

The first round of franchises bundled their public and private documents and the first dozen public documents are not available for consultation.

13. Cheltenham (2) Pursues a two-phase approach. Firstly, in collaboration with the local ILR station – Severn Sound – it proposes a 'purpose-built video-television studio', delivering two news magazine programmes and a sports programme each week. Staffing will consist of a programme director and two community access producers, with a commitment made to provide training. Access is defined as 'programming by the community for the community', resulting from 'individuals and groups who have completed workshop training'. Phase two will see the provision of a purpose built two or three camera production and community access studio. This, however, is triggered 'as build-out progresses', and there is no indication as to the numbers required or any time-scale being applied.

At least two text channels will be supplied, again in collaboration with Severn Sound. The company undertakes to carry third party programming for the local channel 'at cost'. Editorial control is not specified.

15. Wandsworth (2) Two stages are suggested. During the first 18 months, two to three hours of local programming will be delivered per day. The second stage is brought on-line 'as subscriptions increase and funds become available' with the 'aim to build up to 5 or 6 hours a day'. An ambitious range of programmes is indicated, with the intention of using both 'local film and video recording studios' and Wandsworth Cable's own studio (though these are not detailed). Community television is seen as the opportunity for the people of the borough to be involved in the making of programmes, the application draws on the experience of the Swindon Viewpoint project and underlines the importance of training. The approach is therefore seen to be a combination of training and expertise, coupled with 'readily accessible video equipment'. In this way, it is claimed, 'members of the community can become active participants in programme production rather than fulfilling their normal role of passive viewers'. There has been a particularly positive response to the community television scheme from the Asian community.

However, while the intention is to deliver a 'comprehensive local service of three to four hours of original programming to be produced each week', this should be achieved 'utilising comparatively limited technical, financial and staff resources'. Combined with the statement that 'production standards may be to a certain extent lower than that of normal broadcasting', although this is seen as being offset to some extent by 'high local interest value', there is a suspicion that community is being equated with 'cheap television'. This reservation is carried over into the description of facilities. While recording equipment (not detailed) and staff are going to be available seven days per week, editing – described as 'this highly technical and complex process' – will probably be handled by a Wandsworth Cable VTR Editor. Furthermore, due to 'obligations under the Cable Act', Wandsworth Cable claims it must 'retain editorial control over community produced programming'. Training ought to take care of the suggested demands of editing, and the invocation of the Cable Act seems only to matter in the case of local programming, again prompting the conclusion that Wandsworth Cable assumes that local television will be of a relatively low standard. A range of text and interactive services are offered.

17. Camden (3) The application highlights the 'large variety of services', and the potential for some of these to be interactive, as the distinguishing characteristic of cable provision. Cable Camden clearly states that it is not a 'programmer', but indicates that it is 'actively examining the possibility of helping' three locally produced programme strands: a quality film channel - in association with a local cinema and a video distributor – a Hellenic Channel for the Greek community produced by Hellenic TV Channel Ltd., and a daily business programme. Community access is seen to 'depend upon the developing relationship between Cable Camden and its community', and where the 'main elements of community programming seem likely to be' text-based local news and advertising, the Hellenic and business programme ventures and a cultural channel are derived from cultural centres in the franchise area. While a potential collaboration with Westminster Cable is mentioned, there is no reference to provision of facilities or training for the production of this material, nor a time-scale in which it is expected to come on-stream. There is a much better defined commitment to the provision of text and interactive services, which may well derive from the applicant's emphasis on 'the special situation of Camden as a business area'.

19. Preston (3) Offers four local channels, three of which are designated as access, the fourth being a professionally produced and presented news channel, delivering a one hour early evening news programme and carrying teletext during the day. Full training will be made available for each of the access channels, with a full-time Community Access Producer giving guidance to groups or individuals participating. The Community Channel would make use of Lancashire Polytechnic's television theatre, but would also have outside broadcast facilities. It would also carry teletext, and the system technology makes possible 'polling' on programmes. The Learning Channel would be a collaboration with Lancashire Polytechnic, with an emphasis on adult education and 'distance' learning. The Ethnic Channel would be a combination of bought-in Asian and Caribbean programming together with locally produced material. It is also 'envisaged' that teletext services in Asian languages will be made available. All four local channels will be available as soon as the operator begins transmission.

20. Southampton (1) Initially, the local channel will be based on British Telecom's Photo Videotex System with programme inserts. In the first year there will be 4.5 hours of locally produced programming per week, 'hopefully' rising to 7 hours during the second year. Ultimately, the intention is to carry programme services on a separate channel, though no deadline is supplied. The nearest the application appears to get to access is the provision of a 'videobox', whereby people could both comment on programmes and raise issues which might form the basis of future programmes. All local programmes would seem to be produced by the operator's own staff with no indication of training or access to facilities for residents in the franchise area.

21. Luton (2) Initially, local programming will be confined to a nightly news bulletin and 'any community access programming which local organisations may wish to produce'. By the second year of operation 'it is expected that the Community Television Trust will become active in local programme production', delivering news and current affairs, arts coverage, a what's-on service, exchange with other cable operators, particularly in twin-towns, and a videobox. There is a commitment to 'encourage and train new producers and production groups who will have access to the production facilities for the production of work relating to their community'. Community is defined as: 'Communities of Interest, Cultural and Ethnic Communities, Neighbourhood Communities'. It is recognised that such an undertaking will require substantial funds, hence the creation of the charitable trust in order to secure outside sources of finance. There will be three text channels – general, sport and leisure, business – and the capability for interactive provision, though the operator is looking for an experienced party with which to collaborate on this aspect of the service.

23. Andover (1) Andover Cablevision is neither a programme maker, nor is it collaborating with any particular programme maker. Initially, the local service will be in the form of text and graphics service, coupled with promotional material about the operator's other services. 'As the system grows'– no figures are offered to quantify this – the system will be 'upgraded' – again no specifics – to enable local people to make their own programming. Andover Cablevision will offer 'every encouragement and assistance' to ensure this service is a success, and proposes to 'make available some audiovisual recording equipment'– no more details than this vague description are supplied – to enable local people to produce programmes themselves. The provisions outlined in the application are not sufficient to support the applicant's claim that Andover Cablevision is 'highly committed to the development of the Local Channel'.

24. Blackburn (2) Three local channels will be made available in the first two years: Community Channel, Text Channel and Ethnic Channel. The Community Channel will start as a studio-based operation, expanding to include community input to pro-gramme generation – no time-scale is given for this, nor details of what the nature of the involvement would be. The independent production facility ICP and Salford University are indicated as potential collaborators for the studio-based production. The Text Channel will be a rolling-page information and bulletin board service, potentially drawing on the resources of the Lancashire Evening Telegraph. It is hoped that the Ethnic Channel would be operative by the end of the first year, with 'early installation to pass 4,000 ethnic minority households'. East Lancashire Cable 'believes it can organise a programme service which meets the interests and conforms to the strict rules on what is acceptable for entertainment and education' in the ethnic groups identified through research by Lancashire County Council. There is no indication of local access to the processes of programme production, nor of training in the techniques and skills of programme making. The application states that 'East Lancashire Cable will ensure that programmes are in good taste and reflect commonly accepted standards of decency'.

25. Birmingham (2) In relation to community access Birmingham Cable Corporation (BCC) state that they 'will provide studio facilities for local community groups to make their own programmes', and training in the use of facilities will also be made available to build up a 'reservoir of skilled programme makers' in the community. BCC, however, will exercise its 'ultimate responsibility for editorial control of programmes distributed to the public', and the extent of programming in this area will 'depend on the developing relationship between the Company and the community'. BCC feel that early indications are positive in this respect, with a wide range of local groups making what BCC describe as 'good and constructive use of this access'. BCC will also provide a local channel once the system has 5,000 subscribers – out of a potential reach of 465,000. The channel will be a joint venture with the local authorities, newspapers, radio stations and production houses.

26. Southend & 27. Gravesend (2) Drawing on its experience in the American cable market, United Cable's application states 'while local programming is perceived to be of value by a relatively small segment of the cable system's subscribers, those who watch and participate consider local programming highly valuable and a strong motivation for continuing as subscribers'. United Cable concludes, therefore, that 'local programming need not be seen as loss-making window-dressing.' It intends to draw on the success of the 'Crystalvision' channel on its Croydon system, and exploit the opportunities afforded by a multi-franchise approach.

The plan is to develop a replicable local programme channel and production facility format which can be used as a pattern for each local franchise in which United is involved and which will use the various franchise local channels to 'network' locally produced programmes'. This approach has been co-developed with HTV, and the two parties envisage a small cost-effective one or two camera television studio facility located within each franchise area. Parallel to this programme strand would be a local programme coordinator, who would run training courses and workshops to 'stimulate and assist local groups and individuals to use the local franchise production facilities for community public/educational access programming'. The inference is that both the local channel and access provision would be available to some extent as soon as the franchise begins operation, though to what extent, and at what rate it will build is not specified.

28. Hammersmith (2) Community programming provision will begin as text services, which will continue for the 'early years'. This will progress via interactive text to 'fully-fledged productions' made with the help of community groups, organisations and associations throughout the franchise area. Interactivity will be made available 'as the subscriber base develops' - no figures are given - while 'programme production will take place later on', with no more specific schedule supplied. City Centre Cable (CCC - now Videotron) undertake to provide production assistance and training, to work cooperatively on programming ideas, and find necessary funding. Each of the boroughs in the franchise will have its own community channel - 'aimed at communities of interest' – with all the examples provided for programming being almost exclusively text services. Community viewing access points for these services will be provided at a range of public amenities.

29. Bristol (See Southend 26. above)

30. Redbridge (2) East London Telecommunications (ELT) will provide a 'local access or Community Channel' for each of the boroughs in its franchise, though subject to the results of research it is undertaking. ELT undertakes to provide the professional staff, technicians and facilities required to produce such a channel, and to recruit programme coordinators from each borough to liaise with groups wishing to contribute to the channel. Each community channel would only be available to subscribers in its particular borough, and would be part of the basic programme service from day one. ELT will also 'make available on the system time for Public Access', which would again be borough-specific. No charge will be made for distributing pre-produced material on ELT's system, but if ELT's camera or production equipment is used 'a small charge will be made to cover insurance and administrative costs'. ELT's staff will provide training, instruction and assistance free of charge. The same conditions would apply to local authorities, schools, colleges etc. Editorial decisions will remain with ELT, and users of the access provision will have to respect restrictions on content contained in ELT's licence. An advisory group will be established to help in this aspect. ELT is planning to introduce studio facilities 'when subscriber numbers can guarantee a reasonable audience for this type of programming'. No figure is supplied to quantify what a 'reasonable audience' might be, though ELT does state that it 'anticipates that these services will be available during the first 12 months of operation'.

31. Reading (1) The local channel will be 'teletext in vision with opt-outs for access programming'. Pointing to what Cable Thames Valley see as the limitations of realising 'programming of quality at an acceptable cost', it concludes that it will 'begin with a modest amount of local programming (studio-based)', but only when it has 'a network of sufficient size' – no figure is supplied as to what constitutes 'sufficient size'.

32. Northampton (2) The application bares a striking resemblance to that for Luton (21. above). Cable Television (CTV) cites the costs of local programming as the reason that 'it may be several years before regular local programming appears on the screen'.

Therefore, to begin with, small amounts of local programming will appear on specific occasions eg. bank holidays. Programming could also include material made by local people or organisations and there is a desire to foster links with twin-towns. A videobox facility will be provided. As with Luton, a studio facility is proposed as a means to foster an indigenous production community, deploying the same three definitions of community. Again, it is acknowledged that these plans will prove beyond the funding capabilities of CTV 'in the early years', and that 'as a first stage in the development of local programming' a text channel will be employed. There is no reference to the charitable trust approach used in Luton to attempt to attract extra funding for the local channel.

33. Greenwich (see Lambeth 43. below)

34. Crawley (1) Mid Downs Cable (MDC) will make available 'a channel for use by the public and the Local Education Authority'. However, it sees Public Access as having proved 'a difficult service to develop in a meaningful fashion, particularly in small systems' - Crawley has a potential reach of 40,000 homes - and therefore, at least initially, 'can only allocate the channel space whilst discussing the best use of this facility with interested parties'. It sees experience within Harlech TV as helpful in this regard. MDC proposes a news and local noticeboard service – 'Mid Downs Eye' – which would entail a presenter operating in a studio comprised of 'an unmanned camera, electronic news gathering player, still store machine, an ENG camera and editing facility'. In relation to this equipment 'local societies would be invited to produce their own programme with the assistance of MDC staff'. MDC would retain final editorial control, citing the Cable Act as the reason for such a stipulation. The application offers for both business and private subscribers access to the benefits of Mercury telephone connections. Certainly, the application suggests that much greater store is set by interactive and telephony services, and by their future expansion, than Public Access or local programming. There is no indication what facilities or subscriber base underpin the MDC News service, and it is therefore difficult to quantify claims to 'forge closer links with the people and give greater prominence to stories they can identify with'.

35. Greater Glasgow, 36. Motherwell, 37. Cumbernauld, & 38. Dumbarton (1) Cable North will dedicate a minimum of 2 channels in each franchise exclusively for locally originated programming. Cable North will actively encourage local voluntary organisations to provide programming, and will contribute equipment and experienced personnel to this end – what that equipment might be is not specified. 'Both Community and Access channels will start by providing rolling text and photo-videotext services on a 24 hour basis.' The above provisions for local programming however will only be brought into play 'as the system grows and as the demand for full video services grow' – neither of these quantities are specified.

39. Merton & 40. Kingston (2) Very close to the application for Southend (26. above). However, in these applications there is greater emphasis on programming produced for the community, or being provided by the community, rather than a closer relationship around training on, and use of, the operator's own facilities. United Cable Television London South (UCTLS) 'owns video production facilities and employs a producer who currently makes a series of local programmes for transmission on the locally produced Channel 15 service'. UCTLS proposes an extension of this approach into the two franchise areas. Newspaper groups in the various boroughs will be contacted with a view to generating dedicated news services. The statement that UCLTS will offer 'the opportunity for locally based video production units to make programmes for the available public access slots' is ambiguous, in that it does not make clear whether this would involve UCTLS in supplying the necessary facilities and support, or merely accepting already completed material. It also implies, that individuals would not gain similar access to distribution.

41. Cambridge (3) (see account above)

42. Dudley (2) West Midland Cable (WMC) state that its local channel – Black Country Television Ltd. (BCTV) - will be launched from inception of transmissions. In common with Southend (26. above), WMC cite the example of Croydon Cable's Crystalvision. BCTV will be a commercially-supported local television station comprising 'local origination production staff, field production unit and eventual studio facilities'. Although it is implied that the majority of programming will be produced by its production staff, WMC does state that the local channel will be used specifically to 'promote WMC's priority training classes for minority residents interested in television production'. WMC indicates that there has been considerable interest in this scheme. A significant quantity of programming described as being aimed at ethnic minorities, however, seems to be concerned with 'housing, unemployment, health and special educational concerns', which runs the risk of multi-cultural programming being restricted to consideration of 'problems', though this is a perfectly proper, and important, facet of such provision.

43. Lambeth, 44. Peterborough & 45. Norwich (2) In a number of respects – the identification of three formulations for community – the applications bare a striking similarity to that for Luton (21. above). Pointing to the costs incurred in the provision of local programming, both franchises state the intention to 'operate a local programming service as a co-operative venture with other local media operators'. This would include a videobox facility. Again, studio debates are seen as a vehicle with which to 'assist in training new producers and production groups who will have access to the production facility for the production of work relating to the community'. It is expected that this 'ambitious plan' will be implemented relatively soon, due to the high level of local involvement. The first stage however, will be in the form of a text information channel. There are no specific figures as to when the more ambitious facilities will be implemented. The only immediately available interactive service will be a Cable Video Store.

46. Colchester (3) (See consideration of Maclean Hunter applications above)

47. Haringey (2/1) Cable London (CL) will provide several, one-way, local text services. Local programme services might be financed via advertising, but CL argues that 'there is no experience, and little expectation that community channels can be profitable'. Nonetheless, in common with Southend (26. above), CL states that community channels can function as a 'strong attraction for subscribers to other services'. CL also make the important point that as a result of certain widespread standards of professionalism in television, 'local channels will be dependent on the production of material of sufficient quality, range and interest to be attractive to the residents of the area, against the output of professional television producers around the world.' This view contrasts markedly with that proposed by Wandsworth (15. above).

Three broad stages of development are indicated. Firstly, a text and graphics channel. Secondly, cable delivered radio services, building on the existing community radio network. Finally, television services with a primary news and information function. For any specific interest group 'services could build to around 6-8 hours per week of original material'. This figure can be further increased by repeats, and exchanging material with similar operations in other areas.

CL suggest there is the potential for a North London channel, pointing to the work of the Hellenic TV Channel (see Camden 17. above), and the African film and television workshop, Ceddo. However, CL makes clear that it is not in the business of instigating such developments, rather it 'would be a facilitator'. Initially, CL will provide 'seed funding' for production and post-production facilities. These will be established in the existing Camden franchise, but will be made available to Haringey as 'the most cost effective way of providing high grade facilities in the early stages of the cable build' – exact figures are not supplied. The ambition is to progressively secure an ever wider source of funding for an equally diverse range of programming: for example the Hispanic model on New York cable channels, where 'individual groups may set up facilities paid for with local advertising revenues', because the particular community of interest is viable.

49. Leicester (3/2) Offers an ethnic minority programming service in the shape of its Asian Channel, which is possibly the best planned of those available along with Preston (19. above). Initially, the local channel will be a combination of text and photo-videotext together with a live news and information slot throughout the day, and a 'longer, studio-based, current affairs programme each evening'. The proportion of live material will increase as the cabled area grows. The exact relationship is not specified. It is further planned to employ an outside broadcast camera team, which would follow 'the Leicester Sound News Reporters during their day's activities'. The Studios at Leicester Sound and Studio facilities at Q Studios will serve as the other significant resources, and there is an extensive list of information to be supplied by Leicester Sound on the community channel.

'Considerable thought and research has gone into the formulation of a programming structure for the Asian Channel, which compliments the Asian Premium Film Channel, Indra Dhnush'. The programme will draw on the skills and experience of the team working on Leicester Sound's 'Sabras' programme in the form of the Asian Programme supply company. This will deliver six hours of material per day, four of picture and two of text broadcast. Part of the former will include locally planned entertainment programming, produced at Q Studios. There will also be one hour devoted to broad-casting in vernacular languages.

In relation to community access, Leicester Communications (LC) in collaboration with Q Studios, undertakes to 'establish opportunities for interested groups to be trained in the skills of programme making'. Training will be a criterion for subsequent access to the 'full Broadcast quality studio and multi track recording facilities', in order to produce programming for the channel. LC sees the development of this channel as being slow, and 'will be constantly under the control of LC to ensure that the quality of the product is suitable for distribution to the public and equally to ensure that the company exercises its ultimate responsibilities for Editorial Control'.

50. Nottingham (3/2) During the first 2 years of transmission Diamond Cable (DC) will provide one community channel, 24 hours per day, while Radio Trent and Nottingham Evening Post combined will supply a further two. Initially, DC's channel will be text based. During this period DC will also provide 'a local Production Facilities Unit available to local programme producers'. The unit will consist of 'a number of portable cameras, lighting and sound equipment, together with an editing suite in the Cable Centre, where programmes can be assembled, ready for transmission'. The facilities will be available to 'accredited community organisations', and 'professional staff resources will be made available for help and training of qualified users'. It would seem that individuals would not get access to this system. From the third year DC believes it will have reached the subscriber level necessary for the community channel to 'take off and develop a regular audience'. This level of subscription – a precise figure is not supplied – will enable community channel programming 'on a scheduled, daily basis, with permanent slots for each item, reinforced by a regular repeat pattern'. DC undertakes to provide the necessary increase in facilities to enable an expansion of the service, and has set aside space at the Cable Centre 'that could be converted into a studio'– though no indication is given as to when this conversion might take place.

51. Brighton (2/1) Southdown Cablevision (SC) intends to supply a community channel carrying material recognising the different boroughs and towns. Local programme coordinators would be enlisted to liaise with the community, and to develop the channel in each area and 'where appropriate, sponsor local activities'. In relation to public access, SC states that 'a minimal charge will be made for the use of facilities', though distribution and training will be free. In the initial stages, demand for a local information channel will be met 'by the use of graphics and text computers and camera equipment to provide a programme with a mix of video footage and scrolling text'. SC points to its 'extensive panel of local television production companies', as well as its own studio complex, as evidence that it will be able to offer a full local production service to volunteer organisations, or companies wishing to sponsor local charitable organisations. SC undertakes to 'make available its training and hire department to facilitate "self made programmes" in cases where local groups cannot raise the necessary funds to employ production professionals'. The implication here would seem to be that SC would prefer that groups did work through independent production companies, rather than that SC is offering this help as a regular, fixed service. One of the founder companies already operates a television studio in Brighton, and it will be this facility that is used to develop the local services. SC will supply the Community Channel as part of its basic programming package in the first year, with a channel for public and leased access to be 'introduced'.

52. Exeter (3) (see Colchester 46. above)

53. Harpenden (2) (see Northampton 32. above)

54. Watford (3) The Jones Cable Group (JCG) see the community channel, which will be available 24 hours a day, 7 days a week, as being 'at the heart of the new cable system'. JCG will appoint a locally recruited channel coordinator to liaise with local groups and help them develop material. Initially, this will be in the form of text services. 'As the system develops and the number of subscribers grow' – neither quantity specified – 'live and moving picture programming' will be introduced onto the community channel. Such programming would be both studio and location based, with JCG supplying a camera unit for location work. JCG also undertake to 'provide the technical and professional staff to assist local groups prepare and make programmes', not least because it is keen to maintain a 'high standard on the Community Channel'. Importantly, JCG state that 'access to and use of the Community Channel will be free to individuals and organisations within the franchise area'. Extra space will be found to that on the Community Channel for groups wishing to produce unusually long programmes such as drama or sports. A small charge for equipment – not specified – would be levied under these circumstances. JCG also proposes to provide studio facilities for free access programming, together with technical and professional backup. JCG does not anticipate editorial issues being a serious problem, seeing its main responsibility as being to 'schedule programming and maintain technical standards'. If problems do arise, they will be referred to a local advisory group. It states that the various stages of expansion in local provision beyond the initial text service will occur 'as the system develops and audience levels grow' – no specific figures are supplied.

55. Stevenage (2) (see Northampton 32. above)

56. Stoke-on-Trent (3) (see Colchester 46. above)

57. Swansea (2) Cable & Satellite (CS) will provide 3 local community text channels and a local news channel, the latter coming into operation once 20,000 subscribers are on board – out of a possible reach of 110,000. This channel will be supplied by a separate subsidiary company 'with additional local participants'. The creation of Network Vision to operate the local channel is seen as an indication of the degree of seriousness which CS attributes to the channel. It also states that public access programming is a 'key part of Network Vision's local programming'. To substantiate this CS undertakes to 'make studio production facilities available to local societies and individuals. Local programme makers will be given training by our training manager'.

58. Newcastle (2) Comment Cablevision (CCV) points out that the newly expanded independent sector must have outlets for their products in order to override centralisation on London. It is committed to providing 'extensive and responsive local programming' and is exploring a cooperative relationship with Metro Radio plc and other local media to offset the cost. A videobox facility will be established and, in common with Northampton (32. see above), studio-based productions will be used to train new producers or production groups: these groups will then have access to studio and remote facilities for local programming. Ethnic minorities 'will be guaranteed appropriate access to the community channel'. CCV predict that 100% reach will be achieved in 5 years, with 6% (20,000 homes) in the first year and 29% cabled by Year

Two. Once home penetration has reached 'significant levels' – which are not specified – a sports channel will be created.

59. Warrington & 60. Chester (3) (See Colchester 46. above)

61. Stafford (1) Stafford Communications' parent company also runs the Andover service (23. above). The application states that 'Stafford Communications has been set up specifically to operate a cable network within the Stafford/Stone area and it is imperative that the Company becomes integrated with all aspects of the local community'. This is exactly duplicated (but for name and location in the Stort Valley Cable application for Harlow (75. below), and might be taken as marking a certain valuation of local programming. Subscribers will receive two types of local service: visual and audio. Visual material will be predominantly text, with space made available for contributions from local groups. 'It is not thought necessary to operate a live service'. The company will maintain editorial control 'to ensure that both content and quality are legally and socially acceptable'. 'Open access' is said to be an important part of its policy and it purports to encourage the whole community to produce programmes, however, editorial control is reasserted 'to ensure acceptability and quality of all input': one could argue that this could be achieved more effectively through training schemes. A video booth will be located in the public library. The application also suggests an involvement with Sixth Form media courses, although in what capacity is not made clear.

62. Dorchester Public documents not available.

63. Dundee & 64. Perth (3) Tayside Cable Systems (TCS) aims to provide broadband at the lowest price in the UK, and to this end is preparing to waive the connection fee associated with hook-up in local authority housing areas. A charge of £9.95 per month will supply a movie channel and a range of satellite services, with discounts available for old age pensioners and registered disabled. Where possible, both cable and telephone networks will share the same routing and duct structure.

Educational and local programming will be covered by a 50/50 venture with Aberdeen-based independent Tern Television Productions Limited (TTPL), setting up Tayside Television Limited. TTPL has pioneered work on local and community access for Aberdeen Cable Systems Ltd., which will be applied to the running of a 'local studio, training and other services for the community'. It is claimed that 'Tayside Television will provide community groups and others with a valuable means of producing local programming and cable systems will provide an outlet for that programming. This highly successful formula was pioneered in Aberdeen'. The success is at least partly due to the experience of TTPL's managing director, David Strachan, minister of Aberfeldy Church for six years and a founder member of Tay Churches Radio Council. A joint venture between television professionals (TTPL) and cable company (TCS) 'will enable top class training to be provided. Tayside Television will provide equipment and a full time training manager'.

The application claims that the 'best way forward is to set up the concept of Tayside Television in association with dedicated television professionals and the cable company, but largely puts the onus for making programmes and producing material for the channels in the hands of the community'. TCS feels it is 'highly unlikely that sufficient video material will be available for a full transmission schedule on this channel' so the Tayside Discovery Channel will include a high quality teletext.

65. Portsmouth (3/2) Britannia Cablesystems (BC) state that 'community programming will be a modest element of the Portsmouth area cable television system at the beginning'. There are two phases, the first being activated from day one. 'Solentvision Channel' will comprise a text operator who receives, edits and inputs material for text service, using 'fast' digital text and picture systems. The audio component will be provided by Sky radio. Games with prizes will provide a promotional element.

Video productions of a community access nature will be accepted and broadcast, and Britannia will also 'occasionally' commission videos by local producers to demonstrate the Channel's potential.

Phase Two should commence roughly 16 months after the start of construction. BC estimate reaching 11,400 out of 150,000 potential homes by the end of 1991: this is the subscriber level deemed necessary for it to be able to 'provide community television with fuller support'. BC will acquire two 'portable television cameras and recorders, and will establish an edit suite'. A Community Programming Facilitator will be employed to help users and groups to prepare and produce programmes. If there is sufficient demand, extra space will be made available for community purposes.

66. Derby (1) The application by Derbyshire Cablevision Limited (DCL) cites research by Gallup of 400 local respondents, in which '54% said that they were quite/very interested in receiving local programming'. No significant variation in the level of interest was found by age, sex or social class.

It is stated that 'as cable penetration increases and local origination programming develops, companies, educational establishments and local government will be able to communicate directly with people of Derby through cable', yet there is no indication of DCL instigating this communication, merely distributing it. To some extent this is offset by an allocation in Year Two of £60,000 'for the purposes of funding local studio facilities'. Two further channels will be made available at this stage for leased access. The implication of this approach is that access simply means making channel space available and waiting to be supplied with material. There are no references to training, or to supplying equipment beyond the funds of existing facilities. Nor is it clear whether there will be payments beyond this £60,000.

67. Leeds (3) (See Watford 54. above)

68. Wakefield (3) (See Colchester 46. above)

69. Margate (2) (See, for example, Stevenage 55. above)

70. Bromley (1) Telecommunications Network Limited (TNL) will make channels available for community access in both video and text, 'providing for the transmission of news and other material of local interest'. The Company's local policy, it is said, 'will be one of phased growth, expanding services in line with the growth of the network'. An initial monthly subscription service will transfer to Pay-Per-View as technology is implemented. During Year One facilities will be provided for the Council and other local authorities to use the network as an information bulletin board. With regard to access, 'provision will be made for local groups to transmit material they themselves have produced, subject to TNL's legal responsibilities as publisher. It is planned to make available a limited quantity of video equipment and editing facilities for community use'. From the applications already discussed, however, it seems clear that this amounts to merely a token commitment to access or community programming - there is, for example, no mention of training in conjunction with this provision.

72. Mansfield (3/2) (See Nottingham 50. above)

73. Havering & 74. Dartford (3) These applications would appear to be simply slightly altered versions of the Jones Cable Group applications for Watford and Leeds (54. and 67. above). The process of consultation would appear to have taken place this way round, as the Watford franchise was awarded on 3/11/1989 and Dartford's on 16/3/1990.

75. Harlow (1) (See Stafford 61. above)

76. Stratford (3/2) Heartland Cable intends to allocate three channels from its Foundation package to locally originated programmes. The first of these, a Community Channel, will transmit 'television programmes of regional interest to all four towns and individual programmes to each town separately. A two-camera studio will be established at the Warwick control centre', which will be supplemented by location work or by use of Coventry Cable's more advanced studio. The Warwick facility will be upgraded when the 'franchise area's own requirements justify' such provision.

A target for a local channel of 20 hours a week of locally originated community programmes has been established. (No date has been supplied as a deadline.)

From Year Three, a small mobile unit will be required consisting of a truck and two portable camera units. The channel would be used to screen programming resulting from local consultation meetings – Asian and Afro-Caribbean material for example.

An additional local channel will be provided for 'local advertisements and shopping'. This space initially will be supplied at zero or low cost and charges will not be levied until there are a potential 10,000 viewers (out of a figure of 44,000 possible viewers).

A third local channel – in collaboration with Mercia Sound – will be concerned with news, weather and transport. Material which has been generated by Mercia's radio journalists on photo-videotext terminals will also be taken by Coventry Cable and perhaps some other nearby cable companies.

The channel will be supported by advertising revenue collected by Mercia Sound. Once the additional revenue has reached an agreed level, it will be shared between participating companies. A fully-fledged video channel will be established, should interest become sufficiently buoyant although at present no level is suggested to indicate what 'sufficiently buoyant' means.

Two groups of staff will operate to service local programming – playback staff will run facilities and others concerned with community access programming will set up and run training. Cabletext will be available from the system's launch.

77. York and Harrogate (2) There is a planned capacity of 60 channels, 28 of these being planned as a starter package. Four 'community programme services' are also proposed. These are: a local community service with a store front studio in both Harrogate and York and also one main complex; a UK Community Service; a European Community Service; and a Commonwealth Community service. Initially only the local Community service will be available. The other three community programme services will start up once sufficient programme exchanges are under way.

The application announces, 'We propose wherever possible, to be pioneers in the world of community programming, meeting local needs wherever possible'. This is backed up by the promise to 'offer equipment to qualified groups' and to 'train people in the elements of production'.

The application states that local access means:

> A full facility store front studio in the downtown area; a community animator to invigorate, train and assist the people in learning how to 'do' television themselves; a local message centre in the head-end complex; portable equipment which can be used in all of the several sub-centres within the metropolitan districts.

The exact composition of either studio or portable facilities is not specified.

> Our initial commitment has to be to equipment and to the development of the training programmes which will be the key to attracting and maintaining the interest of the citizens.

No timetable is supplied, neither are there figures for the number of staff involved in training and programme provision. The lack of information concerning the exchange channels suggests that they are simply included to give the impression of greater commitment to local programming than is actually the case.

78. Bournemouth (1) The local policy of Bay Cable 'will be one of phased growth, expanding services in line with the growth of the network'. No figures are supplied to allow a clear idea of when these developments will occur, or what parameters are being used to gauge growth as a trigger for 'expanding services'. The paragraph setting out this policy is an exact duplicate of a statement in Telecommunications Network's application for Bromley (See 70. above). It also occurs in Hinckley 86. (below).

The application does say, 'facilities will be made available during the first year of operation for the council and other local organisations to provide information and bulletin boards'.

It also states that Bay Cable will 'make available a limited quantity of video equipment and editing facilities for community use'. It does not say, however, how limited this 'quantity' will be, nor supply details of what it will be.

Bay Cable also state that local groups can transmit material they themselves have produced – but that this would be 'subject to Bay Cable's usual responsibility as publisher'. Bay Cable also seems to lend more weight to provision of air-time, than to provision of equipment and training, in terms of its community access services. These statements also duplicate paragraphs from the earlier Bromley application.

79. Salisbury (1) (See Stafford 61. above)

80. Winchester (1) 'Videotron South does not intend to enter the programme production business'. Local consultations which indicated a 'strong desire for a genuinely local television programme' prompted Videotron South 'to reconsider our plans for local news' and to establish a mechanism which would facilitate 'the earliest practical introduction of local news'. They will supply a text channel and text generator to create 'a local bulletin board'. 'A full television channel, including teletext, will be provided for the exclusive use of local community groups'. Videotron South will 'install an independent telecommunications network, independent of, but connected to, the existing public system'.

The tone of the application, and the small amount of space devoted to local programming provision, tends to suggest Videotron South are more interested in the telecoms aspect of the franchise – 'we will have available the skills and experience of Bell Canada' – rather than television programming.

What is meant by the provision of a full television channel is very unclear. There is no mention of training local community groups, nor is it made clear whether production facilities are to be made available or merely air time for pre-produced material. The fact that Videotron South must, prior to the evidence of local consultations, have had no intention of providing local programming is hardly indicative of an enthusiastic commitment to such provision.

81. Telford (1) Black Country Television (BCTV), will include local interest channels: a regional news and features channel, a public access channel, a classified advertising channel and a jobs channel. A separate Telford local news and information service will also be provided.

Telford Television, in conjunction with BCTV, has established a ten-strong working group of experienced broadcasters and marketers to plan the local service. This group has already agreed that one hour of sport and 15 minutes of news daily would be feasible.

Programming on BCTV is to include: live and taped local sport, material for local schools, coverage of local festivals etc., women's programming, programming for the over 65s, multi-cultural programming, and live current affairs discussions.

Other specialist channels of local interest include 'public access for the transmission of locally produced material by voluntary groups', exchange/home shopping, text and graphics 'What's On', text regional jobs, 24 hour rolling texts in conjunction with Reuters, the Express and Star Group and Beacon Radio - forming a regional news and business service, and regional weather which would be supplied by Midlands based 'The Weather Department Ltd.', who have supplied Sky Television.

Despite the range of 'local' services listed above, there is little suggestion that any production facilities or training in the use of such facilities will be made available to local groups or individuals, nor is there any indication of the intention to commission local programming, rather Telford Television will merely make available air time which they choose to describe as 'public access'. The description of other applications above would suggest that this is a very limited interpretation of 'public access'.

82. Hackney (2) The application should be seen as working in conjunction with Camden 17. and Haringey 47. (above) to establish a North London channel.

Cable London sees the potential for a North London Channel as representing 'an ideal opportunity for the development and demonstration of a locally originated channel' because there are 'a number of well established communities with their own cultural identities and roots, which spread across the whole of North London and are of sufficient size to make a channel viable'.

The application states that 'community groups (of any size from the individual to the branch of a national body) should have access to the cable network to publish their programmes' and 'the North London channel will be provided free in the basic package of services'. The application argues that programme quality 'must achieve levels that the average viewer does not categorise as of a lower standard'. Cable London will ensure programming standards both by 'on-going training of volunteer programme makers' and by a 'consistent guiding editorial hand'.

It is also states that 'the approach which has been adopted to the provision of local programming in Camden will be extended into Haringey and then Hackney and Islington'.

Initially the North London channel will be developed by a founder member of Cable London, to be supported 'in due course' (this time period being left vague) by technical staff responsible for advice and training, as well as Cable London's own programming. Editorial staff will both administer and develop community programming as well as programmer's own activities.

Professional equipment expenses (cameras) have been evaluated at £2,500 - £4,500 and costs of 'high quality editing systems' at £10,000. The application states:

> Start-up of local programme generation can be established in each of Cable London's franchise areas for a reasonable cost. Further facilities can be provided through the central operation shared between all of Cable London's franchise areas.

The figures supplied here point to the facilities being of S-VHS standard video equipment.

The application argues that while 'it remains the intention of Cable London to provide central studio facilities for North London', initially the costs would be prohibitive, and therefore Cable London will use 'existing readily available facilities in the community at large while building a core of trained camera operators and programme producers'.

The timetable for the development of this service is set out in the above table referring to the Hackney example. Clearly the viability of the model will refer back to the experience of Camden which the application makes plain forms the basis of the North London Channel.

83. Doncaster (1/2) South Yorkshire Cablevision (SYCC) states that 'as the subscriber base grows it is committed to providing a community channel in the form of commercially-supported programming', though there is no indication as the time scale or number of subscribers necessary to constitute adequate growth. SYCC will also establish 'its own production centre and studio and will offer training in techniques relating to the use of this equipment'. The local community will be encouraged to take advantage of this facility, but there is no time scale supplied for its introduction or any details as to the specifications of the facilities being offered.

SYCC is looking to develop co-venturing schemes 'whereby programming is made under co-operative plans with local media, financed by local advertising'. Local businesses will be approached to sponsor programmes on the community channel, through low-cost advertising.

84. Rugby (See Stratford 76. above)

85. Nuneaton & Bedworth (See Stratford 76. above)

86. Hinckley (1) N-Com's application carried an identical paragraph setting out its policy concerning local provisions, being 'one of phased growth', to that of Bournemouth 78. (above), and an earlier application for Bromley 70. (above). N-Com also duplicated statements concerning provision of facilities to local councils and policy on access programming. The reason for noting this at all, is that the three applications are ostensibly made by completely separate companies. In this respect it is interesting that while both the applications for Bromely and Bournemouth refer to 'a limited quantity of video equipment and editing facilities' being supplied for community use, N-Com are able to state that it 'will make available two cameras and a basic editing kit' to ensure local access production 'becomes a reality'. It also says it will have a local channel co-ordinator 'to co-ordinate production and provide training to the public on how to use the community channel and the equipment'.

It is worth noting that N-Com's later application for Burton-on-Trent discussed above, is significantly more forthcoming and apparently more committed to local programming.

87. Tamworth (1) In common with N-Com's later application for Burton-on-Trent, this proposal stresses N-Com's experience in providing residents in very small communities with an effective and lively local channel. To this end it states that it will provide both a channel and 'suitable equipment and training to enable responsible residents with sufficient enthusiasm to produce live or taped programmes of local interest and put them out over the system'. However, it does not state what 'suitable equipment' means, nor when it will be made available; so N-Com's declaration that it will undertake the provision of local programme facilities 'with enthusiasm' is not sufficiently bolstered by facts and figures to constitute more than merely a fine sentiment.

88. Grantham & 89. Newark (3/2) (See Nottingham 50. above)

90. Melton Mowbray (3/2) The only addition to the application Diamond Cable made for Nottingham (See 50. above) is the provision of a cable channel for which Radio Trent will supply programming.

91. Manchester (1) (See Derby 66. above) The same criticisms apply for Manchester as for Derby, though it is worth noting that although the potential number of households within the Manchester area is four times that in Derby, Greater Manchester Cable Ltd. is only offering twice as much funding (£120,000) in its first year of operations for local studio facilities.

92. Bury & 93. Oldham (2) Both Bury and Oldham are identical to Newcastle 58. (see above) except for details concerning Newcastle's rate of expansion.

94. Stockport (2/3) Stockport will provide a number of dedicated local services, which will be 'developed as the network expands and will include a channel specifically made available for local groups to access the network'.

Telecable of Stockport will deliver a local channel 'produced by professionally trained media specialists'. The majority of such programming will be undertaken in 'the studio which (Telecable of Stockport) intend to provide'. This will be supplemented by 'utilising a mobile production unit'.

In relation to its community channel, Telecable of Stockport 'undertake to provide ongoing training and assistance to groups of individuals who wish to access the network, and we shall promote the services in order that as many groups as possible are aware of the facilities available'.

Telecable of Stockport also promise to 'take particular steps to ensure that the disabled are provided with every opportunity to learn new media related skills'. The channel capacity will also be made available for services utilising text to focus on Stockport.

There is little specific detail, unfortunately, on time scales or specifications of the studio and mobile facilities mentioned. It is worthy of note that production and training will be handled by 'media specialists', as this seems to be more the exception than the rule.

95. Wigan (3) Cable Communications (CC) adopts a three phase approach which is discussed above.

96. Epping (3) (See Havering 73. above)

97. Dover (2) North Downs Cable (NDC) list six varieties of local community channels, four of which are text based, the other two are educational channels provided in collaboration with the local school system, and a local access programme which will, however, only be 'available to approved community groups'. In relation to its public access channel, NDC states that it:

> will provide a studio and production facilities for the development of a local public access channel intended for public use, and will train community members in local access television production.

There are no details supplied as to the timing of when studio and production facilities will be made available, or indeed, what these facilities will be.

98. Aylesbury (3) (See Watford 54. above)

99. Harrow (2/3) (See Stockport 94. above)

100. Hillingdon & 101. Hounslow (1) Middlesex Cable Ltd. (MCL) already has facilities available with which to generate 'a sophisticated text and graphics channel' for the local community. This channel will also be available to local authorities and community organisations 'from the earliest stages in the development of the network'. MCL also sees local radio as an access point for the community. There is no discussion of programming of a non-text service or indeed of any form of training, even on the text-services provided. Access has been interpreted as making available air-time/channel space and a certain degree of educational programming developed with local colleges.

102. Enfield (2/3) Cable London's application envisages that 'in a four to five year time-scale as many as four local television channels will be available to the community'. This will be subject to three factors: most channels will be text-based - 'such channels form the core of our local and community strategy in the early days'; to undertake training programmes as a way of enabling the community to be involved in programme-making; to combine such initiatives with 'working along side appropriate programme makers to develop a North London television channel'. (See Hackney 82. above)

The application goes on to point out that the nature of the operation will be determined by the number of homes passed and the growth in the number of these homes connected up. The scale of the operation will rely on 'the commitment of the community to cable programming'.

The service build will occur in three stages. At a minimum level there will be a local text channel (information, what's on etc.) and a local news channel (also text). In Year Two, 'our approach is to enable the development of skills, so that commitment to programme making is matched by skills in the community'. Such programming would be part of an ad hoc schedule. This stage will also include the evolution of a service aimed at 'communicating with ethnic communities in their own languages'. Stage three involves the introduction of the 'North London Channel' which will be 'determined by the progress of the whole franchise area'. With the proviso that Cable London is successful in both Hackney & Islington and Enfield (which it was) it would 'expect to reach 20-25 hours per week of original material within three years'.

Cable London make the important observation that 'taken as a whole, the five boroughs that make up our North London strategy include sizeable communities that are large enough to attract common interests and involvement'. (See Hackney 82. above)

Cable London is undertaking discussions with independent providers about how the 'North London Channel' should be structured.

103. Hertford (2) (See Luton 21. above)

104. Sheffield (1/2) Sheffield Cable Media (SCM) undertake to provide a studio in their headquarters at Meadowhall, 'and connections into the network will be offered to other studios, notably those in the city's cultural quarter'.

SCM 'aim to make it realistic to start local production earlier than might otherwise be expected by providing a base of locally-produced educational programmes, including those to be broadcast to a national audience from Sheffield'.

While SCM 'are willing to help local people with developing television production skills', they place more weight on building 'on the considerable skills already available in Sheffield'. The application does not give specific details as to time scales for the start of local production, or of the nature of facilities and training being supplied to enable this.

The SCM approach draws heavily on pre-existing production facilities and training programmes developed by the local production community and city council. It is not clear what the quid pro quo for this will be in terms of air-time/channel space to be made available, or financial support for such services. As has been suggested earlier, local participation under such a regime seems to be fairly low on a list of priorities, where business and telecoms services are seen as being of much greater import.

105. Thamesmead (1) (See Winchester 80. above)

106. Greater Glasgow, 107. Paisley & 108. Bearsden (3) Clyde Cable Vision (CCV) states that it is 'fortunate to have a programming and production department together with full studio facilities with which to create programming such as to appeal to the needs of the various segments of the community'. Such programming is delivered via the Glasgow channel, which comprises programming secured from: in-house production – CCV generated 3,000 minutes plus of local programming in 1989. This material is secured from within the current CCV franchise area 'and highlights community based activities'. CCV describes the output as being 'analogous to the contents of a local newspaper on video'; purchased material – this is currently over 30 hours per month of a 'general entertainment nature' free access to air time – this is provided for material from services such as the National Trust for Scotland, RSPB, and regional tourist boards. Such access is also afforded to local community groups and their productions. 'Additionally, in January 1990, a local programming network was established between cable operators whereby items of wider information are exchanged between UK wide cable operations'; public access and joint initiative material – CCV supplement this interpretation of access with 'a 'public access' service providing training in the use of video equipment and accessing airtime. Joint initiative programming was established by the company in March 1989 allowing individuals and organisations to produce their own programmes using CCV personnel and equipment'. Such programming is under the editorial control of the organisations involved, however material used for the Glasgow channel is subject to CCV's approval on grounds of quality; sponsored programming – for example, crime prevention programmes undertaken with Strathclyde police. CCV also provides a range of local information services on text.

109. Worcester & 110. Sunderland (2) These represent a slightly rearranged version of Bury 92. (see above), which is itself virtually identical to the application for Newcastle 58. (also above).

111. Oxford (1) (See Hinckley 86. above)

112. Barnsley (3) Cable Communications adopts the same three stage approach as that discussed for Wigan and St Helens franchises above.

113. Bedford (2) (See Luton 21. above)

114. Bradford (1/2) General Cable supplies a minimum of information in relation to local services. It states that 'suitable equipment will be installed in the early stages of the network to provide local information via video, text and graphics for one or two channels', the number being determined by 'the needs of the Bradford authority'.

A community access facility will be offered – though this is subject to the approval of the local authority – 'adjacent to, and coordinated with, the studio facility for local production'. General Cable then states that 'in some cases, video equipment could be provided to let residents run specific television broadcasts'. One might ask what an 'access facility' is supposed to mean if local residents are only able to use it in 'some cases'. Moreover, the criteria in operation for selecting these 'cases' are not made available in the application.

General Cable say 'a studio will be built to enable the production of local programmes'. This will be 'equipped with two or three cameras, facilities for picture and sound mixing equipment, as well as recording and editing equipment'. The inference is, however, that this facility will be exclusively for the in-house production of local programming. There is also no specific reference made to training, even in relation to the access facility.

115. Halifax (2/3) (See Stockport 94. above)

116. Huddersfield (2) Kirklees Cable (KC) points to 'a comprehensive programme of community consultation' as the basis for its local programming. KC thinks it, 'likely that the local channel/s will be in the form of text services through which information can be disseminated....' This would be supplemented by a number of 'phone-in' advice programmes. KC also undertakes to develop educational programming with education and training providers, particularly 'programming of local interest which would deal, for example, with local history (social and economic)..... and programmes which would explore the different ethnic cultures'.

The details KC supplies in relation to 'participatory programming', follow very closely the description discussed for Northampton (above), but in addition states it will 'make available portable video recording equipment for registered groups who may wish to make programmes for public access channels'. A full-time co-ordinator will be appointed to administer the access facility and run training courses for people wishing to make use of it.

An 'Asian channel for entertainment' will be provided by KC as part of its basic package. This will be supplemented by production of specific programming from KC's studio facilities in consultation with their 'community action officer'.

117. Burton-on-Trent (2) (See Hinckley 86. above)

118. Carlisle (2/3) (See Perth 44. above) The major change from the Perth model is that the 50/50 joint venture with Tern Television Productions Ltd. to establish Tayside Television Limited, is replaced in the Carlisle application by an 'association with the Cumbrian Newspaper Group'.

119. Corby (2) Initially Northampton Cable Television (NCTV) propose to 'produce and disseminate local text and programmes to either the whole of the area or selected areas within the total franchise area, thereby creating a truly community service'. This material will be supplied from the headend at Northampton.

In Year Two, this will be supplemented by 'two portable cameras and lighting units so that programmes can be injected at selected points on the cable network'. Cable subscribers will be able to 'discuss NCTV's policies with its own senior staff in management talk backs'. NCTV will appoint a programme co-ordinator who will 'specialise in local programme generation'. Such programmes will be 'free of editorial interference, provided they meet the legal requirements applying to television programmes in general'.

The 'community channel' will carry all locally originated programmes to begin with. In addition there will be a simple text based commercial channel for local advertising and shopping information. NCTV observe that such advertising is only likely to become a serious demand once the number of subscribers becomes large enough – a specific figure is not suggested.

120. Darlington, 121. Middlesbrough, 122. North Surrey & 123. Epsom (3/2) (See Portsmouth 65. above) The same approach is adopted in each franchise, however the exact figures vary. In Epsom, for example, phase two will begin about 18 months after construction, or when 15,000 subscribers are being serviced. This compares to 16 months and 11,400 subscribers in Portsmouth.

124. Falkirk (1) (See Greater Glasgow 35. above)

125. Glenrothes (3) (See Dundee 63. above)

126. Greenock (3) (See Dundee 63. above)

127. Great Yarmouth & 128. Wisbech (1) Initially the local service will be in the form of text facilities covering general information, educational material and advertising. 'As cable penetration increases and local origination programming develops', it is felt that the network will become a means through which business, local government and educational establishments could communicate with local inhabitants.

However, figures for the necessary level of cable penetration are not supplied, nor is it clear how local origination programming is to develop. The applications do refer to investment in studio facilities but these are not described, nor is their use (if any) in access programming or training courses made clear.

129. Grimsby (2/3) Alphavision point out that:

> Broadcast television of necessity serves a wide area and it is the cable network's ability to distribute television channels which are about the local area and produced locally which is one of the major benefits the system can bring to an area.

'Access to and use of the community channels will be free to individuals and organisations within the franchise area', with channel coordinators being recruited locally to develop this service. It will initially take the form of text pages, with sections devoted to education, leisure provision and consumer information.

A Public Access Channel will be available to groups wanting to use more time than is usually available on the Community Channel eg. to cover a local play. Time will be provided free, but a small charge may be levied for the use of equipment - figures not supplied.

Alphavision 'propose to provide studio and production facilities as the systems develop'. Technical and professional staff will be made available to assist local groups and ensure high production standards. Alphavision then state:

> It is our general policy that access to and use of the Public Access and Community Channels will be free to individuals, local colleges, schools and other organisations within the franchise area.

These Community Channels will be 'part of the basic services when the systems start operations in 1991'.

The time scale for the studio facilities (referred to above) coming on-stream is not specified ie. no figures are supplied as to what constitutes adequate 'system development'. Alphavision also proposes that mobile camera equipment will be supplied, though when and in what form, is not clear.

130. Haywards Heath (2) (See Burton-on-Trent 117. above)

131. Lancaster No applicants.

132. Lincoln (2/3) (See Grimsby 129. above)

133. Liverpool & 134. St Helens (3) (See Barnsley 112. above)

135. The Wirral (2/3) (See Darlington 120. above)

136. Macclesfield (2/3) (See Stockport 94. above)

137. Newport (1/2) Newport Cablevision (NC) will pioneer three channels of a local and educational nature, two will start with the commencement of the system, the third will be in conjunction with other cable operators in South Wales – Newport News Channel – equivalent to the local newspaper. 'Indeed, we envisage a fixed link camera in the newsroom of the South Wales Argus and reciprocal advertising arrangements with the newspaper'. The stated intention is to deliver programming of a high professional standard, while recognising that the status of its sources may be amateur or impoverished, or both. The News Channel will also 'at regular times' have fixed cameras at Gwent Police Headquarters and NC's shop-window in Newport.

The Educational channel would seek to build towards 'cable in the classroom' for the area's 110 schools and colleges, and encompass distance learning courses.

The Welsh Cable Channel is dependent on the other broadband cable operators in South Wales being established and agreeing to take the channel. It is intended to promote both the Welsh language and senses of Welsh national identity in the English language. The channel would have a fixed camera link with the Western Mail in Cardiff, and would also be able to draw on S4C's massive library of Welsh material.

The rest of NC's programming will be produced by third parties. There is no discussion of access to facilities for local groups, or of training in the use of facilities.

Voluntary Organisation Programming – 'The Church in Wales has a fully equipped video production studio in Penarth, Cardiff, and has offered its facilities to Gwent Association of Voluntary Organisations' associates so that professional quality videos can be produced'.

The application states that NC's business objectives are as follows: to have constructed 850 road kilometres, passing 80,000 homes by 1996; to achieve 22% penetration by 1992, rising to 31% by 1994 and 47% by 2004; to have a subscriber base of 32,000 'in just less than 7 years'; to connect 10,000 telephone lines by achieving 6% penetration for domestic use by 1994 - 10% by 2000; to achieve a 15 year rate of return of some 24% and equity value of over £200 million against an investment of £10.25 million.

References

1. For the European experience of local radio and television a most comprehensive introduction has been published. See Nick Jankowski, Ole Prehn and James Stappers (eds) *The People's Voice, Local Radio and Television in Europe*, John Libbey, London 1992.

2. The Channel Four videobox comprises a sound-proofed cubicle a little larger than a photo booth in which an adjustable stool faces a small window. The user adjusts the stool until his/her eyes match a line on the window. On pressing a button the user is counted down by a clock or lights and usually given a minute to record their contribution. A clock indicates the time remaining. The user can then view their tape and re-record if they choose. The decision to broadcast remains with the broadcaster.

3 Highways Authority Experience of UK Cable Build

Inken Schindler, Institute of Local Television, January 1992

1.   Preface

This study has been put together following a survey of highways authorities in the UK where cabling for television is under way. The experience of cable ranges from several months to seven years, where the build is now completed.

This comparative study of utility operations draws on the advice and comments of those officers involved in supervising and coordinating the plans of cable operators and the other utilities. The study examines the varied experiences of reinstatement, meeting schedules, public safety and the contractor's response to problems and speed of rectification.

Questionnaires were circulated to over one hundred highways authorities only to discover that in many cases publicised optimism about build for 1990-1991 had not materialised. In the end, the survey was able to reach highways authorities with responsibilities in the fifty franchise areas actively building or who have completed their build. Completed questionnaires were received from 79% of these areas. In addition, comments were forwarded by those authorities who, so far, had only experienced cable in negotiation.

Highways Authority Experience of UK Cable Build 1992 is the second highway's survey, and statistics from the first edition titled, *Highways Experience of UK Cable Build 1985-1990*,[1] are included for comparison. In 1990, the sample was much smaller, with fifteen responses from eighteen authorities then being cabled.

2.   Introduction

In February 1992 the Institute of Local Television circulated a questionnaire to highways authorities (or their district council agents) in the towns and cities where cable is being laid for television and telephony.

79% of these highways authorities responded from towns and cities affected by the digging of trenchwork and the installation of plant on the pavements or beneath streets.

Our questionnaire was identical to that circulated in 1990, at a time when cabling had been primed for growth by the Cable Authority's favourable attitude towards overseas investment coupled with secure telephony opportunities for cable operators guaranteed by the Duopoly Review in early 1991. The recession in the United Kingdom and the United States (from where much of the investment was due) reduced the rate of cable building much below that forecast. Nonetheless, despite expectations being trimmed, there has been a very large increase in cabling activity in comparison with the period 1985-1990.

> The new franchises have been built past 1 million homes, but the pace of development is accelerating and the rate of build will reach 1 million homes a year in 1992, with the five millionth home actually being passed before the end of 1994. Over half the population should have cable available to them by 1996. [2]

Laying cable in the UK involves a major civil engineering programme to install underground ducting and co-axial or fibre optic cable to pass 14.5 million homes over the next five years. Of the 135 cable franchises awarded by the end of 1990, cable laying is taking place in 49 districts. Aberdeen Cable completed its build in 1989 and Coventry Cable in 1991.

The 135 franchise holders enjoy the rights of way of the traditional public utility companies: water, gas, electricity and telephone, including both British Telecom and Mercury. While the new Roads and Street Works Act [3] shifts the highways role away from supervision towards that of ensuring the utilities meet responsibilities now passed to them directly, there has been little reduction so far in involvement or concern reported by the highways authorities. This is likely to change in future years as agreements are entered in the light of the new legislation rather than being followed through under the former PUSWA 1950 [4].

Not least, highways authorities are still involved because it is the local authorities to whom complaints are still addressed, while the public adjusts to the changing emphasis of the highways authority duties. As one highways engineer put it, 'because cable is not an essential service like water or electricity, the general public have a lower tolerance to the inconvenience resulting from its installation'.

In the next five to ten years £5-7bn will be spent on bringing cable to the doorsteps of half the homes in the UK. Within local authorities there is limited experience of what cable laying on such a wide scale actually entails. In most large towns and cities cable involves a five year building programme with trench digging for cable ducting, temporary filling and reinstatement of footpaths and roadways and remedial works and rectification and the siting and servicing of footpath boxes for switchgear.

Cable activity will begin by involving local authorities in negotiations with the cable operator, and in many cases already will have involved liaison with the Department of Trade and Industry in determining the acceptable rate and method of build. Throughout the building phase the highways authority as the overall planning body will stay in close touch on procedures and delays to ensure engineering goes as smoothly as possible.

The highways role is not to be envied, juggling a good relationship with the road using public and the many utilities competing for berths and access to the vacant territory under town and city streets. This study has been compiled to pool highways authority experience on cable installation and to provide some practical benchmarks and expectations of performance for those local authorities about to under-go 'the cabling experience'.

- 46% of highways authorities found that cable laying did not go as planned. The main reason for this was that there were disruptions so the work took much longer or the work had to be ceased.

- 11% of highways authorities undertake reinstatement – elsewhere the cable operator reinstates.

- 95% of cable operators are charged a fee – supervision, inspection, reinstatement (Project Management and Wayleaves)

- 81% of cable operators were found to be equal or better than the other utility services when it came to meeting work schedules on time.

- 80% of cable operators were found to be equal or better than the other utility services when it came to speed of response and rectifying problems

- 14% of cable operators were found to be worse than the other utility services when it came to the quality of reinstatement

For comparison, the Summary from 1990:-

- 43% of highways authorities found that cable laying operations did not go as planned. The main reason for this was that the standard of reinstatement was consistently poor, and furthermore deadlines and targets were not readily achieved.

- 28% of highways authorities undertake reinstatement – elsewhere the cable operator reinstates.

- 79% of cable operators are charged a fee – this is divided between supervising the site; for reinstatement and for an inspector to monitor cabling work.

- 93% of cable operators were found to be equal or better than the other utility services when it came to meeting work schedules on time.

- 71% of cable operators were found to be equal or better than the other utility services when it came to speed of response and rectifying problems.

- 46% of cable operators were found to be worse than the other utility services when it came to the quality of reinstatement.

3.   Highways Authority and Cable Operator

Early success for each cabling operation will depend to a great extent on the relationship between the cable operator and the highways authority and the perception of the 'service' by the general public. While cable television is a minority interest a lot of public relations work is necessary in order to convince the majority of citizens that ultimately the inconvenience will be of a general value.

A distinguishing feature of cable in the UK is that it is a delivery system franchised over small districts (mostly between 50-200,00 households). One major confusion that has arisen which the new highways legislation is intended to clear up is the ambiguous division of responsibility between the cable operator and local highways authority. The delegated responsibilities under the new Act do not remove the necessity for planning and full consultation between the cable operator and the highways authority.

From responses received to both the 1990 and the 1992 surveys, positive negotiations and frequent liaison are key factors in ensuring the smooth running of the cable build and in minimising the inconvenience to the public and other utilities seeking to plot berths in the highways and coordinate their own schedules of work.

A F Timms of the Royal Borough of Windsor and Maidenhead advises highways authorities to: 'Keep in close contact with your cable company and sort "problems" at an early stage of the programme', and M J Fuller of the London Borough of Redbridge suggests that 'Redbridge found the need to establish an agreed code of practise for cable TV. The implementation of the code greatly improved control of the work and reduced public complaints'.

Negotiations begun in some highways authorities had reached fairly advanced stages only to find that the cable company failed to start their build. Where this has happened, these highways authorities have been excluded from our analysis but some of their comments are included because the stop-start-stop experience is one that unfortunately many local authorities are likely to face. Comments included:

It was signally anticipated that work would start in the New Year of 1991, there is now no idea of a start date.

No work has started in South Warwickshire. Company long way behind original programme of intent.

Operator has delayed start by 18 months.

The company has ceased operations, (S Morris at Weymouth & Portland BC)

Cable company no longer trading.

Higher degree of local authority supervision required than agreed with cable company, (J W Kelly at City of Bradford Metropolitan Council).

Operator has not commenced programme because of alleged financial restrictions.

Delay in programme - work not yet commenced.

Still no start on the main work.

They have failed to meet start dates.

Whilst the franchise agreement requires 10,000 homes to be passed by April '92, work has yet to start.

We are still waiting for cable work to start. (The company lost one of its major backers last year.)

Devon Cablevision Ltd gained the South Devon Cable Franchise in July 1990. They failed to commence, in accordance with the timing in the license and have withdrawn their operation, (M Webley at Torbay Borough Council).

Agreement was reached that the cable laying would commence in the summer of 1991. There has been no communication from the company for several months.

Detailed negotiations and agreements were almost concluded but the company has had to withdraw.

The franchise operator should be forced to attend 'local meetings' with the other service providers. Deadlines must be enforceable, otherwise the operator should lose the franchise.

Believe nothing.

The Hinkley urban area was to have been substantially covered by December 1990. An entire programme for footway re-surfacing was suspended pending cable work. I am not impressed by the arbitrary and un-announced withdrawal by the operator. Under the New Roads & Street Works Act I would place an embargo on any cable laying within 12 months of the resurfacing of any footway and would not be prepared to discuss compromise.

Cable operator commitments to build have been subject to a great deal of change. Build hurdles have been almost routinely revised downwards over the last two years, in the teeth of the recession. Prior to its merger with the Independent Broadcasting Authority and the establishment of the joint Independent Television Commission, the Cable Authority gave the public assurances that lessons had been learned from the early failures of cabling due to lack of investment. For the 1990s, cable operators would not be awarded franchises until their financing was fully guaranteed. In the majority of cities in the UK cable companies have outstanding commitments way beyond their apparent means. To coin a phrase, the anger in the streets is all too apparent from the highways staff. One authority wrote:-

> The company's organisation was very poor. At preliminary meetings they were unable to make decisions and they did not keep deadlines. It would appear that the franchise for CUC Cablevision may be defaulted on to the extent that they will never start. The cost in staff time on abortive work was considerable.

'We were a bit unsure/suspicious of their intentions. New work has now ceased because of commercial considerations', wrote an engineer from the East Midlands. 'Unprofessional, inexperienced, lack of organisation and forward planning', wrote an engineer from a London Borough. A colleague from a neighbouring authority added that after negotiating funds to pay for site inspectors, the: 'Operator is to cease all work for 12 months'. Another advised:

> Negotiate strongly, be aware of the commercial needs of the operator and the needs of the public and work towards a co-operative agreement.

The effect of the recession upon the long-term investment required for cable has had considerable impact upon forecasts and projections among many if not all of the operators, more so than among the less speculative or more traditional utility companies requiring road access.

Tne lack of funding, and in some case loss of enthusiasm, to meet cabling commitments has led to many stop-start-stop experiences among highway's staff. Many replies contained a simple message; 'Work has stopped!', 'Original schedule of work abandoned.'; 'Bristol was programmed to be completed in 2 to 3 years now more like 5 to 10 years'; 'Rate of build much reduced'; 'The work was proceeding as anticipated then came to a halt through the financial difficulties of [the operator]'; 'Speed of build much slower than expected'; '[the operator] has curtailed activity part way through development' and the second operator in the area 'has not installed progressively but spread their installation activity over a wide area'; 'After considerable problems in the first few months, a reasonable working relationship was established. However, the operator has not been active since December 1990'; 'Took approximately three times longer to complete than the estimate. Policy of first time re-instatement has been abandoned' was the comment from Coventry, where build recently finished.

A comment from one highways authority in London was perhaps suitably ironic:-

> Yes it went as expected. Promises have seldom been kept.

Cable company interest in providing telephony services underpins much of the actual investment in place and this has led in some cases to the development of the cable laying operation in an unexpected way following earlier planning. 'Cable company now returning to areas already ducted for telephone work' wrote A F Timms of the Royal Borough of Windsor and Maidenhead, in an area that has pioneered the telephony service following extensive earlier activity in cable television. The incentive to go for telephony is, as one operator has suggested, because revenue from ten telephony clients equals that from one hundred cable television customers. R Dicken of Bristol City

Council suggests joint work between the authority and the cable operator where possible to overcome the effects of repeated re-working of sites; 'Carry out basic maintenance and footway schemes jointly with or by using cable TV contractors at same time in order to maximise the work being carried out and to avoid returning to same location later on'.

In the two years since our first survey, there has also been considerable turnover in the ownership and personnel running cable operations and some changes in the location of head-ends to take advantage of joining two or more neighbouring franchise areas together into an MSO - or multiple service operation.

Prior to street work being carried out, consultation with highways authorities to determine a programme of work is essential. In this respect, the highways authority must treat seriously each claim to begin work or to start a new phase, despite overwhelming evidence to the contrary that progress is unlikely to go as first planned. Once these programmes have been established it is therefore helpful to locate one or two people within the cable operation who are answerable should any problems develop and who are prepared to keep the highway authority abreast of any delays or set-backs.

In the current financial circumstances in which there is considerable financial restructuring of cable operations taking place it is very difficult, as the highways engineers have suggested themselves, to find examples where commitments made are then fulfilled. When building does start, the confusion is sometimes passed back-and forth between cable operator and sub-contractor. C Tranter of Shropshire County Council advises, 'Ensure ground rules are agreed prior to start of work, establish contact points with cable company and make it clear: they, not their contractors, are the undertakers and the body which should be responsible'.

Safety is an important area where improvements can be made. '[Cable operators and their contractors] could improve on the signing and safety during works operations', (S Long at the London Borough of Tower Hamlets); 'Safety provision for pedestrians has been lacking when installation gangs have followed up into an area – accidents have occurred due to this', (D L Evans at Birmingham City Council); 'Insist on adequate safety training for contractors, cable company and authority staff', (D Fox at the London Borough of Hillingdon).

> The speed of cable laying tends to exceed the ability of the contractors to provide proper signing, remove spoil, take adequate precautions to safeguard the public. In Southwark our experience has been that final reinstatement by Videotron is superior to most other utilities but whilst works proceed much chaos ensues. Tight supervision is therefore essential, (D Eskick at London Borough of Southwark).

4. Smoothing the Cable Build

The supervision (of all works) is one of the key elements in a successful cabling programme. The speed of work makes this essential and it is important not to underestimate the amount of staff time this will take up.

The highways authority should engage at least one full-time officer in the supervision of cable engineering tasks, to monitor progress and to report back on any problems. 'A high level of supervision is required until this cable operation is established', (D L Evans at Birmingham City Council); 'Provide a competent supervisor for every six gangs'.

'To minimize disruption to the public ... keep the number of gangs working in a given area to about 4 or no more than 6', (T Edwards at London Borough of Merton); 'Ensure you have an inspector for every twenty gangs', (J G Edwards at Cambridgeshire County Council); 'In Southampton, large areas of trenching have been left for a considerable time in a temporary condition, as different contractors were employed to do the permanent reinstatements and were not able to "catch-up" with the contractors undertaking the original dig. This has proved most unsatisfactory.'

Furthermore it may be useful to formulate guidelines for installing above-ground equipment and trying to reduce obtrusiveness. 'Ensure they have adequate and effective site management and adequate resources for the (considerable) scale of operations. Prepare for a lot of complaints. Because cable is not an essential service like water or electricity, the general public have a lower tolerance to the inconvenience resulting from its installation'; 'Go into the detail design of manholes and boxes with care; many are not adjustable. Agree a maximum amount of trench that may be in a temporary reinstatement stage. Under the agreement between L. B. C. and Cable London all excavated materials are removed off site. I would suggest that backfilling the trench with E. S. B. or lean concrete has saved many problems,' (N Taylor at London Borough of Camden).

It is possible to avoid unnecessary paperwork by agreeing a system early on with the cable operator. 'A working agreement and enforcement of a code of practice is considered essential'; 'Press on early agreement on wayleaves. Ensure adequate levels of inspection. Hold regular liaison meetings before and during work. Ensure members are involved and invited to presentations. A lot of adverse comment has been received about why the service is being installed in the first place and lack of consultation and publicity'; 'It is necessary to have very clear agreement with operator before start of works. It is also necessary to have extensive supervision – full time inspectorate is recommended and regular meetings at high level'; 'Have a very clear written agreement before works commence'.

It has already been stressed that early and lengthy consultation between the local authority and the cable operator will prove valuable if a good working relationship with the minimum of problems is to develop. It is important that sufficient time is set aside for what may prove to be extensive discussions. It is also worth taking into consideration the practical working hours and the night safety of the sites and compounds.

It is the sheer scale of the cable operation in the next five years – should expectations at last start to become reality – that will lead to problems, should highways authorities not tightly schedule, regulate and police the cabling activity. There will be intense competition for the best engineering contractors, and in the race for digging, experienced engineers will become thin on the ground.

5.   Problems with Reinstatement

Almost half of the highways authorities (46% as against 43% in the study of 1990) who took part in our survey found that the cable laying operation did not go as planned in discussions with the cable operator.

In 1990, in three quarters of these examples the quality of reinstatement was far poorer than anticipated, *this figure was only 21% in 1992.*

In all cases where cabling did go as expected a fee was levied by the highways authority. This fee covered the wages of a full time inspector to regulate the cable operation, often with particular emphasis on monitoring the standard of reinstatement (plus supervision, project management and wayleaves). 95% of the fees were paid by the cable operator, the highways authority paid the fees in the remainder of the cases.

General comments about reinstatement:

> Permanent reinstatement not as expected.

> More problems with reinstatements than anticipated.

> Permanent reinstatement is not being completed (time wise) as agreed. (D Fox at the London Borough of Hillingdon)

> Consider carefully the value of extended guarantees on reinstatement. Perhaps a revenue sum every year from the operator to cover increased highway maintenance costs would make more sense. At present we do permanent reinstatement for most other utilities.

6.   Dealing with the Public

A further difficult area for several highways authorities was the cable operator's relationship with the public.

Problems were generally created by a lack of communication and as the public saw it a lack of information. The public seemed to be unsure of what exactly was happening in their residential streets and they often felt they were not given enough warning prior to sections of streets and pavements being cordoned off. Highways comments included:

> The 'public relations' aspect between the cable operator and the public could be improved.

> Lay down and enforce the ground rules with regard to specification of service and the public requirements from the start and try to develop a good working relationship with the contractor. Ensure the public are fully aware of what is going on by use of letter drops and signing on the job.

> The local operator learnt some hard lessons in early days due to lack of publicity and communication with residents, (D J Ball at Thamesdown BC).

7. Analysis

54% of Highways Authorities found the cable laying operation went as planned, following discussions with the cable operator. *This compares with 57% in the 1990 survey.*

Of the remaining 46% who found operations did not go as planned:-

- 37% found that there were greater disruptions than anticipated and the work took much longer.

- 21% that the work has ceased or the cable operator had not been active for a certain time.

- 21% found more problems with reinstatement than expected.

  of the remaining 21% the highways authorities found a lack of consultation with the public, unprofessional approach among the cable operators, or the original schedule of work had been abandoned.

In 89% of cases the cable operator undertakes reinstatement - *compared with 72% in 1990.*

- In 11% of cases the highways authority undertakes reinstatement.

- In 95% of cases the cable operator is charged a fee for highways authority services – a rise from the figure of 79% found in 1990.

Of the 95% of cases where the cable operator pays a fee:-

- 41% are charged for an inspector (to monitor cable engineering work) - *35% in 1990.*

- 31% are charged for supervising the site - *45% in 1990.*

- 23% are charged for reinstatement - *20% in 1990.*

  of the remaining 5% the cable operator is charged for policing, enforcement, project management and wayleaves.

How did the cable laying operation fare in comparison with the other public utilities?

When it came to meeting work schedules on time:-

- 24% of highways authorities found the cable operator and their contractors to be better than other utilities - *28% in 1990.*

- 59% found them to be equal to other utilities - *65% in 1990.*

- 17% found them to be worse than other utilities - *7% in 1990.*

When it came to speed of response and rectification of problems:-

- 43% of highways authorities found the cable operator and their contractors to be better than other utilities - *21% in 1990.*

- 38% found them to be equal to other utilities - *50% in 1990.*
- 19% found them to be worse than other utilities - *29% in 1990.*

As far as the quality of reinstatement was concerned:-

- 41% of highways authorities found the cable operator and their contractors to be better than other utilities - *16% in 1990.*
- 44% found them to be equal to other utilities - *38% in 1990.*
- 15% found them to be worse than other utilities - *46% in 1990.*

As the comments from highways staff have already amply indicated the statistics confirm an increase in dissatisfaction with the cable operators in meeting work schedules. When work takes place, in the areas of reinstatement and speed of response and rectification of problems there has been considerable improvement since the 1990 survey.

8. Conclusion

We asked the highways authorities to make a comparative study of the overall quality of the cable laying experience with each of the other utility services. We asked them to take into account the quality of plant installation, engineering and reinstatement and minimising the effects on the public.

- How did the overall quality of gas operations stand? (See Figure 1.)

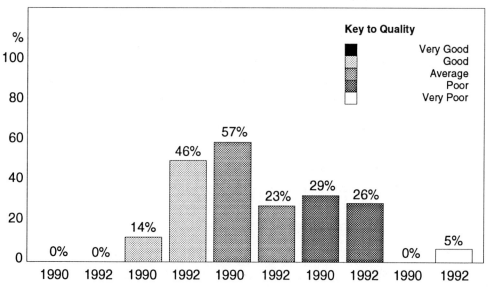

FIGURE 1: How did the overall quality of gas operations stand?

- How did the overall quality of electricity operations stand? (See Figure 2.)

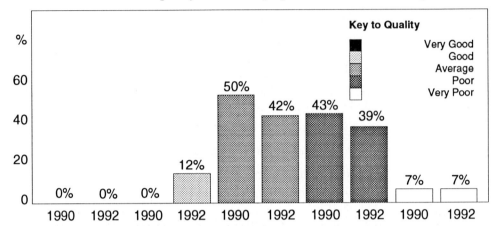

FIGURE 2: How did the overall quality of *electricity* operations stand?

- How did the overall quality of water operations stand? (See Figure 3.)

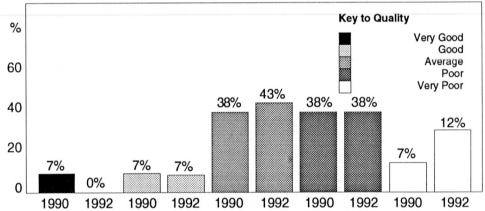

FIGURE 3: How did the overall quality of *water* operations stand?

- How did the overall quality of BT operations stand? (See Figure 4.)

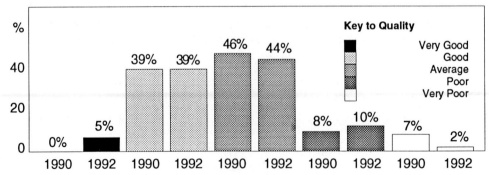

FIGURE 4: How did the overall quality of *BT* operations stand?

• How did the overall quality of Mercury operations stand? (See Figure 5.)

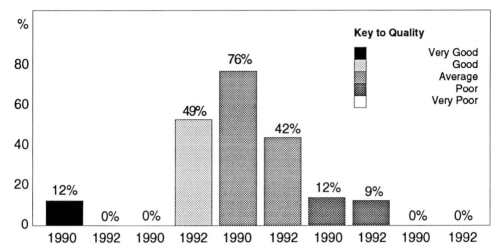

*FIGURE 5: How did the overall quality of **Mercury** operations stand?*

• How did the overall quality of cable operations stand? (See Figure 6.)

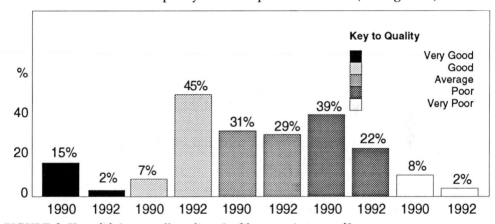

*FIGURE 6: How did the overall quality of **cable** operations stand?*

Totalling the 'very good', 'good' and 'average' performances from the 1990 and 1992 surveys shows Cable pulling up on Mercury and BT the better performers so far satisfying the highways authorities.

• For 1992, general satisfaction with the cable installation for 1990 stood at 53% as against 76% in 1992.

By comparison, Mercury moved from 88% to 91%; BT from 85% to 88%; Gas dropped from 71% to 69%; Electricity moves from 50% to 54%; Water drops from 52% to 50%.

- Cable operators have shown the best overall improvement in highways authority evaluation and have moved up to levels of performance approaching those enjoyed by BT and Mercury.

In spite of the difficult financial circumstances faced by the cable operators in 1990-1992, in comparison with the other public utilities, the cable industry has shown, so far as highways authorities are concerned, an impressive improvement in their overall performance.

Forty nine broadband cable systems were operational on 1st January 1992 , of which four are completely constructed and cover the whole of their franchise areas. The authorities in the towns highlighted participated in the 1992 Survey.

Swindon (Swindon Cable Ltd)
Aberdeen (Aberdeen Cable Services Ltd)
Coventry (Coventry Cable Ltd)
Glasgow (Clyde Cablevision Ltd)
Westminster (Westminster Cable Co Ltd)
Slough, Windsor, Maidenhead etc (Windsor Television Ltd)
Ealing (Videotron Corporation)
Newham and Tower Hamlets (East London Telecommunications Ltd)
Guildford, West Surrey & East Hants (British Cable Services Ltd)
Camden (Camden Cable London plc)
Kensington & Chelsea (Videotron Corporation)
East Lancashire (East Lancashire Cablevision Ltd)
Birmingham (Birmingham Cable Ltd)
Southampton & Eastleigh (Videotron Corporation Ltd)
Luton & South Bedfordshire (Cablevision Bedfordshire Ltd)
Andover (Andover Cablevision Ltd)
Sutton & Merton (United Artists Communications (London South) plc)
Norwich (Norwich Cablevision Ltd)
Bolton (Bolton Cablevision Ltd)
Preston and Central Lancs (Cable Communications Ltd)
Peterborough (Peterborough Cablevision Ltd)
Liverpool (Cable Communications Ltd)
Nottingham (Diamond Cable Ltd)
Tyneside (Comment Cablevision Ltd)
Bristol (United Artists Communications)
Redbridge, Barking, Dagenham (East London Telecommunications Ltd)
Greenwich and Lewisham (Videotron Corporation Ltd)
Kingston and Richmond (United Artists Communications (London South) plc)
Haringey (Cable London plc)
Lambeth and Southwark (Videotron Corporation Ltd)
Northampton (County Cable Telecommunications)
Tayside (Tayside Cable Systems Ltd)
West Glamorgan (Starvision Network Ltd)
Leicester (Leicester Communications Ltd)

West Herts (County Cable Telecommunications)
Thamesmead (Videotron Corporation Ltd)
Cambridge (Cambridge Cable Ltd)
Hackney and Islington (Cable London plc)
Hammersmith, Fulham, Brent, Barnet (Videotron Corporation)
Black Country (Midlands Cable Communications Ltd)
Portsmouth (Cable Comms Solent Ltd)
Enfield (Cable London plc)
Glenrothes (Kingdom Cablevision Ltd)
Derby (Derbyshire Cablevision Ltd)
Harrow (Videotron Corporation Ltd)
Hillingdon (Middlesex Cable)
Hounslow (Middlesex Cable)
Thames Valley (County Cable Telecommunications)

A total of 135 franchises have been awarded, most of which should be starting construction in the next few months. All these franchise areas in total cover about 14.6 million homes. The Independent Television Commission expects to advertise a number of additional franchises in due course.

References

1. Lyndsey Bowditch, *Highways Authority Experience of UK Cable Build, 1985-1990*, Institute of Local Television, 1990.

2. *A Concise Brief*, Independent Television Commission, December 1991.

3. *Roads and Street Works Act*, HMSO, London, 1990.

4. *Public Utilities and Street Works Act*, HMSO, London, 1950.

4   Local Authority Cable Briefing

Lyndsey Bowditch, Institute of Local Television, 1991

With financial support from Edinburgh District Council and Lothian Regional Council.

1.   Introduction

This study was undertaken to monitor the experience of cable and satellite amongst local authority departments across the UK. With over 130 cable franchises now awarded, this briefing offers an overview of local authority involvement with cable and examines some of those local authorities whose departments are in the forefront of cable development.

Practical advice is offered by Housing departments which hold the right of access to council property over the cable operator and are therefore in a strong bargaining position to make financial gains from the cable service or to accumulate tradeable points.

The study looks at:

> Economic Development departments which have developed strong telecommunications links through the advanced fibre optic cabling linked to local cable television franchises. The expectations that the scale of electronic messaging and information transmission will treble over the next four to five years, helped by the with the greater carriage capacity of Integrated Services Digital Network (ISDN) telephone systems. Economic Development departments have a major role in developing information economy strategies dependent upon the cable infrastructure to provide easy to use and cheap electronic communication.

> Public Relations departments on the whole tend to be held responsible for any problems the public might encounter during the installation of cable networks. Those local authorities which have gained access to the cable network to broadcast public information services have found that cable was a more valuable communications tool than any other local media in presenting local authority services.

> Departments of Recreation and Leisure in general tend to have little experience of practical development in cable, perhaps because although these departments are able to make gains from the system they have little to trade in return.

Cable television's potential for education and training is rapidly becoming realised amongst local authority Education departments. This report examines one of the first major studies to be undertaken by the Educational Broadcasting Services Trust based on Coventry's cable pilot channel.

Research was undertaken in late 1990 and early 1991 into the cabling experience amongst local authority departments across the UK. Questionnaires were sent to a number of departments, some of which were then followed up by telephone.

We looked at the experience and opportunities taken by local authorities in respect of the following departments:

Housing – questionnaires were sent to 136 Housing departments in the UK to monitor their experience of cabling, including installation, maintenance, safety and security. A follow up phone survey was conducted amongst selected departments to establish the affect of the Sky/BSB merger.

Economic Development – we looked at Economic Development departments in Manchester, Tyneside and Norwich and their plans for investment and economic gain, advanced telephony and joint project development via the cable system.

Public Relations – questionnaires were sent to those local authorities where cabling was complete or was nearing the end of the build. These asked to what extent cable television was used for informing the public of council events etc, and also looked at the public relations involvement during cable installation.

Recreation and Leisure – plans for the use of cable for library and information services are still in their infancy. We looked at the Dunston Community Television experiment undertaken by Gateshead Metropolitan Borough Council.

Education – we looked at Coventry Education department's response to using cable for community and formal education in primary, secondary and further education establishments.

2. Summary

- 36% of councils charge a fee for cable access to council property mainly to cover the rectification of damage.

- One council charges the cable operator for the salary of a consultant to manage the project.

- Another council has secured an agreement for way leaves including a fee.

- One department replied that they were still in negotiation with the cable operator but that way leaves were to be paid and all damage made good.

- 26% of councils said that the cable operator could utilise any services belonging to the council, mainly access trunking and to a lesser extent cabling.

- 12% of cable operators will, as far as was technically practical, use existing ducting and wiring, although some of this was for CATV and some for MATV.

- In one case the cable operator would make use of the existing piped aerial system.

- One council found it favourable to remain in close contact with the Highways department.

- One department urged effective liaison with the Area Managers and Valuers section before agreeing the go-ahead for work.

- 10% of councils undertake a policy to follow up and monitor the mainte-nance of cable after installation.

- Some housing departments have reached an agreement where the cable company maintain cabling for a nominal fixed fee.

- One council where cabling had not yet started found difficulty in finalising agreements on SMATV systems with the cable company.

- One council reported poor standards of reinstatement on council estates – lower than in normal footways and highways and also delays in rectifying damage.

3.1 Housing Departments and Cable Experience

Questionnaires which asked about the experience of satellite and cable were circulated to over 130 Housing departments in September 1990: of these 46 responded, although 4 departments were at the time unable to complete the questionnaire. Most of the respondents wished to remain anonymous. In the following statistics n = 42.

The questionnaire asked about the experience of satellite and cable throughout Hous-ing departments. Housing departments have a direct involvement with installation and may anticipate financial gains from the service or may accumulate tradeable points with the cable operator for the benefit of other departments.

3.1.1 Advice from Housing Departments

Where the take up of cable is slow, an interim SMATV solution should be considered to combat DTH problems. One council advises close liaison, especially at the start of the contract, and also the importance of establishing how the council's land or property will be affected, with particular attention to houses and flats which have been sold.

Another council gives the advice, 'do not accept the first offer and be prepared to negotiate at length. It is our view that companies in the business are under-resourced in terms of having experienced manpower to provide the systems in the short term – which is what we need to prevent [installation of] individual dishes'.

Advice given from other departments includes: 'ensure that cable routes are agreed before work commences on each type of block or house'; 'it is essential for the council to provide clear design and operating specifications'; inter-departmental working was also seen as very important as was a clear allocation of responsibilities.

One department found that it was beneficial to work with the cable operator to ensure that the cable company is active and financially sound.

Some practical experience from another council was that by installing satellite dishes through communal aerial systems they were able to break the monopoly that the cable franchise company would have had on council customers' viewing choices.

One council was concerned at the DTI's method of awarding licences, although they did value initial communication with the DTI. Subsequently there have been changes within the cable company who hold the franchise and the council are currently waiting to see whether work carried out is of a higher standard than has been achieved prior to this change.

One council felt that the basic idea of cables instead of satellite dishes would prove far better for the council. However they warned that unless cable companies are willing to cooperate more with local authorities, restrictions which the local authority has the power to wield regarding access etc could lose the cable company a potentially lucrative market.

Another council saw possible advantages of cable over and above television services, such as the use of cable for security camera systems, heat monitoring etc.

3.1.2 Satellite

1. Does the council provide guidelines for householders on satellite reception?

> 48% of councils provide guidelines.
> 12% of councils did not respond.

2. Do unapproved satellite dishes present special problems for your council?

> Unapproved satellite dishes present special problems for 79% of councils.
>
> 2% of councils did not respond.
>
> Of those 79% of councils who responded that unapproved satellite dishes did present problems, in 49% of cases the cable operators offered short term solutions.
>
> 65% of councils facing problems with unapproved satellite dishes favoured providing satellite master antenna television (SMATV) systems as

an interim measure. Unapproved satellite dishes on multi-storey blocks also proved to be problematic – in these cases proposals to 'part wire' or again install SMATV systems were seen as short term ways of dealing with the problem.

Other councils found problems with areas where there was no communal system and where the householder had not requested permission to erect a satellite dish. Solutions were sought by up-grading existing communal aerials, by the addition of satellite channels to existing community antenna television (CATV) systems, by the possible purchase of the dish if owned by the householder, or by 'conditions of tenancy'.

3. Does your council own local cable networks for delivering BBC/ITV etc in some of its council housing?

57% of councils own cable networks for delivering BBC/ITV etc. (See Figure 1.)

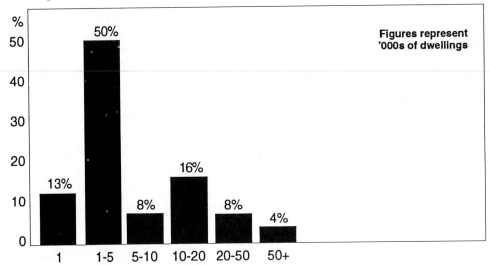

FIGURE 1: Representation of size of council owned cable networks.

4. Have you been approached by BSB, SKY or other satellite systems operators to install an alternative system to individual satellite reception by each householder on the council's cable networks (a system usually known as SMATV)?

91% of councils have been approached.

Of these 91%,

40% are likely to take up the offer.
35% are unlikely to take up the offer.
25% are unsure whether they will take up the offer.

Approaches ranged from free equipment and provision of channels for dwellings over a certain number of households (usually 30-40). In other cases a varying number of channels were offered free, with other channels paid for by subscription. Other offers included free installation only; the addition of Sky and BSB to most CATV systems; the conversion of existing CATV systems into SMATV systems. In one example the council were considering becoming a SMATV licensed operator to 7500 dwellings providing Sky and BSB. Another department replied, 'we are enhancing existing communal aerial systems to provide four BSB channels direct in partnership with Telefusion Ltd, at a cost to tenants of 10 pence weekly from 1st April 1991, with a similar deal to be finalised to supply Sky Television'.

One council found that they were unable to take up the offer as television would be distributed through communal aerial systems which they did not own. Four departments which responded were still negotiating offers.

5. Will the cable operator/SMATV operator pay for access to the housing cable networks?

In only 30% of cases does the cable operator pay for access to the housing cable networks. One council had negotiated that the cable operator would pay for access as part of the overall housing and cable company agreement. In another instance the cable operator does not pay for access but will assume all maintenance and development costs.

6. Will tenants be offered favourable channel rental terms for satellite operator access to the housing cable networks?

64% of councils said that their tenants would be offered favourable rental terms. In one case lower rental terms were not offered but two free VHF channels on BSB were proposed instead (with Sky verbally agreeing to similar conditions). In another case lower connection charges were offered to council tenants than to other areas.

3.2.2 Cable

One council, who did not fill in the questionnaire, responded that direct cabling was unlikely to be provided for approximately two years. In an effort to provide multi-channel facilities, they were developing networked communal satellite television systems with the cable operator. The first such scheme has been completed (650 dwellings) with a further 2000 homes in the pipeline. These systems are directly compatible with cable and those receiving television in this manner can simply be 'plugged' in when cabling reaches the district.

1. Is the cable laying operation taking place much as your department expected following discussions with the cable operator?

In 76% of cases cabling had not started and local authorities had no experience in this area. In the 24% of cases where cabling was under way or had been completed, half found the cabling operation was taking place as expected following discussions with the cable operator. The remaining half had found the operation: 'rather slow', 'delays in operation' and 'long delays due to arguments with the County Council on pavement reinstatement'.

2. Is the cable operator charged a fee for access to council property (eg.) for project management, way leaves, rectification of damage?

> 36% said that the cable operator was charged a fee for access
> 48% did not respond

16% of councils charge a fee for access to council property to cover rectification of damage. One council charges the cable operator for the salary of a consultant to manage the project. Another council has secured an agreement for way leaves including a fee, and yet another has arranged for a fee to be paid as part of their agreement with the cable operator. One department replied that they were still in negotiation with the cable operator but that way leaves were to be paid and all damage made good.

3. Does or will the cable operator utilise any services such as trunking, cabling or maintenance belonging to the council?

Only 26% of councils said that the cable operator would utilise any services belonging to the council. 27% of these said they would, in the main, access trunking and to a lesser extent cabling. 45% said that they would, as far as was technically practical, use existing ducting and wiring, although some of this was for CATV and some for MATV. In another case the cable operator would make use of the existing piped aerial system. One council found it favourable to remain in close contact with the highways department. 50% of councils did not respond.

4. Does the cable operator make cable television available free of charge or at a reduced rate to council tenants?

14% of councils said that the cable operator would make cable television available free of charge or at a reduced rate to council tenants. One council said that this would be available only on SMATV systems. In some cases negotiations were still underway on these proposals. 50% of councils did not respond.

5. Does the Council issue a standard design brief or guidance notes for installing cable in new/existing sites?

17% of councils issue a standard design brief or guidance notes for installing cable in new/existing sites. 50% did not respond.

6. What provisions does the Housing department make for security and safety during cable installation?

72% of councils did not respond. In 5% of cases there are currently no provisions made for safety and security, although some of these are considering what measures may be taken. Other councils have more comprehensive provisions ranging from supervision by council officers, to 'comprehensive specifications backed-up by a full-time on-site supervisor employed by the city engineers' department to protect the council's interests. The post is funded by the cable operator'. Another department stated that no specific standards are set other than that the method of installing must comply with Highways Standard requirements.

One department stated that contractor cards would be issued and standard contractor conditions would apply. Others state that safety and security are the responsibility of cable installers or that the cable company has to comply with standard safety guide-lines. Another department urges effective liaison with the Area Managers and Valuers section before agreeing the go-ahead for work.

7. Does the council employ a follow up policy to monitor and maintain cable after installation?

Only 10% of councils undertake a follow up policy to monitor and maintain cable after installation. Many believe that monitoring and maintenance is the responsibility of the cable operator. Others have reached an agreement where the cable company maintain cabling for a nominal fixed fee. 62% of councils did not respond.

8. In the experience of the Housing department, have the cable operator and their contractors provided a good, average or poor service in installing cable through council housing and adjacent land?

Many councils have had very little experience of cable to date, and as a result only 14% of Housing departments were able to comment on the standard of cable installation through council housing and adjacent land.

2% of departments found that the cable operator and their contractors were good at meeting work schedules on time and 10% found them to be average.

2% found the cable operator and their contractors were good as far as speed of response and rectification of problems were concerned, 7% found them to be average and 5% found them to be poor. One council where cabling had not yet started found difficulty in finalising agreements on SMATV systems with the cable company. One council reported poor standards of reinstatement on council estates – lower than in normal footways and highways and also delays to rectify damage.

14% of councils commented on the quality of workmanship of the cable operator - of these 2% found the quality to be good, 7% found the quality to be average, and 5% found the quality of workmanship to be poor.

A sample of Housing departments were consulted following the Sky/BSB merger, to find out what affect this had within their department.

Dundee District Council

No offers were taken up with either Sky or BSB prior to their merger. Dundee has a policy to deal only with the cable operator, Tayside Cable Systems Ltd. As a result the cable company have agreed to install a temporary system of satellite dishes which will be replaced when the cabling is installed.

Stevenage Borough Council

The Sky/BSB merger had little effect on this department since contracts had not been signed with either of the companies. They still retain Sky, although they no longer have the Super Channel.

The original cable company, Maxwell Cable TV pulled out in late 1990, and Cablevision

Communications have since taken over the franchise. This has set operations back and negotiations between the cable company and the Housing department are currently underway, although to date no technical details have been established.

The council plan to retain control over the cable ducting initially, but once it has been laid the cable company will oversee and maintain the cables. The council are not planning to make any charge for access to their property.

Dover District Council

Again this council felt the Sky/BSB merger would not affect their policies. They had taken a decision to deal only with the cable company – North Downs Cable. In this district it is the responsibility of the cable company to maintain the cable as they own the ducting. The council do charge a nominal fee for access to council property for way leaves.

As far as satellite dishes are concerned, the Planning department's guidelines are followed, these allow satellite dishes to be erected on houses but forbid satellite dishes on blocks of flats. The Housing department is not involved in enforcing this.

Bolton Metropolitan Borough Council

This Housing department found the Sky/BSB merger had a considerable effect on their operations. 75% of BSB satellite dishes had already been installed prior to the merger and consequently all operations had to stop, which provoked many customer complaints. Currently the council are trying to arrange a deal via Telefusion, whereby all dishes will be replaced by Astra dishes. However the right of distribution is currently under debate.

Since the BSB/Sky merger the cable company has had to revise its plan for installing cable throughout the city – previously it was able to rely on the availability of both Sky and BSB as a selling point. The cable company has now come into direct competition with the SMATV distributor.

Council dwellings and communal flats will not be cabled up – instead these homes will receive communal satellite dishes. As the cable company employ the same contractors as the highways department, this has encouraged a fairly smooth relationship.

Birmingham City Council

In early 1990 Birmingham City Council began negotiating with the cable operator. The council was approached by both Sky and BSB and by the middle of 1990 BSB pushed for a deal to be secured.

SMATV systems are installed by the cable operator in new and rewired blocks of flats and the signals are sent down the council's existing cables. However the council maintain the MATV system.

The council charge the cable operator a fee for access to council property. The cable company also fund two permanent full-time posts for monitoring the cable laying process. The council do not retain any control over the ducting.

Glasgow District Council

At the time of the Sky/BSB merger, BSB SMATV systems had been installed in 68,000 out of a total of 75,000 homes. The remaining homes received satellite on the MATV system, over which the council retain ownership. After the merger, council tenants received two channels free (the Sports channel and BSkyB 1) via the CATV system. The council are finding that increasingly tenants wish access to additional channels, such as the movie channels. As a result the council is currently negotiating both with Clyde Cablevision, the present cable operator, and with a private operator to establish a better and cheaper service for Council tenants.

The cable franchise was awarded in 1985, however the local authority is disappointed at the level of uptake in the past 5-6 years, and feels uncomfortable that residents buy DTH dishes even in areas which have been fully cabled. As a result the council very much welcome competition from private SMATV operators.

The council cooperated with Clyde Cablevision during cabling and gave the company right of way leaves, and insisted on reinstatement being performed to their specification.

There have been problems in cabling some high rise blocks. The council's Engineering department provide a specification for cabling routes through the building which must be adhered to by the cable operator, although this may not always be the most cost-effective route for the operator.

London Borough of Ealing

In this borough the satellite merger presented a slight problem as a contract had been signed for BSB to install SMATV systems, however there had been no SMATV installations carried out prior to the merger.

Videotron, the cable operator makes use of existing trunking belonging to the council. The council are currently negotiating with the cable operator for a fee in return for access to their property.

About one third of the franchise has been cabled, and operations are going 'reasonably well'. The main problems which have been encountered include difficulties in maintaining a proper liaison process with the cable operator, which has led to further problems regarding the flow of information from the operator to the council.

An interim assessment of the cabling operation is planned before the cable operator gains access to council property.

Aberdeen City Council

Aberdeen was the first cable franchise in the UK to complete its build, with cable passing 91,000 homes by 1989. Extensive marketing was carried out, particularly in areas of council housing. There were disruptions to the cable build when the council demanded way-leave payments from the cable operator for passing municipal properties, Aberdeen Cable Services Ltd. This led to an impasse lasting over a year during which time the cable operator was unable to gain access to its most promising subscribers, council house tenants. Eventually an amicable arrangement was reached and a smaller fee, replacing the original demand for £1.00 a metre, was secured. Estimates put the loss of revenue during this period and the additional financial burden placed on the cable operation at around £1 million.

Once Aberdeen Cable secured access to the council estates the take-up looked more promising and reached 18%. However these early problems led to fluctuating subscription charges and the introduction of a basic and add-ons package of channels. The recession in North Sea oil in the mid-80s, the house price collapse and the drop in prosperity and rise in unemployment added further to Aberdeen Cable's problems. With the changing economic fortunes, churn – the rate of turnover in subscribers – became a particular problem in Aberdeen, at one time the annual subscriber turnover was as high as 40%, although in the last year it has been running at around 25%.

The current rapid growth in fibre optic cabling linked to local cable television franchises has provided opportunities for enhanced telecommunications. As a result of this advanced technology, some local authorities in the UK are already developing information economy strategies in connection with their economic development departments.

3.2.3 Interactive Services

Beyond television and home shopping, cable can provide a number of interactive services ranging from public information services to linking networks of community organisations and new start businesses. Schools and colleges are able to link up via cable to gain access to improved language and international television programmes. The cable network also encourages distance learning and training. Cable can also provide a network of telecommunications between libraries (information services) and academic establishments.

Manchester

In Manchester, the opportunities for enhanced telecommunications have already been seized, with the commissioning of the Manchester 'Host' study to investigate the technical and economic feasibility of establishing a low cost, integrated computer information and communications service for Manchester (known as the Manchester 'Host' Computer). The study was commissioned in September 1989, the public version of the final report was made available in May 1990.

The study set out to examine the potential for an integrated service which would offer users access to electronic mail, computer conference facilities, electronic bulletin boards, fax, telex, on-line database storage and retrieval, access to remote database services, and a range of other services including electronic publishing, translation services and on-line software libraries.

The report stresses that the Host should be seen in the wider context of providing an important component of the developing telecommunications structure of the region which includes the forthcoming cable television franchises, the City Council's Telematics training programme involving over a dozen European partners and the proposal to the

European Community's COMETT programme for an advanced telecommunications project.

The feasibility study, in close liaison with the City Council and the Department of the Environment, considered a number of options for the Host corporate structure: the structure has to be capable of running the core Host services in order that it is financially self-sufficient and capable of survival and growth without public subsidy. It should also be of economic and social benefit to the community.

The market for electronic information and messaging in the UK is expected to treble within next 5 years – as a result of the introduction of international communications standards. The spread of ISDN technology will also result in the expansion of services providing on-line facilities to include developments such as interactive graphics and mixed-media messaging.

There are opportunities for the Host to be made available via the cable network. The services which the Host computer can offer include:

- electronic mail – communications from user to user with similar systems throughout Europe, N America and the rest of the world;

- bulletin boards – public and private access boards to enable on-line information for general consumption/special interest groups;

- conferencing – public and private conferencing facilities to enable structured on-line discussions to take place;

- file transfer;

- fax transmission;

- telex;

- databases and information services (high availability of local information services have a local relevance);

- networking facility for schools and colleges – encourage the use of existing computer and communications hardware.

Small and medium sized enterprises (SMEs), universities and polytechnics will have access to the services the Host offers. Telephony services will be established via the Host. The Host will carry: advertising for local companies/ businesses; tele-shopping or networking with suppliers, sub-contractors; printing and publishing services; financial services with banks, financial consultants etc; property information; news services – this is an important potential source of information provision (examples in Boston, USA and Odense, Denmark indicate that newspaper services are very popular with network users. In Odense these include classified advertising, general and sports news, a 'What's On' guide, chatlines and games).

It is important to establish cooperation with the local press. In the case of Manchester, the *Manchester Evening News* felt that if competitors started offering on-line services the pressure to follow suit would be considerable (comparable to pressures for full colour printing). They were keenest to offer advertising (as opposed to editorial) sections of the newspaper. They were also willing to make listings and information available.

Uses of Host system within the City Council Architects Department –

provision of a coordinated and efficient information and communication system: information on educational literature, health and safety in the home, construction of housing and roads can be made available via the system. The Host is compatible with the computer-aided design system.

Careers Office –

lists of all employers in area, careers offices and services available via Host.

Education Department –

most primary and secondary schools already have the necessary computers and modems for accessing the system. As Information Technology becomes increasingly important in the national curriculum - the Host provides a low cost entry point and a focus for Information Technology activities.

Further Education –

electronic mail is seen as an important developmental tool allowing joint authorship and conferencing between staff and students at remote sites. Information can be published via the system on services which colleges etc provide. The system can also provide interactive links between colleges.

Environmental Health –

source of information on topics such as, atmospheric pollution levels, consumer protection database, lists of legislation.

Housing Department –

information on rent, rebates and benefits, property details, rehousing, accommodation for the elderly etc.

Tourist Information Centre –

provide database on tourist information, including city's attractions and events, food and drink and hotel guides, also statistical information about the region.

Planning Department –

information on planning applications, land availability, land checks, sites available for development, ordinance survey maps of region, census information, register of community facilities.

Social Services Department –

the system can provide the department with communication links to enable quick and effective liaison with a dispersed set of organisations.

Details of services which the department provide and how the public can get access to them information on child care, care of the elderly, mental health services etc. - can also be published via the Host.

Libraries –

computer terminals located in libraries would help lessen the number of face-to-face enquires for information. An on-line system would also allow computers to be up-dated more efficiently.

Economic Development Department –

this department can offer information on grants available for companies in the city, a list of land or property which the council have for sale or lease, statistics on the local economy, and a directory of companies in the city. And perhaps more importantly, Economic Development departments have strategic planning and coordination to trade in exchange for enhanced local industry and possible information economy advantages.

In terms of its contribution to the local economy, the report concludes that the Host project will :

- provide local businesses with an innovative and useful communications facility.

- generate commercial opportunities for new services to be provided via the Host.

- create new jobs in the city, both through the Host organisation and the related services that will be based around the Host.

- provide a valuable new service for non-commercial organisations in the city.

- provide links with Europe - also funding opportunities and related projects.

Norwich

In Norwich, the local authority is also developing strategies to deal with the 'information economy', dependent upon the cable infrastructure to provide new opportunities for growth and improvement in the collecting, processing and transmitting of information and data.

In Norwich, the infrastructure of telecommunications satellites together with fibre optic cabling linking to television/telecoms, will make this sort of electronic communication easier and cheaper. Norwich currently suffers isolation as a result of poor physical links which can be overcome through cable and satellite networks.

Some of the potential aspects of fibre optic cabling include:

Teleworking – where a worker is based outside the headquarters of an organisation but is connected by a telecommunications/cable link attached to a computer, which enables them to send work via the cable network to a client/employer elsewhere in the country.

There are obvious advantages of teleworking for employees - it provides flexibility, especially for people who are tied to the home; it may provide an easier form of employment for those with disabilities; and it can act as a focus for community activity.

Additional benefits from teleworking include a reduction in commuting which means less traffic on city roads, increased employment prospects of people who have disabilities or caring responsibilities, and teleworking may be advantageous to employers who currently face restrictions on office space and equipment. Norwich Union are believed to be acting on this already.

Norwich City Council have drawn up guidelines for teleworkers in the city, which include - teleworkers being given the choice of whichever legal form of employment best suits their needs; training to the same level as Head Office employees; additional training and advice relevant to home-working – eg. health and safety, time management.

Local Networking – the cable network also allows the exchange of compu-ter based information (similar to Manchester's Host computer).

Teleports – the cable infrastructure enables the development of a teleport where a full range of modern information technology, telecommunica-tions and audio visual systems can be installed on a shared use basis. (This may also encourage the growth of small scale firms.)

The combination of teleworking, local networking and local television are seen to provide important resources and work in the Norwich area.

Tyneside

Tyneside is perceived as a geographically disadvantaged area as far as its communica-tions infrastructure is concerned. A report entitled *The Information City* published by the University of Newcastle Upon Tyne in August 1989 [1], argues that the cable infrastruc-ture is the most potent instrument in the area's development as an 'information city'. Cable development can also offer the 'image-engineering' industries more scope for business growth. The report states, "A strong modern image of Tyneside, which cable and local cultural industries would undoubtedly help to create, is essential to the entire local economy - from the financial sector to tourism".

Cable developments in Tyneside are expected to have a positive impact upon the area's image by bringing new technical and communications developments and economic growth to an area which has been traditionally dependent on blue collar industries. This aside, the University of Newcastle's research has pinpointed three areas where cable could serve the needs of Tyneside's information economy: it would help upgrade the quality of the present 'information environment' which is directly dependent on the infrastructure underpinning it; the cable network would enable firms within the city to link up more easily than ever before; and 'the localised and interactive nature of the cable system would create new target-marketing and advertising opportunities for Tyneside businesses'.

Global networking capabilities will depend to a large extent upon an advanced cable infrastructure. The cable infrastructure also provides the potential for a teleport which relies on the sophisticated head-end and advanced satellite facilities to link users with the rest of the globe via satellite links.

The development of video-conferencing is seen as a potential means for attracting new and relocated businesses into the area.

Teleworking on the telecommunications network where information processing tasks are sent along a 'wire', accessing remote computing facilities, data bases, or transmitting text to a remote receiver is another derivative industry of cable. Teleworking creates employment opportunities and provides productive employment for those who cannot easily leave home to work.

Within the production industry local television services obviously provide outlets for the local production sector while retaining expertise and programme-making talent which otherwise may drift south.

Local cable television services should also provide disadvantaged and marginalised groups within the community such as the unemployed, the disabled, the elderly and ethnic minorities as well as others who are normally denied access to conventional broadcast medium, with considerable potential to become directly involved with programme-making.

Small and medium sized enterprises, many of which currently lag behind in their use of telecommunications and the information economy, can benefit from the cable infrastructure 'both to enable them to participate in the networked value-adding partnerships, and to help them respond to the opportunities and challenges of an increasingly open European and world economy'.

The local authority, one of the major information technology users within any city, is likely to reap benefits from the cable network as advanced communications become crucial to managing, coordinating and planning the delivery of public services. Interactive cable services are capable of collecting feedback information from customers in real time, targeting complex markets for services, and integrating retrieved information into computerised data base systems used for managing, coordinating and running services.

The report cites some existing examples of cable's potential for communication between the local authority and the city's residents. These are:

- rolling screen 'bulletin board'.
- announcements of council meetings.
- advertising council initiatives in social services, local economic development etc.
- consumer research to identify public service demands.

- reservation services for public facilities such as recreation and sports centres, meeting rooms etc.

- opinion polling to monitor performance in services delivery.

- job advertisements for council departments.

- delivering information, opening and closing times for public facilities; emergency services for disabled people, the elderly etc.

- social services in health, recreation, housing etc.

Education and health services can also find the cable system beneficial in a variety of applications. Cable's two-way nature enables the development of interactive learning – the University of Newcastle's Education Department's Interactive Learning Project is developing software for use with interactive video discs. The report suggests that advanced cable systems will be an extremely cost-effective method for accessing interactive learning systems both in schools and in the home.

Cable will also provide easier means for education authorities to monitor the performance of individual schools - allowing a two-way information flow between the school and the education authority, and thus enabling easier management of the local education system.

The health service too is able to utilise the cable network in the development of new services and in more effectively employing existing resources. The report states that, 'improved resource management is regarded as one of the central issues facing the health service ..... the need to communicate large volumes of regularly updated information (for example on patient and treatment referrals) lies at the heart of effective resource management'. The cable network can make this information accessible to General Practitioners and other health service outlets across the city.

Teleshopping services are also available on the cable network which will particularly benefit those whose mobility is limited.

4.   Public Relations

Questionnaires were circulated to 20 local authorities where a cable service is up and running or nearing completion of the build.

Of the five departments which replied, three (London Borough of Tower Hamlets, Berkshire County Council, and Slough Borough Council) said that the council receives complaints from the public concerning the engineering, installation or road works involved in laying cable. Of the others, Surrey County Council responded that the cable operation was not far enough ahead to assess, and Leicester City Council replied that it was too early to comment as cable laying would not start until January 1991.

The Public Relations department of the London Borough of Tower Hamlets, Berkshire County Council, and Slough Borough Council found that the public held the council responsible for problems concerning cable and that the public expected the council to provide a solution. In Slough's case the cable operator and their contractors responded quickly to prevent follow-up complaints. In the other two cases the cable operator responded to complaints only after further complaints and local authority pressure.

Neither Berkshire County Council nor the London Borough of Tower Hamlets receive provision from the cable operator to broadcast a local public information service on cable television. The cable operator provides access for Slough Borough Council to transmit a local public information service on cable but currently this is run on an ad hoc basis by the Town Clerk. Although there is no cable in Leicester's ground, the Information Services department does intend to run local information programming.

The cable operator offers Slough Borough Council a daily local news/magazine programme on one cable channel which the council find a valuable way of distributing information involving the public. There are provisions made for councillors and officers to receive training in television presentation.

Leicester's case is based on projected services which will be available when the cable system is up and running. However it is proposed that the council will have access to a complete channel showing video and teletext. The teletext information will be compiled and edited by council employees and it is intended that the information will be able to be broadcast within the hour.

While the amount of time allocated to Leicester City Council for weekly programming on video remains to be negotiated, the council will use their own staff and equipment - the cable operator does not provide equipment for programme making. It is proposed that the council will use television time weekly, and eventually they hope to include studio-type interviews, location on-the-spot material, news items, cultural and leisure items, educational items, health items, and also to involve the public as both an audience and as interviewees. At the moment the staff involvement in terms of time is not known. Leicester have negotiated a contract with the cable company to provide information on a cost and profit basis.

It is also intended that the cable operator will offer a regular news/magazine pro-gramme on the cable channels. Two channels will be available for local/community use. A professional production company Q Studios, who are also shareholders in the Leicester franchise, will be involved in these services. As far as training is concerned, Leicester Council intend to train specifically for cable - although they already put officers through an intensive course on radio and television interview techniques.

All those who responded saw cable as a good means to put across the local authority message with conviction.

Berkshire County Council said that the council would like to set up information/ education channels but the costs involved precluded this.

Slough Borough Council thought that their news service was good but found that the quality of local videos were often poor.

The view of Leicester is that cable has the potential to offer a better presentation of the council and its services than other local media.

Coventry City Council's Public Relations unit produces videos for all the council's departments and puts together a weekly news programme for the city's local cable television network.

Coventry City Council became involved with cable early on, after an approach by Coventry Cable TV. The cable company were planning to set up a local programmes channel called COLT - Coventry's Own Local Television - and were keen that local organisations and community groups should write and produce their own programmes. The cable operator felt that if the local council took the lead in this, other local groups would follow.

The City Council were keen to become involved. Despite an initially small audience, the council saw their involvement as a valuable investment for the future. They were aware too of cable's potential as a local communications medium, and were keen to take maximum advantage of this as early as possible.

The first input which the Public Relations department made was to produce a weekly ten minute news programme called 'Contact'. Initially the programme was presented as a simple talking head with occasional still pictures which provided information and updates on the services available 'from your City Council'. This programme continues today in a more sophisticated form.

A trainee from Coventry Cable TV was given a placement within the City Council's customer relations unit. With the spin off for video production the City Council were keen to take the placement on full-time as a cable/video technician and producer. The council also agreed a set hire charge with the cable company for facilities – including camera, edit suites and studio time - of £1000 a month.

These facilities allow the video producer to make professional quality promotional and informative videos at minimal cost for the council's service departments – many of these videos are also broadcast on COLT. For about £30,000 a year the council are able to produce material to a high standard which would otherwise cost four or five times that amount using outside companies.

The weekly news programme is produced in a relatively short period of time: the Press and Publicity Officer puts together a script, based on issues of the week which are usually already written up in press release form; an Officer then spends a morning presenting the programme, while the video producer may stay all day in the studio filming and editing the programme and may also film additional material throughout the week. The programme goes out on COLT three times on one evening each week.

The council's involvement in local cable television has since opened up many other opportunities, particularly in the education field.

As a result of their interest in cable Coventry City Council participated in the first local cable and education steering group in the UK. This group comprised, Coventry City Council, British Telecom Education, National Council of Education Technology, West Midlands Further Education Council, The Cable Authority, Coventry Cable and the Educational Broadcasting Services Trust.

The group undertook a study into ways in which the cable television network could help Coventry schools, FE colleges, and the home learner. It was thought that educational groups could produce their own programmes – a learning opportunity in itself – and then broadcast the end result as part of a given curriculum. Subsequently all Coventry schools and educational facilities have been cabled up.

Coventry Cable TV had originally planned for three television programmes - however the initiative sparked off forty-three programmes, including ten from the 'Open College'.

The Elmbank Teacher Centre produced three programmes, and the careers service one. Hereward College produced a programme on rock music, Coventry Polytechnic one on language for engineers, in particular with German, and as part of the Council's policy of assisting parents back into the job market, Tile Hill College produced *Go For Access* looking into careers for women. Henley College produced a programme called *What Did You Do At School Today Mummy?* which reported on women returning to Adult Learning based at local primary schools with their children in preparation for a return to work.

In most cases these programmes were produced by students at the schools, colleges and institutions involved with their own equipment– Coventry Cable offered them studio, edit suite use and air space free of charge.

The cable company envisage this as a long term investment, in that the more young people get used to using cable television, the more likely they are to use it for entertainment, education and other services when they are older.

Coventry Cable also employ satellite links to pick up foreign language channels which are useful for language tuition under the guidance of the Language TVE Group.

Another service which the council has taken up is the use of teletext pages. These are used to convey a wide variety of local information, such as roadworks, refuse collection details and bus timetables. These are broadcast on COLT and other cable channels when they are not broadcasting video programmes. This service has been particularly useful for residential homes for the elderly, most of which are cabled up.

The City Council see many advantages in cable, not least that it is environmentally friendly. Cable is also seen as the main information highway in the city - a developing communication system that impacts on every aspect of city life, information, education and entertainment.

Overall the departments of Recreation and Leisure were uncertain of the implications and potential of cable, and where there was an interest and an awareness of the potential of cable there was little actual practical development.

On the whole Recreation and Leisure departments are able to make gains from the cable system but have little to trade in return.

Coventry Cable and Education Steering Group

In July 1989, Coventry's Cable and Education Steering Group undertook a study to assess the potential of cable television for education and training looking in particular at adult, continuing and further education.

The study set out 'to discover how cable television could promote access, respond to local needs and support flexible learning'.

From early January 1990, Coventry Cable began broadcasting educational pro-grammes on its local channel. Training courses in television production were run by the cable company for teachers and education advisers which meant that there was a number of people interested in educational television production.

Through cable television programmes as learning resources could be delivered to and from schools, colleges and companies. Cable offers unique characteristics for education and training, in particular the availability of channel time and the potential for interaction.

Education and training trends in the 1990s are focusing on 'learner-centred' rather than 'teacher-centred' learning with education and training reaching new groups of people. The demand for learning in smaller groups, possibly with tutors not always present has resulted in a need for useful and adaptable resources.

The report states,

> The 1980s saw a development away from learning in fixed places at fixed times in fixed groups. This was across all areas of education and training but probably most marked in further education colleges and employer training departments.

During the 1980s there was a growth in the home use of microcomputers and video recorders resulting in a wide variety of learning packages being used in the home environment. The report predicts that during the 1990s the number and sophistication of computer learning packages will again increase. Flexible open learning and indi-vidualised learning combined with increased home technology requires structured presenter led television programmes, as well as computer packages, print and audio support. The trend towards local responsiveness has proved strong:

> It is likely that significant finance would be available for a delivery method that could respond quickly to particular local needs and also likely that significant finance would be available from a number of local areas which joined forces to meet particular widespread needs in a cost effective way.

Adult learning has in the past been seen as a social activity - again new possibilities are beginning to exist with participation in live programmes and link ups between adult learner groups. 'Leisure learning at home' can be advertised in a much more systematic way through cable television in the home or college. The nature of television learning also has a specific effect in the understanding of technology, science, language and communication. As schools and employers seek greater contact, television links are a new way of bringing these groups together.

> Up until now higher education has not made significant use of open learning facilities but it is likely that the 1990s will see a development in

this area with, again, the need for flexible resources that can be adapted for various individual needs. It is likely also that universities and polytechnics looking for new types of activities will consider distance learning programmes much more seriously than they have in the past and will be looking for television opportunities to support and also to present learning.

The study suggests that work related education areas include: basic literacy, communications, numeracy, European languages, Information Technology, health service updating, pre-retirement training, problem solving, stress management and assertiveness.

Currently with the exception of BBC language programmes there are few educational television programmes which take people through a course of learning. 'Local educational television has not been explored in the UK simply because the resources to provide this have not existed.'

The report concludes that there is 'considerable audience interest in more factual television programming particularly in local issues, environmental issues, child/ student education and leisure activities and opportunities'.

The interactive nature of cable also provides opportunities for enrolment, enlisting help, for ordering support resources, or for joining in a discussion. [2]

5.   Dunston Community Television Project

Dunston Community Television was a community-based project to set up and run a local television service on the cable network, initiated by Dunston's local librarian with the support of Gateshead Metropolitan Borough Council. The project was carried out using borrowed camera and video equipment and it received minimum funding.

In 1980 a group called the Social Arts Trust began meeting, at the invitation of the local librarian of Dunston, a village on the outskirts of Gateshead, Tyne and Wear. From these meetings a subsequent group evolved who felt that the village lacked an exciting community focus – this group resolved to develop a demanding and challenging project which would provide opportunities for people to work together and prove technically and organisationally demanding. What emerged from these meetings was a decision to set up a community cable TV project to be run by the local community.

The project was undertaken on a small scale basis, reaching only 900 homes (the equivalent of 2000 people), and a decision was taken to broadcast initially for one month only, from September 1981. The project was regarded as a mini-television station, subject to the same regulations as national television. In January 1981 Rediffusion, the cable operator, was contacted, and after checking the Social Arts Trust's credentials – proven by the screening of a tape – the project was given the 'go ahead'. Throughout the experiment a good relationship was maintained between the cable operator and the local community.

The Home Office Broadcasting Department were contacted next and were willing to issue a licence once they were convinced that the project had local support and the cable company's permission. Dunston Library agreed to provide studio space for the project's needs.

Having secured a licence, studio space and access to the cable network the group then had to fund raise. This was undertaken by the Social Arts Trust. £2000 was secured from Northern Arts and a variety of camera equipment and tapes were loaned from Tyne Video, Tyne Tees Television and Gateshead Libraries. The local community was invited to a series of open days at the studio, a month before programmes were due to go out, and gradually the public became involved in helping to establish and run the station.

Publicity was sought both locally and on a national level. A programme strategy was adopted whereby the same pattern of programmes was transmitted at the same time each week, and a decision was taken to avoid competition with prime-time viewing, and instead programmes were screened where there were 'gaps' in national television viewing. Four hours of programmes went out weekly from Friday through to Sunday on an existing cable channel, which prevented difficulties of retuning television sets. The programmes were prepared by the group on half inch black and white tape and were transmitted by Rediffusion from a sub-station. Considerable technical help was provided by Rediffusion in getting the tapes out on cable – it was not, the group commented, just a matter of sticking a tape into the system and running it.

Several weeks after broadcasting ceased a survey was carried out in a random selection of homes within the receiving area. 75 households, 8% of the total number, were visited and answers represent the views of 211 individuals.

65% of interviewees received Dunston Community Television, of these

> 31% watched regularly
> 45% watched occasionally
> 24% watched once

Of these viewers,

> 66% watched the Variety Programmes
> 48% watched the news
> 45% watched the quizzes
> 39% watched the Children's programmes
> 27% watched the pre-school programmes
> 21% watched the Breakfast show

When asked why they enjoyed the programmes,

> 82% said because the programmes were local
> 24% said because the programmes differed from those they normally viewed
> 15% said because the programmes were interesting
> 3% said because the programmes were broadcast on Sunday evenings

When the interviewees were asked if they would like to see the experiment repeated,

68% said yes
21% said no
11% did not know

If the experiment was repeated,

34% would like broadcasts to be more widely available
24% would like better quality transmission
19% would like broadcasts to be longer
19% would like the broadcasts in colour
16% would like better programmes
50% would like better advertising
12% did not want the experiment repeated because they did not receive cable television

After the four week transmission period, a public meeting was held to discuss the future of the cable station. From the discussion which took place it emerged that the priority of the people of Dunston was to secure jobs. As a result Dunston Community Workshop was set up - an independently managed project to promote employment and productive leisure in the area. A member of Dunston Community Television commented that the television project had been a good starting point for the work which they currently undertake, but that the group could not afford at the time to get sidetracked into running a cable television station.

References

1. *The Information City*, University of Newcastle Upon Tyne, August 1989.

2. Copies of the report entitled, *Educable* are available from the Educational Broadcasting Services Trust, 1/2 Marylebone High Street, London W1A 1AR.

5 Reading the ITC's *Mapping Regional Views*

Dave Rushton, Institute of Local Television, 1991

Introduction

In November 1988 the Government announced in its White Paper *Broadcasting in the 90s: Competition, Choice and Quality* that 'the regional basis of what will become Channel 3 is crucial' ...... so begins the ITC's Study, *Mapping Regional Views*.

The IBA/ITC were given the responsibility of deciding the geographical division of the UK into regions for whose particular interests the Channel 3 licensees will need to cater 'within the statutory framework'.

In this analysis, we provide an interpretation of the findings of the ITC Study and highlight the implications for the future of local television broadcasting.

Three factors were taken into account which informed the decision to advertise the fifteen regional Channel 3 licences with the same broadcasting hours and areas as the ITV contracts, including .....

> maintaining the stability of Channel 3 in transition form from ITV by retaining the existing regional map in the light of increased competition from satellite and cable, a free standing Channel 4 and the development of Channel 5.

an agreement by the existing ITV companies to supply the bulk of network programming on a financial basis that did not penalise the economic prospects of the smaller less wealthy regional services. The ITC decided to enhance this agreement by requiring a minimal figure for the competitive Channel 3 tender for the smallest areas.

> The research was designed around the existing transmitters, which form the building blocks of the present ITV map and of the future Channel 3 map.

The introduction of a greater number of regions was excluded from consideration before the ITC Study was begun.

This latter decision may have been tempered by the view that smaller regions would not be viable since the present small regions relied on support from within a network

116

including larger more profitable regional networks. In addition, creating smaller regions would have led to greater transmitter expenditure and problems of demarcation. Yet, 35% favoured bigger regions with 42% against (with 25% don't knows). Can interest in larger and smaller regions be reconciled?

Would you prefer more localised regions?, could not be asked, since on practical as well as economic grounds it would not have been possible to meet the demand. But the question stands, of the 76% who wished to remain within the present ITV region how many would have actually preferred a smaller regional focus? The viewers answers to more detailed questions in the Study indicate a large percentage in favour of such an option.

Despite the serious constraints that retaining the transmitter building blocks imposed upon the Study, the research revealed considerable evidence calling for a more localised form of television than the ITV/Channel 3 regions can actually provide, certainly without more sub-regional opt-outs.

The authors of *Mapping Regional Views* believe that 'the best prospect of sustaining the highly regarded regional programme service within the coverage areas known and appreciated by viewers' lay in 'keeping the existing map'.

Mapping Regional Views presents a most valuable snapshot of public interest in local television drawn from across the UK. Yet it presents a level of local news interest especially that goes beyond the limitations imposed upon the research and reduces the face-value of 'the best prospect of sustaining the highly regarded regional service' lay in 'keeping the existing map'.

The evidence at the disposal of the authors of the ITC Study shows that by no means (in a less transmitter restricted scenario) could regional television be termed an ideal platform to accommodate viewer demand. It is in fact a relatively poor 'best prospect'. The transmitters as building blocks do not meet the demands of the public for localised services.

The questions that will be raised here are whether in view of a widespread interest in a more highly localised form of television efforts should now be made by the ITC to meet those demands as an adjunct to the Channel 3 and Channel 5 assessments. For example, to take greater control of ensuring that a local channel on cable fully meets the demands of public service broadcasting.

Through no fault of their own, the regional television services are not able to deliver the specific service the viewer would most like.

By hiding this deficiency local television prospects are systematically ignored by regional services and pose as something which demonstrably they are not. The ITC Study is itself the victim of the semantics of regional television, in which local can even mean national in the marketing of a regional television service.

The Institute of Local Television would like to see the demand for local television that the ITC Study has revealed become as real a priority for the ITC as it clearly is with the public.

With cable, the technical means already exist or are being put into place to better meet those public aspirations, at least in urban areas. Public service television should not be left off the local channel agenda in the assessment, encouragement and support shown for cable. The ITC's ad hoc approach to regulating local channels is simply inadequate and the ITC is engaged in double standards in promoting quality in one department (terrestrial television) and a free for all in another (cable television).

The ITC Study confirms that the public demand for localised television is far too important a public service to be left to the market and the vagaries of North American investors.

An Analysis of Mapping Regional Views

The ITC Study 'concentrates primarily upon viewers perceptions of what it means to live in a specific part of the UK, the role of regional broadcasting, and the implications of these perceptions for the present ITV regional structure'.

Local television has become a confusing term and its ambiguity is perpetuated in Mapping Regional Views. Some examples of how terms are confused appear in its Summary of Key Findings. What do the researcher's mean by region? :-

Regional Attachment

Most people surveyed had lived in *their area* for 10 years or more years, while only a small proportion had been resident for less than two years. The great majority felt they belonged to and liked living in *their area*, with many having a distinct sense of their *region* being 'special'. Most people interviewed said they would miss *their area* if they had to move away from it. (*page 4*)

Regional news

Television has a dominant role to play as a source of news at the national and international level, but it is not so widely regarded as the main source of *regional* or *local news*. (*page 4*)

General Regional Programme Preferences

There was widespread support for *local* programmes and a degree of interest in seeing additional non-news *regional* programming in peak times. (*page 4*)

The most popular *regional* programme topics, in terms of what people said they would be most likely to watch, were *local* news, *local* weather forecasts, and programmes dealing with *local* countryside or *local* environmental issues. (*page 4/5*)

In these examples drawn from the Summary of Key Findings substitution of *local* for *regional* or *area* for *regional* is possible. But is *local* a synonym of *regional* in day to day use? How are *local* and *regional* used in the ITC Study questions?

In a particularly detailed part of the ITC Study the researchers consider the very problem that conflation of *regional* with *local* has given rise to, so far as viewers are concerned:-

> Viewers living in and around Gloucester have complained in the past about the fact that, as part of the Central West ITV *region* rather than part of HTV west, they did not get sufficient news about *their part of the country*. (*page 5*)

Otherwise throughout most of the ITC Study, the ready confusion of *local* with *region* or with *area* leads to conclusions about capacity or expectation from the regional TV service. This is at odds with the research evidence. Regional TV services, especially news services, are not highly prized as suggested. They are useful sources of a form of news that the public generally does not find especially important (news from neighbouring counties and districts).

> **Opinions about Broadcasting Changes**
>
> Relatively few people were aware of any changes to the ITC system which will arise from the new legislation. Under one in ten spontaneously mentioned the new licence bidding procedure. Most were in favour of their regional company retaining a studio presence in their region. However, feelings were mixed on the issue of whether or not larger ITV regions were a good or bad thing for the future.
>
> Finally, over the UK as a whole, 76% of viewers wanted to remain within their present ITV region with only a minority (17%) wanting a change. The survey results clearly show the central role ITV plays in UK broadcasting, both at the national and, particularly strongly, at the regional level.

The Study's claims for regional programming are somewhat circuitous. The hegemony of the transmitter building blocks puts pressure upon the conclusions to ignore the prospects of a service, or services, that would more adequately capture the local priorities apparent among the public that were interviewed.

What the regional broadcaster understands by local television may be very different from what a viewer in any one part of the region might wish to actually see compared with a viewer in another part. The 'viewer' for the regional broadcaster an anonymous if not entirely spectral being who lives nowhere special except somewhere out there in the region.

Attachment

The ITC Study seeks to consider the attachment people have to the area in which they live. Under a number of headings it explores how a regional television service can contribute to this attachment.

Under the headings of **Stability & Belonging** (*page 7*) we find that the variations on the use of 'local' and 'area' are intended to be understood to mean the same as 'region(al)'.

Yet it is far from clear that anyone has any affinity for an otherwise arbitrary area coinciding with the map of transmission of a regional television franchise!

> A clear factor in the success of any *regional* television structure is people's interest in and attachment to *where they live.*

Where they live may be an *area*, a *part of the country*, or it might be *local*.

> all viewers were asked how long they had lived *'in this area'* .

> The overall pattern proved to be very stable, justifying the claim that there was a great deal of residential stability.

> **Belonging**

> Another measure of *regional* attachment is people's feeling about their own *area*; where there is a sense of liking and belonging to *where they live.* Nearly nine in ten (88%) felt they belonged and liked living in their *area*. For many people there is also a distinct sense of their *region* being 'special' and anticipated regret at the prospect of having to leave it. Over seven in ten respondents (73%) said they would miss their *area* if they had to leave, while four in ten (41%) saw their *area* as very different from other parts of the UK. (*page 7*)

This surely expresses a measure of attachment to an *area*, not *region* or *regional* attachment – unless *region* can be slipped loose from its coincidence with the geographical spread of the television region, whose scale does not readily conjure association or affinity.

Clearly there is no reason why we should chop and change between *region* and *area* in this outline. *Region* and *area* are in danger of being confused and we may be led to conclusions about the value of a *regional* television service by assuming it to be about a *region/area* with which we actually identify or feel belonging.

The assumption that there could be coincidence between the closeness of attachment to an area and the representation implied in a regional TV service is not capable of being drawn either from the evidence presented or from common (or any other kind of) sense.

The Scottish Television region is one with which the writer of this study is reasonably familiar. It is quite obvious that a television *region* corresponds to nothing much beyond its own invention and those associations which a viewer makes through the medium of watching programmes. The sudden leap of imagination whereby our immediate *region* or *where we live* might come to be equated or represented within our regional television service and its accident of transmitters is not at all straightforward.

As we shall see, there is no generally publicly shareable political cultural 'will' that lurks behind the arbitrariness of the regional television footprint. It is perverse to imply otherwise.

How might a feeling of belonging to one place be related to the regional television service? Only through satisfaction with the way that the immediate area to which the viewer is attached, its life and activities, are portrayed or represented. But this is not what the ITC Study sets out to show. It would lead to a denial of the value of the regional service to show such a good service being provided for one *area* with which some viewers have attachment through living there since this would palpably be at the expense of other *areas* and their attached viewers getting any airtime at all!

Looking to the example of Scottish Television, it is evident from its presentation that it is in fact adopting a national role. This competes with the regional/national service provided by the BBC in Scotland.

Scottish –*your local service* – is essentially playing the Scottish card and throwing up its hands at a more localised distribution of signal, which the transmitter building blocks may readily exclude from being an option in the Scottish region.

But the authors of the ITC Study do not consistently confuse local or area with region or regional. The distinction between local and regional is not lost altogether.

Where a distinction can make a point it is made, while it is quietly glossed over or ignored elsewhere.

Interest in the Region

Attachment to the *region* is also expressed in people's interest in and active attempts to find out more about *where they live*. One way in which this tendency is expressed is the extent of readership of *local* newspapers. Over three in four (77%) people interviewed across the UK claimed to read a *local* free paper while four in ten (42%) regularly bought a *local* paper. Despite this fairly high consumption of *local* printed news, three quarters (74%) of the people sampled still said they would 'like to know more about what is happening in their area'. (*page 7*)

We might draw the conclusion from this paragraph that *'where they live'* or *'in their area'* is broadly understood to be the area covered by local free or bought newspapers. There is nothing here that confirms an attachment to the region, unless that region coincides with the catchment of interests and geography served by a local paper. [1]

The reader's own conclusions can be drawn as to the inability not the ability of the *regional* television news service in meeting this *local* need.

Are the ITC and the regional companies guilty of belittling or reducing the significance of the *local* demand for (especially) news in favour of what the building blocks are actually best able to deliver, ie. *regional* news?

Importance of News

The majority of people across the UK have a clear sense of attachment to and interest in *where they live*. This is reflected in their assessment of the relative different news types (see ITC Table 1 [2]).

The majority of people interviewed regarded all forms of news as important. However news about a person's own *locality* or *district* was seen as being of primary importance by most people (88%).

ITC Table 1. Importance of News

	Important %	Not Important %
Your local area	88	12
Your county or district	88	11
Neighbouring counties and districts	66	33
The rest of England/Scotland/Wales/ Northern Ireland	79	21
The whole of the UK	84	16
European countries	68	32
World news	82	19

With the addition of our own county or district, a number of neighbouring counties and districts best coincides with the catchment of regional TV services. More often than not this means the news is about somewhere else, a place towards which the viewer has no great attachment.

Across the UK it would seem the viewer finds more important the news from within a country setting England/Scotland/Wales/Northern Ireland (79%) than from the collection of neighbouring counties and districts (66%). Scottish Television's efforts to portray itself as a national service, to drop STV in favour of Scottish, and perhaps to prepare itself for a larger role when legislation permits, are encouraged by the ITC Study. But surely – a *national* and *local* television cannot be passed off as one and the same service?

The *area* and the *place we live* are not exhausted of meaning by equation with the regional television service area. In fact, we might well have a positive feeling towards the regional television programming *in spite of* rather than *because of* its ability to serve our apparently important local needs by way of news. An example of the public preferring a TV region in spite of it not meeting local demands is no more apparent than where a service straddles the border of England and Scotland. This was given particular attention in the ITC Study.

Border is favoured over Scottish as the regional service by the people in the Scottish part of the region. But more programming was wanted about Scotland's capital, to which some loyalty attaches among people living in the Scottish Border towns. How can this presently be delivered to the occupants of just those towns?

Table 2 in the ITC study, not reproduced here, draws attention to the relative priorities for sources of news. Television features very high for news about the UK, European Countries and the rest of the world but not about the place we live or our area. (Table 1)

> At the local level the press is the main source of news for most people. However, TV rapidly comes into its own at the wider level of neighbouring counties and districts (see Table 3).

ITC Table 3. Sources of Regional News

Get most news about:

	TV	Press	Radio	Other source*
Your local area	37	64	25	19%
The county or district you live in	44	58	25	12%
Neighbouring counties and districts	61	40	22	6%
The rest of England/ Scotland/Wales/Northern Ireland	84	38	21	2%

* Almost all these replies relate to 'other people' as news sources. Note: Percentages total more than 100% since viewers were free to name more than one source of news. (*page 9*)

Table 3 is of interest for two reasons.

Firstly, it confirms that the country card is a significant one for a regional TV service to play where possible. Table 3 shows us that for large scale sources of super-regional or country news, regional television are favoured as a source of news over press, radio and other sources – that is for news about the rest of England/Scotland/Wales/Northern Ireland. But for local news it is not a significant player compared with the press.

Secondly, the supposed merits of 'TV rapidly coming into its own' for 'news about neighbouring counties', is not a particularly positive recommendation. This is not an especially valued service among viewers (see Table 1). People find news about their local area (88%) and then about their county or district (88%) more important than their neighbouring counties and districts (66%).

Local papers stubbornly remain the preferred source of news over television for the most important news, and for news about an area to which people are most likely to feel some attachment.

So far as news in concerned we can conclude from the ITC's figures, that regional television is not very good at providing the news that people want, unless it projects a role larger than its region in order to provide or portray itself as providing a country based service. We can see here why a significant number of people favoured an enlarged regional service while the option of smaller regions was not on offer.

In an assessment of the relative merits of regional TV news between one channel and the next we must remember that 'television is not the main source of local news'.

ITC Table 4. TV Channel Choice for News

Get most news about:

	ITV	BBC	% naming C4	BBC2
Your local area	74	43	2	1
The county or district you live in	73	44	2	1
Neighbouring counties and districts	68	47	2	1
The rest of England/Scotland/Wales/ Northern Ireland	61	59	3	3
The whole of the UK	61	60	4	3
European countries	60	60	5	4
The rest of the world	61	60	5	4

Note: Percentage total to more than 100% since viewers were free to name more than one source of news

An apparently impressive comparison (in Table 4) favours ITV as the source for most news about the local area and county and district – 74% ITV to 43% BBC and 73% ITV to 44% BBC1 respectively. It is not what it seems.

The regional BBC and ITV services cover different territory and do not mirror each other. The BBC regions being much larger.

The impressive differences between the services (Table 4) occur for a part of the news provision for which television is currently not highly regarded, for the provision of news at the local and district levels.

In addition, where both viewer interest and provision of service do coincide, in news from 'the rest of England/Scotland/Wales/Northern Ireland', the difference between the BBC and the ITV offerings is only 2%, which statistically is not worth a candle.

Most viewers (over 60%) feel the amount of regional news currently shown on ITV and BBC is about right, although around one in four in each case feel there is too little. Hardly anyone believes there to be too much regional news. This balance of opinion was found across all ITV regions (see Table 5).

ITC Table 5. The Amount of Regional News on ITV and BBC1

	ITV %	BBC1 %
Too much	1	1
A bit too much	3	3
About right	67	62
A bit too little	18	19
Too little	7	7
Don't know	5	8

Two questions beg to be asked here:-

Do people think that the amount of regional news is about right because they couldn't take much more material that is generally unimportant to them?

Do those who think there is a bit too little regional news, want more of something the system cannot readily deliver, a local form of news which they would find important?

In short, *would you like more news about your town or area?*

The first question above may seem a trifle perverse, but the very large volume of extra hours being offered for regional news among the Channel 3 bidders is not consistent with the ITC Study's conclusion that the number of hours currently on offer is about right.

What the Study reveals is a demand for more quality (ie) relevance or importance not more quantity, or irrelevance or unimportance.

The large increase in regional news hours that the Channel 3 bidders promise presumes that among greater quantity there will be something of more local interest to more viewers. But this is just a pearl for each viewer among a bucket of oysters.

Increasing quantity does not seem a very sophisticated approach. Viewers will in proportion to finding a few things of importance to themselves, find many more things of importance to others - to those living in a neighbouring county or district the news about which each viewer finds least interesting. (see Table 1)

Having previously differentiated local and regional – by associating local with a catchment equivalent to the local newspaper – on page 11, the ITC Study returns to confusing *local* and *regional* news once more.

At the time of the survey both ITV and BBC showed a main *regional* news programme in the early evening on weekdays between 6pm and 7pm. Both channels also provided regular *local* news bulletins during the day, at the weekend and after their main evening networked news programmes (ITN's News at Ten and BBC 1's 9 O'clock news). People were asked how often they watched these *regional* news services.

As was the case with *local* newspapers, most people sampled across the UK exhibited an appetite for *local* news. Around two thirds of the people interviewed throughout the UK claimed to watch an early evening news programme (69%) and late evening news headlines (64%) three evenings a week or more. Indeed, almost half (48%) claimed to view early evening *regional* news programmes every night (see Table 6).

But we already know the people watching these programmes were not watching them because they found the regional TV services an important source of *local* news (see Table 1). *Their appetite for local news is not being satisfied by regional television.*

We can confirm that people have an unsatisfied appetite for *local* news, (from the evidence of the Institute's two city based studies in 1989 and 1990) moreover they appear to have an appetite for *local* news on a local television service, an appetite not satisfiable at all by *local* newspapers.

Unfortunately, there is no local television service available.

Local television news is a service in high demand. Regional television presents its services as more local than they can possibly be, and the ITC Study serves to gloss over and bury the distinctions.

With the exception of regional TV city opt-outs, which may come close to a sense of local news provision with which people can have some realistic expectation of attachment, the regional service is not a local service at all.

A triumphal note is expressed (following Table 6, not reproduced here) that

> ITV's regional supremacy was once again demonstrated (over the BBC) when viewers were asked which early evening regional news programme they most often watched.

For the news most people find important - local news - the viewers' heads were just as likely to be found buried in the local paper, whether or not while watching regional news.

The amplification of the competition between the two dominant public service television providers (BBC 1 and ITV) is clearly not helpful in a research study of viewers' interests. It reduces the provision of a public service to a competition between services on offer, rather than consideration of services in demand. (Neither the BBC nor the TV regional service does the job being claimed.)

While a general confusion of *local* and *regional* has been at play, a pointed distinction emerges briefly:

> Almost half of those sampled watched daytime *local* news bulletins on most weekdays (49%) and over two thirds (68%) viewed on weekends. Only 8% of viewers never watched a weekend *regional* news bulletin, while less than a third (30%) never watched *regional* bulletins during the day.

Here, the positive figures (49% & 68%) refer to viewers of local news bulletins, the negative figures (8% and 30%) are the percentage of viewers who never watch regional news bulletins.

We know that viewers value *local*. But both *regional* and *local* news bulletins are *regional* news bulletins and are no more nor less regional for being watched or for not being watched!

Regional news is what we get on television. We call it *local* because it is as near as we are getting to really *local* news. When we like it (or when we watch it) it is *local*, when it is less relevant (when we don't watch it) it is *regional*. Or so it might seem.

There is nothing sinister in the authors of the ITC Study responding to what they see on television as any viewer might respond. But there is something of concern when this process permeates rather than informs the Study.

The ITC Study perpetuates rather than explains the myth-making that is part and parcel of regional television marketing.

It is a necessary and acceptable commercial activity on the part of regional broadcasters to embellish the *regional* news bulletins with the positive associations, of *local* and *area we live in* and so on. No company markets its own irrelevance (for long).

Cable, for instance has the capability of providing a local service more in keeping with public demand. By not regulating cable as the legislation permits the terrestrial service will continue to provide a failed service without the public actually sighting a better quality alternative.

Should one television service that cannot deliver the goods be favoured by the ITC over one that can? Should public service television meet public demand or compromise the public's demands to suit the service that it can only poorly offer?

Upon such considerations, of the Orwellian uses and abuses of local, a marketing strategy for a commercial television company might well be based. Such a strategy plays upon the confusion and entrenches the abuse, rather than seeks clarity. Is this the ITC's job too?

The Scottish in Scottish Television is stood next to the public presentation of its service as the local service. This reconciles two news arenas in which the viewer feels psychologically comfortable - the local and the national. In this case, the viewer particularly values news from Scotland and from their local area. In any realistic sense each viewer regularly gets neither. A limited number of transmitters and a diverse region present very real problems in reconciling demand with supply.

Scottish Television's national mantle leaves scope for national ambitions to be played out which are now set-up to carry the regional viewer along at some later time. But whither then and now the truly local service that in word if not in deed the ITC Study would have regional television provide?

Whatever else Scottish Television may be doing, it is certainly not stressing its *regional* credentials. The service Scottish is actually offering is not promoted, only the service it would like to offer (national) and the service the viewer would like to receive (local).

Loyalty to Scottish Television is despite either the ITV service or the BBC service meeting certain perceived needs by way of important news. It is not that one is better at its service role than the other.

BBC Scotland is even more stretched than Scottish Television to fulfil its role as a regional news provider when literally, rather than through wishful thinking, it actually does serve all of Scotland.

From this example, and there will be regional differences we would hope throughout ITV, the regional television service is torn to maintain the identity of the station in competition with rivals (notably the BBC) and to ensure that the service does not emphasise one part of its region in favour of another.

In the process it names the *regional* output *local* and provides a service that nobody really wants that much for what it purports to be.

Regional Programming

While regional news amounts to two thirds of *regional* output, there is other programming provided by the regional ITV companies.

The ITC Study draws the following points to our attention:-

> The remainder of the *regional* output - ie programmes especially made to reflect the tastes and outlook of people in the *region* - include current affairs, documentaries, religion, arts, help for job seekers, documentaries, sport and community service announcements. (*page 12*)

> The importance of *local* and *regional* programmes was demonstrated when seven in ten (71%) people interviewed said they would like to see a good many more (20%) or rather more (51%) programmes about *their area* on ITV in the future. (*page 12*)

> The majority of viewers (72%) were interested in seeing some *regional* programmes in peak viewing time. (*page 13*)

> The majority of viewers wishing to see *regional* programmes during peak time (57%) wished to do so only two or three times a week. (*page 13*)

> The most popular *regional* programme topics were *local* news, weather forecasts, local countryside and wildlife programmes, and programmes dealing with *local* environmental issues. (*page 13*)

If *area* [with which the viewer relates] is taken to mean *local* rather than *regional*, as several of the earlier uses had implied, then these figures indicate that 71% of people want to see more *local* (not *regional*) programmes - *they want programmes about their area that they are not able to get much of.*

ITC Table 8: Popularity of various regional programme topics - the proportions of viewers who said they would definitely or probably watch.

	UK Tot %	M %	F %	Age 16-34 %	Age 35-54 %	55+ %	Social Class ABC1 %	C2 %	DE %
News	93	92	93	90	94	95	94	93	91
Weather	90	90	90	86	91	92	90	90	89
Countryside/ Wildlife	80	81	80	69	85	88	82	81	79
Environmental issues	80	80	80	73	86	82	87	78	73
Views of local people	75	73	77	68	78	80	71	77	78
History & Geography	73	74	72	61	78	81	79	74	66
Consumer advice	70	64	74	63	75	62	71	69	68
Other parts of UK with local links	67	67	67	61	69	71	69	68	63
Other parts of World with local links	64	64	64	58	67	69	66	64	62
Hobbies	63	62	64	58	63	67	61	66	62
Community services	61	55	66	55	65	64	61	62	61
Welfare and social services	59	55	62	51	55	72	46	60	73
Public transport	58	56	58	54	56	62	52	59	63
Educational programmes for adults	54	54	54	52	58	52	60	55	47
Tourism	52	51	53	45	57	55	54	53	48
Events eg. Jumble sales, fetes	49	40	55	39	51	56	44	49	53
Council politics	48	50	46	36	52	58	53	47	44

continued/

/continued	UK Tot %	M %	F %	Age 16- 34 %	35- 54 %	55+ %	Social Class ABC1 %	C2 %	DE %
Listings/ What's On	48	45	52	64	50	29	55	49	40
Sport	45	63	31	47	43	46	43	49	46
Business	45	53	38	43	52	42	54	43	35
Job vacancies	42	40	43	58	47	18	34	46	46
Parliamentary politics	37	39	36	24	38	50	41	33	35
Bands & pop concerts	33	34	33	62	26	9	32	38	33
Religion	33	29	37	17	31	55	34	30	35
Arts	32	30	34	25	34	39	47	24	21
Educational programmes for schools	28	25	32	31	34	19	29	29	27
Farming	24	28	20	14	25	34	24	23	24
Ethnic minority interests	16	16	16	17	16	15	16	17	15

This table provides further justification for a more *localised* form of television than *regional* television can provide.

We are already (well) aware that local news (93% interest above) is unsatisfied by the present regional service.

City studies have shown a similar level of interest in a high quality local news service to that found by the ITC across the UK. [3]

If we scan the list of other programme topics listed in Table 8 a good number can be qualitatively better for having a *local* rather than a *regional* focus.

Weather (90%) can vary markedly across regions.

Views of local people (75%) is self evidently better handled on a more local basis. *Links with other parts of the UK/World* (67% & 64%) would often be town to town or district to district links.

Community and welfare services (61% & 59%), *public transport* (58%) and *education for adults* (54%) and especially *jumble sales* (?) (49%) and *council politics* (48%) are all far more highly localised than a television sized region and are usually organised on a county or district or town, or with jumble sales on an even more localised basis.

In addition to the above contenders for being better serviced on a *local* basis, some less obvious programming with a high audience interest, could work equally well at local or regional levels.

> Countryside/wildlife and environmental issues could form the topic of more localised programming and the basis for programmes involving a high degree of public participation.

The findings of the ITC Study are consistent with the pattern and especially levels of interest found in the Institute of Local Television's studies in Norwich and Edinburgh for local (ie) city programming. For example, Edinburgh:-

---

Interest in Different Types of Local Programming [4]

News	92%
Special Interest Programmes	81%
Current Affairs	80%
Amateur and Professional	
Sporting Events & Meetings	60%
Local Entertainers	75%
Participating in Local Television	56%

ILT TABLE 1: Edinburgh Study 1989

Local television research

The Institute's research in 1989 and 1990 not only established an interest in local news and other programming for television delivery but also found enthusiasm among the public for participation in programming and in their local television service.

Participation was not characterised just as a 'hands on role', though this was not excluded. People were asked whether they would like to be involved in a television programme about their hobbies or interests, and thereby to contribute to programming whose subject they were already interested in. There was a very high (56%) interest in this broad approach to participation.

A charity, Edinburgh Television Trust has been set up in Edinburgh to promote local television literacy and to involve local people in the television and broadcasting processes as they become available in Edinburgh. Similar groups are being formed in other parts of the UK.

For the most part a regional TV service provides vicarious television, for the vast majority of its potential viewers. Yet the credentials of the regional service are largely founded on its experiential offerings - or experience related topics, news about an area which the viewer knows and in which they are involved.

In the ITC Study this experiential role is interpreted as 'regional attachment'. The ITC

Study fails to establish an association between the area the viewer lives in and the television service provided to that area.

Such ambitions prove to be beyond the scope of transmitter bound television with its present building blocks. A ersatz bonding emerges between viewer and broadcaster only by evaporating local of its more useful and common meanings and substituting it with regional.

In the ITC Study, news is the main contender for examination.

The regional TV service is unable to provide the detail of news information each of us appears to find important. Generality and greater regional emphasis, including attempts to sell regional news as the local news, are made instead.

While the UK may not achieve a highly localised news service on television for some years to come, there is no escaping the issue that the current ITV/Channel 3 transmitters fail to deliver a service that the public considers important throughout two thirds of its programming output (news) or more. Yet, Channel 3 bidders are offering an increased volume of regional coverage. Without breaking that material down into far more localised bulletins for transmission, which some proposals favour, the evidence in the ITC Study points to more rather than less public alienation with the service.

Who wants more news from the neighbouring counties and districts? Not as many people as would watch a local or national news alternative it seems. The ITC should look beyond their transmitters and start to reconcile the delivery of a quality local television service with the public demand for the service.

References

1. This is far from a pointless semantic exercise. In 1989 a study in local television was conducted in Edinburgh by Peter Kitchenman. In 1989 there appeared a very strong requirement for a high quality local news service among the people interviewed (92%). Local here was taken to be the city [of Edinburgh], the 183,000 homes of the local cable franchise, an area slightly smaller than covered by the local evening and free newspapers.

In a subsequent smaller study, undertaken in both Edinburgh and Norwich in 1990 evidence was sought to see if subscription payments for a local news based channel (ostensibly for cable delivery in these two cities) would undermine interest in purchasing the local newspaper. It seemed that it would not, and the researcher concluded that there was a demand for more local news and a desire to see this on television, even if paid for through subscription. (Researched by Lyndsey Bowditch, the findings were published in *Making Local Work*, and reprinted here in Part Two.)

2. Relevant Tables have been reproduced with their original reference numbers as they appear in Mapping Regional Views.

3. Edinburgh and Norwich studies conducted respectively by Peter Kitchenman in 1989 and Lyndsey Bowditch in 1990.

4. Peter Kitchenman, *Edinburgh Study*, ILT, 1989, (reprinted here as Chapter 1).

6   Survey of Local Channels on UK Cable, 1992

Julie White, Institute of Local Television, 1992

1.   Introduction

As part of the Feasibility Study on Edinburgh Television conducted in the summer of 1989, Peter Kitchenman visited all the UK cable operators then offering a local or community channel. (The earlier study is reprinted as Appendix Two.)

So far as we know the 1989 survey was the first commissioned to establish the extent of local programming offered by cable operators under the terms of Section 7 of the Cable and Broadcasting Act 1984. By 1989 eleven cable franchises were in operation. By July 1992 this number had risen to fifty five.

Because of this lapse of time and increased cabling it has become necessary to update the earlier study. We also thought it was necessary to anticipate changes in policy affecting local services arising from the implementation of the new Broadcasting Act of 1990 which makes no provision for local commitments or even local consultation.

The 1992 survey was undertaken using postal questionnaires and telephone interviews as a follow up where required. The written questionnaire followed the pattern of the 1989 survey with the addition of questions on training for local broadcasting.

This new survey is introduced with a commentary on the policy towards regulating local and community television services on cable. The Independent Television Commission have adopted the former Cable Authority's interpretation of their duties without significant change of personnel or emphasis. Although the new Act contains no local obligations, the terms of old Act remain in force for the majority of franchises. Nonetheless, some uncertainty surrounds the regulation and implementation of local services.

So far as this side of cabling is concerned, the ITC's line is quite different from that of Oftel, cable's co-regulator. [1] Our commentary compares the guidance given to franchise applicants by the Cable Authority with statements from Oftel. For explanatory material we have drawn upon a lengthy file of correspondence with Edinburgh Television Ltd and the Institute of Local Television as well as upon discussions with officers at the ITC.

2.   Commentary

In January 1991 the 1990 Broadcasting Act came into force and replaced the 1984 Cable and Broadcasting Act. In the new Act cable is one possibility among a range of local delivery technologies that might be used to deliver services over local areas. As yet no new local delivery franchises have been granted but cable franchises established under the 1984 legislation can choose to operate under the terms of the new regulations. Only one company, TeleWest has chosen to do this. For the majority of cable operators the terms of the 1984 Act continue to prevail. Whether cable operators who choose to convert to the new Act, which contains no local or community obligations, will be required to make provision for local and community services is not clear from the Act. However, in a recent article in the ITC's *Spectrum* magazine Jon Davey, Director of Cable and Satellite at the ITC, maintains that:

> All the licences held by cable operators under the 1990 Broadcasting Act require that the licensee should provide a local service in accordance with a statement annexed to the licence. These will be designed to reflect what was included in the franchisee's approved application.

Mr Davey continues:

> the preparation and adoption of which [the above annex to the licence] is only just starting. [2]

Section 7 of the Cable & Broadcasting Act 1984 (reprinted as Appendix One) is most explicit about creating conditions to encourage programming from community and voluntary organisations. Section 7 suggests that commercial programme suppliers *not* associated with the cable company might expect to be able to provide services to subscribers on the network. Section 7 amounts to a small reduction in the cable operator's monopoly on programme supply and delivery and would appear to be a fair exchange by the operator who by their licence gains the rights of way required to lay cable in the highways and footpaths of each city. These rights of way protect the operator to a significant degree from hindrance by personal or civic objectors to the passage of cabling across their properties or the construction of pavement boxes and trunking throughout their boroughs. [3]

If cable does not provide these local and independent services then the service remains a purely commercial and non-local operation benefiting from the rights of a traditional public utility – such as water, telephone or gas – to gain access to potential subscribers via the properties of non-subscribers and the public streets. When utility status involves the supply of essential services in monopoly supply to the majority, utility status is not contentious and is most surely in the public good. The majority of people clearly believe that essential services should not be obstructed in their passage to the majority of households seeking them. Yet with cable devoid of local forms or significant public demand, the utility status provides purely a commercial advantage and not a public fulfilment. Is it not an infringement of the rights of the majority that do not want cable that it should enjoy utility status and fail to provide local and independent services? Even when local services are not being supplied by the cable operator, the rights of the franchise exclude potential competitors from the supply of local television services:

services which are evidently in public demand. Cable operators can deny a service, refuse to supply that service and instead supply services that are not in public demand under the power of their utility rights of way. Moreover, the locally defined services fitting into the boundaries of districts and city authorities are regulated nationally with little or no effective local control by citizen or local elected body. Standing at almost 70%, an increasing percentage of the companies and the investment behind UK cabling is North American in origin. On the face of it cable is a gross infringement of civic accountability and the rights of citizens to determine their own local communications.

Without a significant local element, cable provides neither a unique service nor for that matter a service of general public benefit. Less than 25% of homes that are able to receive a cable television service choose to take television on cable. Yet in the legislation it is clear that cable was conceived to have unique benefits and to provide a community good as well as a commercial good.

Section 7 of the Cable & Broadcasting Act 1984 requires the applicant:

> (a) to include a range and diversity of programmes;
>
> (b) to include in the programmes matter which originates within the European Economic Community and is performed by nationals of member states;
>
> (c) to include in the programmes an increasing proportion of such matter;
>
> (d) to include programmes of an educational nature, programmes calculated to appeal specially to the taste and outlook of persons living in the area and programmes in which such persons are given an opportunity to participate;
>
> (e) to include programmes provided otherwise than by himself or by associates of his;
>
> (f) to include programmes provided by local voluntary associations and to assist such organisations in the preparation and production of programmes;
>
> (g) to include in the programmes matter which is calculated to promote the understanding or enjoyment of programmes by persons who are deaf;
>
> (h) to provide, or secure the provision of, related services.

If complied with, Section 7 would ensure that each service contained significant elements unique to each community. No other programme supplier is currently in a position to make community provisions or to provide services that are sensitive to local demands. Yet cabling is under way in many parts of the UK without evidence of local commitment or anything amounting to this level of resources for community services being provided. Has its uniqueness been thrown away or merely overlooked? The ITC wrote regarding one city in a letter in May 1990:

> The Authority will, in its licence, not yet issued in the case of Edinburgh, require the applicant to provide a local service, the form of which will be

agreed in writing with the Authority and this will become a term of the licence. The local services to be provided may be based upon the propositions in the franchise application.

Here is only the 'possibility that local services *may be* based upon the propositions in the franchise application'. This would suggest that the local parts of the service supplied by cable are not a significant factor in deciding whether or not to award a franchise. Once a franchise had been awarded by the Cable Authority the applicant required two licences before work on constructing the network could begin;

a) a licence under the Cable and Broadcasting Act 1984 covering the programming carried on the network; and

b) a licence granted by the Department of Trade and Industry under the Telecommunications Act 1984 covering the installing and running of the network.

The telecommunications watch-dog Oftel is responsible for monitoring and enforcing the latter licence. The DTI has issued 119 licences to date. Licences are issued provided the franchisees can satisfy the DTI that they have the necessary finance to build the networks. Oftel's role is to encourage widespread use of the cable infrastructure and to ensure that the cable operators do not retain a monopoly in the supply of new telecommunication services in their own efforts to break the old monopoly previously enjoyed by BT in providing telephone services. Condition 10 in each cable operator's DTI licence echoes Section 7 of the Cable and Broadcasting Act. Trevor Single, Section Head for Cable at Oftel described Section 10 of each telecommunications licence as requiring:

The licensee to permit anyone using approved telecommunication apparatus to provide any service by means of the cable network. The intention of this condition is to ensure that people are free to develop value added services, such as banking, financial information, and local television, and to use the cable network as a means to offer these services to potential subscribers. The licensee is obliged to provide access and capacity on the network unless the service or services to be offered are likely to impede the sound commercial development of the cable network, and the Director General has not expressed a contrary opinion. It should be noted that the ability of a cable operator to deny the provision of a service only applies where development of the whole network could be impeded and not for example where access is sought to offer a competitive service.

Oftel continue:

In summary, the Telecommunications Act provides a mechanism whereby people can use the cable networks as a means to offer a wide range of services, including local television, to others. Oftel will investigate any breaches of licence conditions, including the one relating to access to the cable network. [5]

Oftel's determination to encourage open access to the new cable networks is reinforced in a letter from Oftel's Director, Sir Bryan Carsberg of the 28th January 1991,

> I would be willing to conduct an investigation if a provider of local television services was unable to reach a reasonable agreement with the local cable operator for the carriage of those services.

Oftel's position appears in stark contrast with that of the Cable Authority and the ITC. The latter has removed community demands and independent access from licence provisions and anticipate stipulating these in some later annex. But Section 7 stands at the heart of the 1984 Act, the sole justification for franchising local areas is the provision of local services. Guidance provided by the Cable Authority to each franchise applicant in 1987 makes clear importance of fulfilling the local obligations and of being responsible for implementing the commitments that are made.

Guidance Information for Franchise Applicants, published by the Cable Authority in 1987, indicates the Authority's expectations for community programming and stresses in point 2.12, an:

Obligation to provide the promised service

> The Act gives the Authority the specific power to include in its licence such conditions as it considers requisite or expedient having regard to the applicant's proposals in relation to the criteria described in paragraph 1.13 above [a repetition of Section 7 of the Cable and Broadcasting Act 1984]. In this way *any failure by a franchisee to fulfil the plans for services outlined in his application may place him in breach of his licence. The applicant should ensure that his proposals are realistic and practicable.* (our italics)

This paragraph can have left little doubt in the minds of all the applicants that the Authority intended the applicant to make plans that would be realistic and achievable; or to suffer the consequences of a possible breach of licence by not introducing these services. Yet this vital feature of each licence remains unresolved and unspecified some nine years after the Act came into force and after 135 franchises have been issued.

The exclusion of Section 7 from regulation is not an oversight on the part of the Cable Authority and the ITC. Both bodies have invited applicants to ensure these obligations are properly provided for and then discounted these commitments when they have been made. In this process the ITC have withdrawn the public benefits to be provided by each franchise as required by both the Act and their own Guidance.

From a letter of 3rd May 1990 the ITC writes:

> The Cable Authority does not automatically accept statements made by potential franchise applicants in their applications and may indeed take its decision having discounted certain aspects of what the applicant may have said.

The Cable Authority have therefore been prepared to award licences to companies whose plans the Authority has in very significant parts found to be 'unrealistic'. Yet even with these 'unrealistic' elements removed very, very few cable companies have begun building since 1990. What realistic criteria actually remained upon which the

Authority could base the award of each franchise when what was left no longer provided the key services the Act came into force to ensure were provided? With the significant local contribution of cable withdrawn cable is a delivery agent for satellite and a competitor in providing telephony. Is this sufficiently new or essential for cable to warrant having utility status? The majority of cable services remain unstarted. Why would the ITC focus especially on discounting those parts of the commitment which make an obvious social contribution to each community and which our studies show is of most interest to the public? It is upon Section 7 that cable's utility bargain and the Authority's regulatory responsibility clearly hangs.

The ITC's willingness to take Section 7 out of the cabling commitment extends their regulatory inconsistency to the absurdity of protecting the cable companies from the obligations that they have already made in order to conform to the Act and the Authority's earlier guidance.

A letter dated 21st February 1991:

> It [also] needs to be stated that the Cable Authority's approval of a franchise application does not necessarily entail the Authority's acceptance of or belief in everything contained in the application. The Authority tended to discount or attach no importance to some proposals [while still awarding those applicants a franchise].

The ITC are denying the public services which legislation encourages and awarding franchises to companies whose proposals are inadequate. This would suggest a fundamental flaw and possibly bias in regulatory application of the Act. Such an approach might be explicable if it was clear the Authority had no obligations towards taking account of the public's interest in cable services. Yet Section 5 1.4 of the 1984 Act requires the Authority to take such steps as they consider appropriate:

> to ascertain the opinions of the public in the area ... and ... to encourage the making of comments and suggestions about those services by members of the public ... and shall take account of those opinions.

For the Authority and ITC to present their duties in such a convoluted way they have created the distinct appearance of being unconcerned that they are awarding a franchise to a body whose approach they have identified as being be misleading and even deliberately false. Was local and community television discounted because the service the companies intended to provide unlikely to live up to public expectations? Or was it simply because the local services would add a financial burden to the cable companies which they privately presented themselves as being reluctant to fulfil? Was the quiet removal of the burden of local and commitments and independent access a bargain to attract reluctant cable investors? If the Cable Authority and the ITC interpret their primary duty as protecting companies from obligations that are social but expensive in order to provide services that are purely commercial and profit centred how do they differ from the Cable Television Association whose legitimate interest is surely to represent the cable companies' commercial interests? The Cable Authority write in their 1988/89 Annual Report that:

The Authority's aim is to give to those it regulates codes and guidelines which are easy to understand and clear in their application and interpretation, in order to minimise errors, encourage consistency and preserve respect for the rules.

If this were so then the franchise proposals that have been discounted as unrealistic by the Authority should suggest clearly to the Authority that these applicants have not followed the Authority's Guidance to take particular account of Section 7. If clarity is all it is portrayed to be then this failure to be 'realistic' has already suggested to the Authority in the logic of its public documents that these companies lack an ability to build a £50m cable network. If these companies would have been in breach of licence if they had been allowed to go ahead with the local options in the form proposed then the more obvious course of the Authority should have been not to award the licence at all. From exactly what are these companies being protected? The answer is that the cable companies are being protected by the Authority and ITC from the very terms of the legislation the Authority was introduced to implement and the ITC obliged to follow! Removing altogether the local service seems to negate the purpose of the legislation – which was to provide local services of local public interest within a commercial framework but not exclusively dictated by commercial criteria.

In Cable Company Franchise Commitments (Chapter Two) Adrian Friedli outlines the local components of each franchise. It is difficult to see how the very general promises made by the franchise applicants in their applications can be dismissed as 'unrealistic' by the Cable Authority and ITC. 'Inadequate' would be a more suitable term since 10% of the franchises awarded by the Authority were awarded to *identical* applications. The centralisation of local television regulation has led to a deeply cynical and dishonest approach towards public demands and legal expectation, public interests and local accountability.

Finally, the ITC suggest in a letter of 18th September 1992 that:

> more local and community services have been provided (by cable operators) than were ever required under any licence mandate.

The ITC cites United Artists (Croydon), Leicester Communications and Videotron as examples of companies:

> developing local services ... typical of the industry's expanding interest in this genre (of local television).

It is because there *never was a mandate* applied to the licence to ensure an even standard of local services were scheduled that services are at such a low level. Terrestrial television by comparison is much more highly regulated. Of course it cannot approach the level of localness that the public demand. The ITC would have the public believe that due to their own deliberate negligence more local services have arisen without a mandate than have arisen when a mandate was never enforced. What evidence is there to support the ITC's contention that more has arisen from no regulation than would have arisen from appropriate regulation?

3.   Survey of Local Channels

Local services have expanded in the last three years by 100%, with 10 operational franchises offering local television programming in 1992 compared with 5 in 1989. Over the same period the number of active franchises has increased from 29 in 1990 to 55 in 1992. There are a further 64 franchises that are dormant. Even so, these have been awarded licences on *the evidence that funds were available to build*. A further 14 which have yet to obtain a licence or have been have withdrawn.

In July 1992, aggregated across all 55 operational broadband cable franchises there are 1,567,599 homes passed by cable in the UK. In these cabled areas, 330,630 people subscribe to the cable service. The percentage of homes taking cable where the service is on offer is 21.1%. [6]

This is a rise in penetration from 18.9% over the year from 1991. Although the general rate of cable growth has actually fallen behind ITC expectations with only 225,000 extra homes passed in the first half of 1992. [7]

Out of the 135 licences awarded by the ITC in 1990, by mid 1992 119 have taken up telecoms licences with the DTI.

Of these 119, there are now 43 operating cable companies serving 55 franchise areas. 32 of these franchise areas have 2500 plus subscribers. [8] It is three years since the last of the franchises have been issued under the 1984 Act and in less than half of the franchise areas has cable been started. Nearly half of Britain's towns and cities lie within a dormant franchise which denies the occupants local services while preserving for the cable company a monopoly of supply to the franchisee pretty much at their leisure. Relatively few franchises have been withdrawn.

Currently, only 10 of the 55 operational franchises provide locally made television programming. These are Croydon (United Artists), Merton and Sutton (United Artists), Kingston and Richmond (United Artists), Swindon (Swindon Cable), Coventry (Coventry Cable Ltd), Aberdeen (Aberdeen Cable Services), Blackburn/Burnley (East Lancashire Cablevision Ltd) Camden (Cable London Plc), Haringey (Cable London Plc) and Enfield (Cable London Plc).

Just six companies covering ten franchise areas offer a local service to the customer. For the most part a single service is offered by these Multiple Service Operators across their adjoining franchises.

Windsor Cable Communications are in the final stages of setting up a full local service as this publication goes to print and Leicester Communications and Midlands Cable Communications anticipate launching full video programming on a local channel before the end of 1992.

The above operators all provide a local video text service, as indeed do all 25 companies covering the 33 franchises who took part in this research. The exceptions are Diamond Cable Ltd who are not due to begin broadcasting until November 1992 and Birmingham Cable Ltd who have no local programming at all.

Andover Cablevision do offer a local text service but did not feel it extensive enough to enable them to answer questions. However, for accuracy Andover will be included in the as providing a local text service. Nynex Cable Communications are not included in the final figures, as their local text service is still in its infancy.

3.1   Cable Company Profiles

Where a cable company's local proposals were made public before the franchise was awarded, an extract of this has been included within the profiles. Where applicable, the numbers (1), (2) or (3) appear at the end of the extract to indicate the rating Cable Company Franchise Commitments attached to local programming intentions for each franchise applications. The three rating indicates as follows:

> **Group 1** there is virtually no evidence to substantiate the applicant's pledges of commitment to local provision on the local channels, there are few, if any, provisions for training and only the vaguest offers to make equipment available.

> **Group 2** generally takes the form of a phased development approach; where the applicant either waits for subscriber numbers to reach sufficient mass to sustain an expansion from the original text channel, or where operators seek to collaborate with existing media concerns to accelerate the process.

> **Group 3** there is a firm, substantial commitment to resourcing the local channel in advance, so that it is in a position to generate both access and local programming almost immediately.

It should be kept in mind that this Group Number relates to proposals made up to eight years ago and that the summaries of each cable operation should also be considered.

Aberdeen Cable Services Ltd

303 King Street, Aberdeen, AB2 3AP. Tel: 0224-649444
Contact - Marc Macrae
Franchise area - Aberdeen and area
Premises in franchise - 93,231
Homes passed 30/9/92 - 93,422
Homes connected - 14,897
CTV penetration - 15.9%

Aberdeen began broadcasting in May 1985. As an early entrant into cabling, the Aberdeen bidder was not obliged to provide an outline of its proposals for public consultation. The commitment to local television programming was unspecified at the beginning of 1991, although Aberdeen provided a comprehensive service at the outset.

Staff

Aberdeen employs thirty staff in total, five of whom are employed in sales and marketing.

Text

A local video text service is supplied in-house.

Programming
Local video programming is carried on a separate channel and broadcasts approximately 1.5 hours of fresh programming per week.

Broadcasts are mainly documentaries and leisure interest. Programmes are made by national production companies (50%) and local voluntary and community groups (50%). lo-band equipment is used. Local programming is funded solely by the station with a budget of up to £250 per hour.

Community involvement
Local programme making and planning are improved by community involvement but Aberdeen was uncertain about involving the public in local editorial policy-making.

Advertising
Aberdeen does not broadcast any local advertisements and feel that interest from local companies in cable advertising is low at present. However, Aberdeen believe that this is an area which has much potential for growth.

Summary
In 1989 when the previous research was undertaken, Aberdeen produced 2-5 hours per week of local television programming. Unfortunately, the scale of their local programming has had to be greatly reduced since then due to high running costs. Aberdeen now only produce 1.5 hours of fresh programming per week, although they do offer good access for the community by broadcasting programmes produced by voluntary/community organisations and by providing training in television production for the public (see training section). Aberdeen Cable are a relatively small company yet are one of the very few to have completed their build. Their commitment to local access has been strong but they expect there will be a need to look towards expansion of the services in the future.

Bolton Cablevision Ltd

25-30 Queensbrook, Bolton Technology Exchange, Spa Road, Bolton. BL1 4AY. Tel: 0204-365111

Contact - Frank Mundy
Franchise area - Borough of Bolton
Premises in franchise - 130,000
Homes passed 30/9/92 - 26,158
Homes connected - 4,565
CTV Penetration - 17.5%

Bolton started broadcasting in July 1990. As an early entrant into cabling, the Bolton bidder was not obliged to provide an outline of its proposals for public consultation. The commitment to local television programming was unspecified at the beginning of 1991.

Staff
Bolton employs approximately thirty seven staff, twenty of whom are employed in sales and marketing. Bolton foresees the need for extra marketing staff in the next two years.

Text
Bolton offers a local text service which is supplied in-house. This employs two people part-time.

Summary
Bolton are a reasonably small operation who have been broadcasting for a little over two years. Allowances could be made for this short broadcasting period if they had provided much hope for the future, but with no date set to begin local television programming and no need indicated for production staff over the next two years, Bolton do not offer a very progressive outlook for the community for the near future anyway.

Cablevision Bedfordshire Ltd

Cablevision House, 20 Cosgrove Way, Luton, Bedfordshire. LU1 1XL. Tel: 0582-401044
Contact - Richard Rodiss
Franchise area - Luton/South Beds
Premises in franchise - 97,000
Homes passed 30/9/92 - 10,000
Homes connected - less than 2,500

Cablevision Bedfordshire (C Beds) started broadcasting in February 1990. The commitment to local television programming in their original franchise application was described as 'to encourage and train new producers and production groups who will have access to the production facilities for the production of work relating to their community'. C Beds recognised the need for substantial funds and planned to broadcast, initially, only teletext *(Cable Company Franchise Commitments*, group 2).

Staff
C Beds employs twenty staff in total, six of whom are employed in sales and marketing. C Beds foresees the need for extra sales staff within the next two years.

Text
C Beds offers a local video text service, in conjunction with their local newspaper - *The Bedford Times* - the service details local news and events. The channel employs one person. The two companies share equally the revenue and advertising.

Summary
Cablevision Bedfordshire are another example of a small operation, broadcasting for

approximately two and a half years, but yet to establish a full local television service for the community. They have adhered to much of what was proposed in their franchise application, as their initial plans were for a local text service which indeed they have provided in conjunction with a local newspaper, building some links with the community. Cablevision Bedfordshire are very keen to develop local television programming in order to meet the needs of the community, but have no start date set so far.

Cable London Plc

Centro House, Mandela Street, London. NW1 0DU. Tel: 071-911-0111
Contact - Alison Pugh
Franchise areas - Camden, Haringey, Enfield, Hackney/Islington
Premises in franchises - 258,000
Homes passed: 30/9/92 - 58,328
Homes connected: - 16,646
CTV Penetration - 24.4% (Camden)

Cable London began broadcasting in December 1989. The commitment to local television programming in their original franchise application seemed promising. Cable London stressed the need for quality and a high standard of programming and pledged to 'develop the relationship between Camden and its community'. No time scale was given but Cable London gave a clear commitment to the provision of text and interactive services (*Cable Company Franchise Commitments*, group 3).

Staff
Cable London employs two hundred staff in total, fifty of whom are in sales and marketing and one of whom is employed in television production. They foresee the need for extra staff in both of these areas within the next two years but it is not known how many.

Text
Cable London offers a local video text service which is supplied in-house. This employs 1 person.

Programming
Cable London has local video programming which is carried on a separate channel and broadcasts up to 5 hours of fresh programming per week. Cable London broadcast mainly current affairs, documentaries, sports, comedy and ethnic programmes of variable length. These are produced by the station (70%), local production companies (10%), local film/video workshops (10%) and gained on general acquisition (10%). Cable London use S-VHS and Hi-Band equipment. Local programming is funded solely by the station and the channel has a budget of up to £250 per hour.

Community involvement
Cable London believe that local programme making and planning are improved by community involvement, but do not feel that involving the public in editorial policy-making is beneficial.

Advertising
Cable London has no local advertising at present.

Summary
Cable London has been something of a local programming success story. They have been broadcasting for only three years, yet produce up to five hours per week of local video programming offering a wide ranging selection of material to over 10,000 people. They broadcast the local channel to three of their four franchises.

Cable London have a good relationship with the community, broadcasting programmes made by local groups in addition to funding and training individuals and organisations in the basics of television production. An increase in local television programming is foreseen although the company are not currently budgeted to increase their staff. It should be kept in mind that Cable London are a large company, perhaps in a better position to resource projects than smaller operators, but they are still very much an illustration of how local programming could develop in the not so distant future.

The addition of recent services for ethnic minorities on offer from Cable London are an important and original contribution.

Coventry Cable Ltd

Whitely Village, London Road, Coventry, West Midlands. CV3 4HL. Tel: 0203-505345
Contact - Maria Beck
Franchise area - City of Coventry
Premises in franchise - 119,000
Homes passed 30/9/92 - 117,078
Homes connected - 10,001
CTV penetration - 8.5%

Coventry began broadcasting in September 1985. As an early entrant into cabling, the Coventry bidder was not obliged to provide an outline of its proposals for public consultation. The commitment to local television programming was unspecified at the beginning of 1991, although broadcast facilities, including sophisticated editing and signal routing, the envy of many local production companies, were installed for local programme production in the mid-'80s.

Staff
Coventry employs forty staff in total, eight of whom are employed in sales and marketing and one part-time in television production. Coventry foresees the need for extra staff in both areas but only if finances allow.

Text
Coventry offers a local text service which is supplied by a voluntary organisation - a local college.

Programming
Local video programming is carried on a separate channel and broadcasts approxi-

mately three hours of fresh programming per week. Coventry broadcasts a variety of programmes which are made for them mainly by the local college (above) which produces the text service (over 90%), but Coventry also broadcast United Nations material. Coventry use hi-band equipment. Local programming is funded solely by the station and Coventry has a budget of up to £250 per hour.

Advertising
Advertising at present is limited to charitable organisations. Coventry feels that the area they cover is not big enough to meet with the expectations of their prospective clients and foresee limited opportunities for expansion. They do feel there is a great deal of potential for local cable advertising but only if larger companies can be persuaded to use it as a viable means of promoting their product.

Summary
Although Coventry have been forced to dramatically scale down their local service since being set-up in 1985, they still offer particularly good access for the community with most of their programmes originating from local sources outwith the station.

They have established strong links with a local college and encourage community involvement both through the college and by offering free advertising for charities and voluntary organisations. Unfortunately funding is a problem at Coventry, therefore there are no resources available for training and there is a degree of uncertainty regarding the development of local services in the near future.

Derby Cablevision Ltd

Unit A, Chequers Business Park, Derby. DE2 6AW. Tel: 0332-200002
Contact - Rachel Turner
Franchise area - Derby/Sponden
Premises in franchise - 96,000
Homes passed 14 June 1992 - 5,950
Homes connected - less than 2,500
CTV penetration - N/K

Derby started broadcasting in October 1991. The commitment to local television programming in the franchise application was ambiguous. Derby pledged that 'as cable penetration increased they would use a local channel to communicate directly with the people of Derby'. They also spoke of an allocation in their second year's budget to allow for a local channel, however the meaning was slightly vague making no reference to training or equipment beyond existing facilities (Cable *Company Franchise Commitments*, group 1).

Staff
Derby employs forty three staff in total, sixteen of whom are employed in sales and marketing. Derby anticipate the need for extra sales staff within the next two years in addition to the possibility of local broadcasting staff.

Text

Derby offers a local text service which transmits school news, community notices, miscellaneous sales and business information.

Summary

Derby Cable Vision are a relatively young company who have been broadcasting for just one year. With regard to local programming at present, they seem to be adhering to the vague proposals reproduced in Cable Company Franchise Commitments as their service is teletext only. This said, Derby are currently negotiating new ownership, therefore plans and projects for the future are at something of a standstill. Derby received a favourable response in recent market research towards local programming and hope to be able to offer television programming to their customers in the future.

East Lancashire Cablevision Ltd

Glenfiels Park, Site 2, Blakewater Road, Blackburn, Lancashire. BB1 5HQ. Tel: 0254-680094
Contact - Milton Haworth
Franchise area - Blackburn/Burnley
Premises in franchise - 168,000
Homes passed: - 30/9/92 - 40,500
Homes connected: - 4,030
CTV Penetration: - 10.7%

East Lancashire Cablevision (East Lancs Cable) began broadcasting in November 1989. The commitment to local television programming in their original franchise application pledged three local channels in the first two years of transmission, however no indication was given of local access to programme production, nor to training in the techniques and skills of programme making. (*Cable Company Franchise Commitments*, group 2)

Staff

East Lancs Cable employs thirty four staff in total, twenty six of whom are in sales and marketing and four of whom are in television production. East Lancs Cable foresees a need for extra staff in both areas within the next two years.

Text

East Lancs Cable offers a local text service which is supplied in-house. This employs two people.

Programming

Local video programming is carried on a separate channel and broadcasts approximately seven hours of fresh programming per week. East Lancs Cable broadcasts mainly current affairs, leisure interest, religious and sports programmes which are produced entirely by the station. East Lancs Cable use hi-band and broadcast quality equipment. Their budget is unspecified and local programming is funded wholly by the station.

Advertising
Advertising is teletext only, divided equally between products, services and retailing. At present East Lancs Cable feel that local companies are not particularly interested in using cable to advertise but they think that there is most definitely potential for growth.

Summary
East Lancashire Cablevision are a positive example of a cable operator offering the services in demand from the public equally if not better than the larger companies. The commitment from the original cable operator, the Canadian company Maclean Hunter drew heavily on their North American experience which indicated that local programming helped stabilise audience interest in cable. ELC have been broadcasting for almost three years and employ thirty four staff yet manage to produce up to seven hours per week of new programming covering a variety of subjects.

The station have forged strong links with the local technical college and also offer comprehensive training in all aspects of television production for up to six local people per month. One area in which they could improve community access is by broadcasting material other than their own to give local voluntary groups the chance to reach a wider audience, as emphasised in Section 7.

This aside, East Lancs. Cablevision are clearly well on the way to fulfilling the proposals made in their franchise application and instill much confidence for the future of local programming on cable.

Encom Cable TV & Telecommunications Ltd

Limeharbour Court, London, E14 9TY. Tel: 071-895-9910
Contact - Ian Bennett
Franchise area - London Boroughs of Newham and Tower Hamlets
Premises in franchise - 145,000
Homes passed 30/9/92 - 57,228
Homes connected - 9,385
CTV Penetration - 16.3%

Encom (formerly) East London Telecommunications (ELT) started broadcasting in April 1987. The commitment to local television programming in their original franchise application proposed to provide a 'local access or Community Channel' which would initially run as a text service. They hoped within twelve months of operation to have full studio facilities and complete local programming. Encom undertook to provide professional staff, technicians and programme coordinators to liaise with groups wishing to contribute to the channel. (*Cable Company Franchise Commitments*, group 2)

Staff
Encom employs twenty staff in total, six of whom are employed in sales and marketing. ELT foresees the need for extra sales staff within the next two years.

Text
Encom offers a local text service, but offered no specifications.

Summary
Encom have been broadcasting for over five years but still run a text-only local service. They have most certainly not introduced the proposals made in their franchise application, as there was clear indication of television programming, mentioning facilities, staff and community liaison.

At present, Encom are a small operation looking to expand in sales and marketing and seem little interested in growth in other areas. They do have plans to launch the local text service at their Redbridge franchise in the near future, but can this really be seen as expansion for a local service which after five years should be offering the viewer more than text?

Leicester Communications Ltd

28-29 Oswin Road, Leicester. LE3 1HR. Tel: 0533-554000
Contact - Jenny Ludlam
Franchise area - Leicester, Loughborough and Shepshed
Premises in franchise - 200,670
Homes passed 1 April 1992 - 25,439
Homes connected - 5,876
CTV Penetration - 19.7%

Leicester started broadcasting in April 1991. The commitment to local television programming in their original franchise application proposed a very well planned Asian Channel. Initially a text and photovideotext service combined with a live news and current affairs slot was planned although the proportion of live material was to increase as the cable area grew. In relation to access, Leicester proposed to 'establish opportunities for interested groups to be trained in the skills of programme making'. (*Cable Company Franchise Commitments*, group 3/2)

Staff
No totals were given but two staff are devoted to local programming. Leicester foresees the need for extra staff in both sales/marketing and television production within the next two years.

Text
Leicester offers a local text service which is supplied in-house. This employs one person full-time and two trainees.

Programming
Leicester expects to launch full video programming in November 1992.

Advertising
None at present, but Leicester feel local companies are very interested in using local cable to advertise and believe that it is an area of great potential.

Summary
Leicester are still a reasonably young operator and have been broadcasting for approximately eighteen months, yet things are moving in line with commitments. Leicester are

149

set to launch local television programming in November 1992. Their plans for training have also being fulfilled, they have trained twenty people so far in the technicalities of television production. If all goes according to plan and television programming is introduced, Leicester will bear the communities proposals in mind and offer the community good access to a quality service.

Midlands Cable Communications Ltd

Cable House, Waterfront, Merry Hill, Dudley. DY5 1XJ. Tel: 0384-482448
Contact - Lynne Smith
Franchise Areas - Wolverhampton/Walsall/Dudley/Sandwell/Cannock/
Kidderminster/Bromsgrove
Premises in franchises - 545,000
Homes passed 30/9/92 - 29,208
Homes connected - 5,378
CTV Penetration - 17.8%

Midlands Cable Communications (Midlands) started broadcasting in August 1991. The commitment to local television programming in the original franchise application proposed launching a local channel and planned local production staff, a field production unit and eventual studio facilities. The application implied that the majority of programming might be produced by the station, although the intention was to promote training classes for residents from minority communities. (*Cable Company Franchise Commitments*, group 2)

Staff
Midlands employs approximately one hundred staff in total, forty of whom are in sales and marketing. They foresees the need for extra staff in sales/marketing, in addition to possible production staff.

Text
Midlands offers a local text service which is supplied in-house and employs one person.

Programming
Midlands are set to launch video programming at the end of the year.

Advertising
Text advertisements only.

Summary
Midlands are a young station who have been broadcasting for only a year. They have kept closely in line with the proposals made in their franchise application. They stated their intention to launch a local channel, but gave no time scale. At present Midlands operate a local text service but have plans to begin video programming before the end of 1992 which would be in keeping with their proposals. Midlands' commitment to community access seems to be consistent, although the introduction of local television programming should further their develop relationship with the public as participants in the provision of services.

150

North West Cable Communications Ltd

Cable House, 2-8 Frenchwood Avenue, Preston, Lancashire. PR1 4QF. Tel: 0772-832888
Contact - Tony Williams
Franchise areas - Central Lancashire, Preston, South Liverpool, Wigan
Premises in franchise - 339,000 (total)
Homes passed 30/9/92 - 138,633
Homes connected - 31,844
Central Lancashire and Liverpool South only, no total available for Wigan.
CTV Penetration - 24.1% (average).

North West Cable Communications (NWCC or Cable North West) started broadcasting in May 1990. The commitment to local television in the original franchise application was very encouraging. The operator was to offer four local channels; three local access and a professionally produced and presented news channel. These were all to come into action as soon as the operator began transmission. Close links were made with Lancashire Polytechnic regarding a Learning Channel with an emphasis on adult education. (*Cable Company Franchise Commitments*, group 3)

Staff
Total staff numbers were unspecified but thirty five are employed in sales and marketing. NWCC foresees the need for television production staff within the next two years.

Text
NWCC offers a local text service which is supplied in-house and employs two staff.

Programming
NWCC are set to commence providing video inserts very soon but are not in a position to forecast when they will actually start to produce programmes.

Advertising
NWCC broadcasts text adverts.

Summary
North West Cable Communications have been broadcasting for over two years and there are no moves towards implementing the proposals made in their franchise application. It is most disappointing, considering how promising their commitment seemed to be, to find that they operate only a local text service. The company are set to commence video inserts soon but were unable to specify when actual production would begin. Video inserts are, of course, a step in the direction towards programme making capacity but this is some way off the proposed professionally produced and presented news channel.

Norwich Cablevision Ltd

32a Whiffler Road, Norwich. NR3 2AZ. Tel: 0603-787892
Contact - Hazel Campeny
Franchise area - Norwich

Premises in franchise - 83,000
Homes passed 4 June 1992 - 16,195
Homes connected - N/K
CTV Penetration - N/K

Norwich started broadcasting in May 1990.

The commitment to local television in their original franchise application was cautious. Norwich proposed to 'operate a local programming service as a cooperative venture with other local media operators'. They planned to begin their local service as a text service and no dates were given for video programming beginning. (*Cable Company Franchise Commitments*, group 2)

Staff
Norwich employs forty staff in total, approximately twelve of whom are employed in sales and marketing. Norwich foresees an increase in sales staff dependant on growth rate.

Text
Norwich offers a local text service which is supplied in-house and employs one person.

Summary
Norwich have been broadcasting for over two years. Their commitment to local programming in their franchise application was cautious. No dates were given although they suggest there will be no need for programming staff within the next two years. [Research was undertaken by the Institute of Local Television and jointly funded by Norwich Cablevision, Norwich City Council and Eastern Arts. Local service proposals were made, but shortly after Massada the cable component in the franchise withdrew and earlier this year PacTel, the telephony component, put all their UK franchises on the market. PacTel's interest totals some 10% of UK cable. The Norwich network has the most cabling in place.]

Nynex CableComms Ltd

Wimbledon Bridge House, 1 Hartfield Road, Wimbledon, London. SW19 3RU. Tel: 081-540-8833
Contact - Graham Pitman
Franchise areas - Portsmouth (Solent), Brighton (Sussex)
Premises in franchises - 373,000 (total)
Portsmouth figures only available
Homes passed 30/9/92 - 46,923
Homes connected - 9,504
CTV Penetration - 18.2%

Nynex started broadcasting in September 1991. The commitment to local television programming in their original franchise application was favourable. Video productions of a community access nature were to be accepted, broadcast and occasionally commissioned by Nynex to demonstrate the potential of a local channel. In the long term, equipment was to be acquired and a Community Programming Facilitator employed to help users and groups to prepare and produce programmes. (*Cable Company Franchise Commitments*, group 3/2)

Staff
Nynex employ approximately six hundred staff in total. Nynex foresees the need for both sales and marketing staff and television production staff within the next two years.

Text
Nynex are in the initial stages of setting up a text service presently. This service will initially be contracted out to another company, but will eventually be carried out in-house.

Advertising
Only free text advertising is broadcast at the moment but they have extensive plans for a quality television programming service. Nynex feel that local interest in cable advertising is high. They are planning to work closely with local newspapers and take time to develop good advertising, learning through the mistakes made by other companies.

Summary
Nynex are a fairly new company who have been operational for almost a year. They are presently establishing a local text service for two of their franchise areas (named above) and are keen to expand to full video programming as soon as finances allow. Nynex appear to be honouring the proposals made in their franchise application and have recently appointed a Head of Local Programming who is based at their head office in London but is responsible for overseeing development of the local services at all their franchises. Nynex are very excited about the possibilities for local television programming although they stress that development will continue at an appropriate pace to ensure that quality is not lost.

Peterborough Cablevision Ltd

Unit 29, Metro Centre, Shrewsbury Avenue, Peterborough. PE4 OBX. Tel: 0733-230303
Contact - Sara Haydoke
Franchise area - Peterborough
Premises in franchise - 58,000
Homes passed 30/9/92 - 21,356
Homes connected - 4,175
CTV penetration - 19.0%

The company started broadcasting in August 1990. Commitment to local television programming in their original franchise application was cautious. Peterborough proposed to 'operate a local programming service as a cooperative venture with other local media operators'. They expected to implement their local plans relatively quickly, however no specific dates were given. (*Cable Company Franchise Commitments*, group 2)

Staff
Peterborough employs approximately fifty staff in total, sixteen in sales and seven in

marketing. Peterborough foresees the need for five to ten extra sales and marketing staff within the next two years.

Text
Peterborough offers a local text service which is supplied in-house by two administrative staff part-time.

Advertising
Advertising on the local channel is all locally produced and targeted specifically to the Peterborough cable area. Advertising rates differed according to duration of the advert, offering discounts for cabled customers and businesses. Services account for all of the advertising.

Peterborough feel local companies to be very interested in cable advertising and believe that, in general, there is much potential for growth.

Summary
On the whole, local programming seems to take somewhat of a back seat at Peterborough. Efforts are currently to be found concentrated around sales and advertising which they see as expanding in the future and little interest was shown in local services. The company have been broadcasting for two years and have, to a certain extent, fulfilled their initial franchise application proposals as they did not specify whether their local service would be text or television programming. They offer a text local service at present, but give no dates as to when they expect to expand the service to video programming.

Swindon Cable

Newcome Drive, Hawksworth Estate, Swindon, Wiltshire. SN2 1TU. Tel: 0793-615601
Contact - David Gosling
Franchise area - Swindon
Premises in franchise - 65,000
Homes passed 30/9/92 - 60,342
Homes connected - 17,918
CTV Penetration - 29.5%

Swindon started broadcasting in September 1984. As an early entrant into cabling, the Swindon bidder was not obliged to provide an outline of its proposals for public consultation. The commitment to local television programming was unspecified at the beginning of 1991.

Staff
Swindon employs forty eight staff in total, fifteen in sales and marketing and 1.5 in television production. Swindon foresees the need for 2.5 extra staff in television production within the next two years.

Text
Swindon offers a text service which is contracted via an agency.

Programming
Local video programming is carried on a separate channel and broadcasts up to five hours per week of fresh programming. Swindon broadcasts mainly local news, sports and arts/entertainment programmes which are between ten and thirty minutes in duration and are produced entirely by the station. Swindon use hi-band and broadcast quality equipment. Local programming is funded wholly by the station but the budget was unspecified.

Community involvement
Both editorial policy-making and programme making are improved with community participation but Swindon was uncertain about involving the public in programme planning.

Advertising
Swindon offers videotext advertising divided between products 60%, services 20% and retailing 20%.

Swindon have received much interest from local companies and feel there is certainly much potential for growth.

Summary
When the previous research was undertaken, Swindon was broadcasting up to six hours per week of local programming and the situation has changed little since then. This can be read two ways; as positive because they have not been forced to cut back on programming but negative as they have not managed to expand in three years despite greater take-up.

Also, Swindon have been broadcasting for almost eight years and are still only showing their own material. It would surely be a appropriate for a company with such extensive local programming experience to accept material from, and perhaps even offer training to, local community and voluntary organisations.

Tayside Cable Services

Tay works, Brown Street, Dundee. DD1 5EF. Tel: 0382-22220
Contact - Derek Smart
Franchise area - City of Dundee/Broughty Ferry/Monifieth/Carnoustie
Premises in franchise - 79,000
Homes passed 30/9/92 - 25,,569
Homes connected - 8,993
CTV Penetration - 36.9%

Tayside started broadcasting in November 1990. The commitment to local television programming in their original franchise application was encouraging. Tayside planned to set up a company called Tayside Television Ltd to provide community groups with the means of producing programmes. They pledged to provide equipment and a full-time training manager and stressed that the onus was on the community to make the programmes but felt it "highly unlikely that sufficient video material will be available for a full transmission schedule on this channel." (*Cable Company Franchise Commitments*, group 3)

Staff
Tayside did not supply staff totals in any form although they did intimate that extra staff would be needed in both sales and marketing and television production within the next two years.

Text
Tayside offers a local text service which is supplied in-house and employs one person.

Advertising
Tayside feel there is much potential in their area although they have not yet canvassed the market.

Summary
Tayside have been broadcasting for almost two years and still there is no sign of possible fulfilment of proposals made regarding community access in their initial franchise application. Far reaching promises of a separate production company providing training and equipment were made but as yet, none of this has come to fruition. They offer a local text service at present and intimate that programme production staff will be needed within the next two years, although no dates are given for the commencement of local television programming.

United Artists Communications (Avon) Ltd

700 Waterside Drive, Aztec West, Almondsbury, Bristol. BS12 4ST. Tel: 0454-612290
Contact - Allan Robertson
Franchise area - Bristol/Bath and area
Premises in franchise - 392,000
Homes passed 1 June 1992 - 66,382
Homes connected - 13,321
CTV Penetration - 20.5%

United Artists (UA (Avon)) started broadcasting in this franchise in September 1990. The commitment to local television programming in their original franchise application was promising, though ambiguous. UA (Avon) proposed to draw on the success of the Croydon franchise (see next profile) and 'develop a replicable local programme channel and production facility format which could be used as a pattern for each local franchise'. UA (Avon) aimed to provide a local programme coordinator to run training courses and workshops to stimulate community interest in access programming. No time scale was mentioned for these plans. (*Cable Company Franchise Commitments*, group 2)

Staff
UA (Avon) employs one hundred and eighty seven staff in total, thirty in sales and marketing. UA (Avon) foresees the need for additional staff in both sales and marketing and television production within the next two years.

Text
UA (Avon) offers a local text service which they receive directly from their Croydon franchise (see next profile).

Programming
UA (Avon) foresee an increase in their local programming in the near future.

Advertising
UA (Avon) have none at present but feel local companies are very interested and there to be much potential for growth in this area.

Summary
United Artists have been broadcasting in the Avon franchise for two years. They are a sizeable operation and a major interest in UK cable employing many people and serving a large franchise area. However, this has not accelerated their progress in local channel development. They offer a local text service which is received from the Croydon franchise but as yet, do not have full video programming like their sister franchise.

United Artists are keeping to the proposals made in their franchise application as they had extensive plans but offered no time scale, therefore. They foresee an increase in local programming in the future hopefully this means they are set to follow Croydon's example and begin local television programming.

United Artists Communications (London South)

Communications House, 5 Factory Lane, Croydon. CR9 3RA. Tel: 081-760-0222
Contact - Deborah Ward
Franchise areas - Croydon, Merton and Sutton, Kingston and Richmond
Premises in franchise -369,000
(figures for Croydon and Merton and Sutton only)
Homes passed 30/9/92 - 221,481
Homes connected - 38,023
CTV Penetration 24.5% (average)

The Croydon franchise began broadcasting in December 1985. As an early entrant into cabling, the original Croydon operator was not obliged to provide an outline of its proposals for public consultation. The commitment to local television programming was unspecified at the beginning of 1991.

Staff
UA employs two hundred and fifty staff in total but were unable to specify a break-down. UA foresees a need for extra marketing staff within the next two years if programming hours increase. They also employ twenty five people freelance to deal with local programming.

Text
UA offers a local text service which is supplied in-house. This employs two people.

Programming
Local video programming is carried on a separate channel and broadcasts approximately 4.5 hours of fresh programming per week. UA broadcasts mainly magazine, religious and sports programmes, produced by both the station (70%) and local voluntary and community groups (30%). UA use hi-band equipment. UA do not specify the local programming budget, however it is funded mainly by the station (90%) but aided by sponsorship (10%). From experience, UA believes that the type of company most likely to sponsor would be computer or communication based.

Community involvement
UA believe that levels of involvement from the community are greatly dependant on the amounts of time and money available.

Advertising
The advertising on UA's local channel is locally sourced, although 10% of it is modified national/regional material (i.e. voice-over). The type of company likely to use this form of advertising are large multi-nationals such as jewellers or car manufacturers. Advertising rates vary according to time of day broadcast and length of advert, as did advertising packages. UA's local advertising is concentrated around retailing (60%), products (20%) and services (20%). UA anticipate phenomenal growth and believe that the surface has just been scratched, while accepting that it may take months, or years, to establish local cable advertising as an acceptable alternative to radio and the press.

Summary
When the previous research was undertaken in 1989 Croydon was broadcasting up to 2.5 hours of fresh programming per week. This figure has now risen to 4.5 hours covering a wider variety of subjects therefore definite progress has been made since 1989. Also, three years ago, Croydon was producing most of the material from within the station, whereas now, 30% of broadcast material is made outwith the station by local voluntary and community groups. This is very a positive step for community access, something which Croydon believe to be very important so long as there are adequate amounts of time and money allocated to local programming. United Artists have succeeded in steadily furthering local television programming at their Croydon franchise and broadcasting this channel to their two other London franchises. All that remains now is for them to keep building on the quality of the material, consider offering training for community volunteers and begin actual production at the two franchises currently receiving Croydon's local programming rather than their own.

Videotron - West London Division

Parkways, 179-181 The Vale, London. W3 7QS. Tel: 071-740-4848
Contact - Lorna Glickman
Franchise areas - Ealing, Kensington and Chelsea, Barnet/Brent/Hammersmith/Fulham, Harrow, Greenwich, Lewisham, Lambeth/Southwark, Thamesmead Town, Wandsworth
Premises in franchises - 1,008,000 (total)

Homes passed 1 April 1992 - 226,257
Homes connected - 54,075
CTV Penetration - 26.3% (average)

Franchise areas in South London division - Greenwich/Lewisham, Lambeth/South-wark, Thamesmead Town, Wandsworth.

Premises in franchises - 318,000 (total).

Videotron first started broadcasting in these franchise areas in January 1987. The commitment to local television programming in the original franchise application was ambiguous. Videotron proposed to offer local text services in the 'early years' progressing to fully fledged productions made with the help of community groups, organisations and associations throughout the franchise areas. Videotron also suggested production assistance and training would be made available although no time scale was indicated for any of the plans. (*Cable Company Franchise Commitments*, group 2)

Staff
Videotron employs around six hundred staff, approximately one hundred of whom are in sales and marketing. Videotron foresee the need for three to five television production and two to four sales and marketing staff within the next two years.

Text
Videotron offers a local text service which comprises council and borough information supplied direct from local authorities and is produced in-house, employing one person.

Programming
In September 1992, Videotron are launching Multicultural Television which consists of five new ethnic channels; Persian Television (Iranian), Channel A/Culturebeat (Asian), Hellenic TV (Greek and Cypriot), Better Vision TV (Afro-Caribbean) and Anadolu Radio TV (Turkish). These will be free channels transmitting on week-ends from 6pm-11pm and will attempt to reflect the multi-cultural market Videotron serves.

Advertising
Videotron are soon to begin broadcasting advertising. Videotron are aggressively involved in developing the London Interconnect 1 project, with local advertising expected to play an important role.

Summary
Videotron have been broadcasting for more than five years and are now beginning to offer local television programming. They offer a local text service at present which is broadcast to all eight of their London franchises. They do not appear to be in a great hurry to comply with the proposals made in their franchise application as there is still no mention of training. However, the Multicultural Television Channels they are in the process of launching make great advances in the direction of productions made in conjunction with the community. Videotron also foresee the need for three to five production staff within the next two years, therefore a good deal of expansion must be anticipated in the local programming sector.

Westminster Cable Co Ltd

87-89 Baker Street, London. W1M 1AJ. Tel : 071-935-6699
Contact - Vicky Hanbury-Williams
Franchise area - City of Westminster
Premises in franchise - 120,000
Homes passed 30/9/92 - 56,314
Homes connected - 11,138
CTV Penetration - 20.4%

Westminster started broadcasting in September 1985. As an early entrant into cabling, the Westminster bidder was not obliged to provide an outline of its proposals for public consultation. The commitment to local television programming was unspecified at the beginning of 1991.

Staff
Westminster employs approximately fifty staff in total, ten of whom are employed in sales and marketing. Westminster foresees the need for extra staff in sales and marketing within the next two years.

Text
Westminster offers a local text service which is supplied in-house and employs two people.

Advertising
25% of their advertising is nationally/regionally sourced with the other 75% being targeted specifically to the cable area. Of this specific advertising, most of it is locally produced (75%) but Westminster also broadcast 25% modified national/regional material. Companies who have modified their advertising locally include American Express, London Electricity and British Gas. Interest in cable advertising from local companies has increased steadily over the past year and Westminster see definite potential for the future.

Summary
Westminster are a reasonable sized company who have been broadcasting for almost seven years. Why then is their local programming still text based? Westminster appear to be another operator who give much weight to the sales, marketing and advertising side of the operation and less to local programming in order to gain public support. Their commitment in the past to local programming has gone unspecified and indeed they do not appear to have extensive plans for it.

Windsor Cable Communications

Cable House, Waterside Drive, Langley, Berkshire. SL3 6EZ. Tel: 0753-810810
Contact - Sally Allen
Franchise area - Windsor/Slough/Ashford/Staines/Stanwell/Heathrow & Iver
Premises in franchise - 113,800
Homes passed 30/9/92 - 90,546

Homes connected - 15,839
CTV Penetration - 17.6%

Windsor started broadcasting in December 1985. As an early entrant into cabling, the Windsor bidder was not obliged to provide an outline of its proposals for public consultation. The commitment to local television programming was unspecified at the beginning of 1991.

Staff
Unspecified.

Text
Windsor offers a local text service which is supplied in-house and employs one person part-time.

Programming
Windsor are in the process of launching full video programming. This will comprise three hours per week of original programming providing a comprehensive assortment of sport, local news and local interest programmes. Windsor will use hi-band equipment.

Advertising
Windsor have planned comprehensive advertising.

Summary
Windsor are another operator whose commitment to local programming has long been unspecified. However, now after almost seven years on air, they are set to begin local television programming. They have been operating a local text service for some time but are presently in the process of launching a full video channel covering a wide range of subjects. Community access and involvement on this project is unspecified as yet, however it is hoped that this will develop over the months and soon Windsor will be in a position to offer training and extend their programming hours.

4.   Training

Providing television training for the public is an important part of the provision of community access. Simply allocating a slot in the broadcasting schedule for local programming does not solve the access problem for organisations or individuals with no production experience or equipment.

Four of the companies contacted for this research offered training for prospective local programme makers; Aberdeen Cable Services, Cable London Plc, East Lancashire Cablevision and Leicester Communications. Each of these companies conduct comprehensive in-house training courses covering all aspects of television production including camera work, editing, script writing and programme planning. The training is fully funded by the cable operator in all cases except Aberdeen where small charges, paid by the trainees or their organisations, are made to cover costs.

The number of individuals trained in the above skills varies from one operator to another. Aberdeen trains, on average, eight people per month; East Lancashire trains six per month; Cable London varies from month to month according to resources and Leicester has trained twenty people to date.

When the previous study was undertaken in 1989 both Coventry Cable and Clyde Cablevision were also able to provide training for would-be local programme makers. However resources are no longer available for training at Coventry and Clyde Cablevision were unable to comment on any aspect of this research due to their local programming sector being terminated.

5.   Local Teletext Services

In order to gain a general overview of local teletext services from a source outside the operational side of the cable industry we contacted Picture Applications in Ware, Hertfordshire, who are contracted to provide a Channel Guide service for many of the major cable operators.

The Channel Guide is an information channel giving each cable viewer an overall summary of all cable programmes available to them at any one time, making it simpler for them to plan their viewing.

Picture Applications also supplies a local teletext service to cable companies which is generally divided between:

What's On and Sports	30%
Local News	20%
Messages/personals	20%
Advertising	20%
Information about cable	10%

The news and current affairs items are updated between twenty and thirty times each day in order to ensure their content is always accurate. Picture Applications feel that the fact the information is constantly updated is one of the features which makes local cable news so attractive for prospective subscribers.

Picture Applications find a limited interest in national advertising, and the advertising that they do carry is generated within each local area. Cable provides a cost-effective way for small businesses to cover their local area whilst gaining access to a larger urban area if the cable operator happens to be working as part of a group of franchises.

The service sector seems to make up the predominant section of local cable advertising although both products and retailing feature regularly.

In assessing the future for local text services and indeed the future of community television on cable, Picture Applications have experienced renewed interest in text recently. Although this is not necessarily the best indicator for local television in general, Picture Applications believe that the cable operators are coming round to the realisation that community programming is the unique kind of service that the viewing public in Britain is interested in.

6.   Conclusion

Where cable companies are currently providing local services this is being undertaken on a purely ad hoc basis. The technical standards of equipment and training vary from franchise to franchise. Newer franchises have mostly opted for industrial standard equipment often S-VHS while older franchises installed broadcast standard studios and editing facilities or the BVU sub-broadcast format.

While local and community provision remains un-regulated it is not surprising that there is an inconsistent level of service being provided. East Lancashire introduced local services from the outset of their build; Windsor have take seven years to introduce a local service and Clyde have terminated their local operation.

The inconsistency in the regulation of terrestrial services delivered over transmitters in comparison with those delivered by cable is most apparent for the cable subscriber who encounters both services and will not know the history which explains why terrestrial television receives is of a higher technical and mostly professional standard. With a variety of technologies available in the '90s to deliver television regulation must move away from criteria based on the way the signal is delivered to criteria based upon the nature of service supplied. Or regulation can be formally abandoned altogether as in effect it already appears to have been abandoned informally.

Cable is able to deliver a higher quality signal to the home than the transmitter and yet its programming by being effectively unregulated ensures that poorer signals leave the cable company than those leaving the terrestrial broadcasters.

Local services for local populations should be of the same high standard as other forms of programming and most importantly be of a consistent standard across the country.

When our research was undertaken between June and September 1992 it was assumed that there would be a significant difference in the local services available in comparison with results found in our previous study in 1989.

We know that many changes have occurred in the cable industry within the last three years, and would expect that this increased development would be reflected in the level and richness of the local services on offer. We were wrong.

The ITC contends that local services are expanding citing Croydon (United Artists), Leicester and Videotron as examples.

Some services - Coventry, Aberdeen and Clyde - to name but three are smaller in scale and local involvement than they were even three years ago. The Clyde service is no longer responding to calls; the Aberdeen service is on a much reduced scale than either at its outset or even in 1990 and Coventry no longer uses its production facilities to provide the regular local authority service.

If local services are indeed expanding, it is difficult to see by what measure this expansion is assessed. If local channels continued and developed at the current rate of 5 franchises every 3 years, all 135 franchises should be able to offer a local service by 2067.

Cable has struggled for eight years to be of interest to barely 20% of the homes it passes.

Satellite penetration exceeds cable at a ratio of 5:1 and has pulled further ahead from 3:1 in the space of little over one year.

Cable in its presently regulated state is not the answer for local television seeking to reach all members of the local television audience. For communities in London and Leicester and areas with a mix of distinctive cultures the community of interest channels are however making a distinctive contribution. But audiences remain small and do not seem set to rise above 30-40% for some considerable time. (See Chapter Seven.)

Studies carried out in Edinburgh in 1989 and 1990 found extremely high levels of interest in local programming, especially in local news. In a small pilot survey in 1990 83% of people interviewed were willing to pay a monthly subscription of £2.00 or more for a 'quality local television service with an emphasis on local news.' The apparent willingness of people to pay a subscription for local television is an indication of the enthusiasm for this 'missing' element in television broadcasting.

Another 'missing' element in broadcasting is that of community involvement. The 1989 survey found that as many as 56% of the people questioned were interested in participating in the production of local programmes. A widespread demand for greater participation in local television raises some far reaching questions about the current limitations and deterioration of public service broadcasting. On whose behalf is cable being regulated - the public's or the operator's? A parliamentary review of the purpose and regulation of policy towards local television services is required immediately.

References

1. Oftel administer the Department of Trade and Industry Telecommunications Licence awarded to each cable company and ensure the building of each cable franchise meets agreed targets in passing a specified number of homes.

2. *Spectrum*, ITC, Autumn 1992, London

3. The Director of Planning, Edinburgh District Council, wrote to amenity groups in Edinburgh's New Town drawing attention to fact that the telecommunication's licence granted cable companies the right to 'enable cables to cross adjoining properties'.

4. Trevor Single, *Regulatory Requirements of the Telecommunications Act Licence, Local Cable Television Conference Delegate Briefing Papers*, ILT, June 1991.

6. *New Media Markets*, 10th September 1992, Vol 10 No 17.

7. *Television Week*, 18th September 1992.

8. Figures in this section are derived from *Who's Who in Cable and Satellite*, January 1993, WOAC Communications Co. 1992 and *UK Cable Performance, New Media Markets* December 1992, Financial Times Newsletters, London.

9. *Noisy Channels: A Local Government Report on Cable, the Local Economy and Local Television*, ILT, Edinburgh, 1990. This publication provides several accounts of cabling experience in Britain and Northern Europe.

7   A Local Future on Cable?

Dave Rushton, Institute of Local Television, 1993

Whether it will be possible to run local television services on cable independently of the cable operator's desire to retain control over channels depends upon Oftel's willingness to enforce Section 10 of the Telecommunications Licence. This is currently being tested. [1] Meanwhile, Oftel has indicated that the clause in Section 10 of the Telecommunications Licence which enables access to the network to be made by alternative service suppliers is to be redrafted in favour of the cable companies; strengthening their monopoly.

But is cable in the foreseeable future capable of reaching the high percentage of subscribers that are required to make a local service worthwhile no matter who provides that service?

1.   Measuring the Number of Subscribers

The number of subscribers in a cable area is usually expressed as a comparison between homes *actually* taking the service and homes *capable* of taking the service. In terms of this ratio, cable subscribers have risen year by year from 16.5% in October 1990 to 18.9% in October 1991 to 21.5% in October 1992. [2] While this suggests that there is a slow rise in the overall interest in cable across the country subscriber percentages are not evenly distributed between new and older franchises.

In our table in Appendix Four instead of the more usual comparison we compare the number of *households that subscribe to cable* with the total *number of households allocated to each franchise*. This may seem perverse – many if not most households in each cable town are unable to take the service because cabling has not passed their door-step. But for a local service it is this relationship between the number of subscribers and the total franchise population which actually describes cable's local potential. If cable has no foreseeable local role then what useful purpose does it serve being franchised district by district?

Cable companies are required by their telecommunication's licence to pass all the households in their franchise area within a stipulated period of time. It would seem to follow that cable companies will endeavour to recruit and maintain an increasing percentage of subscribers in order to support the cost of this commitment. Upwards of half the total cost to set up a franchise – running at >£50m per 200,000 homes – is spent on digging the holes and laying the trunking. Our table in Appendix Four shows how far away each cable operation is from becoming locally useful. How long might it be before a significant number of homes in each area is reached that would make a local service worthwhile?

2.   Moving Forwards or Dropping Back?

As new franchises get started a picture of slow growth across the country disguises the reality of standstill and even decline in the older completed or near-completed areas – at least on the television front. The level of take-up nationwide is distorted by the higher than average penetration at the start of each build. Cable operations mostly begin by providing services to those communities that are likely to be high television users. This early growth can be explained by a mixture of favourable access to council house trunking and the use of SMATV and narrowband cable systems in council owned residential areas – finding cabling and customers together who can both be favourably converted to the new channels. [4] It is not surprising that relatively high percentages of subscribers become difficult to maintain when cabling moves among the less interested households further afield.

Franchises that have been under construction for five or seven years have had difficulty reaching a 30% take-up let alone moving beyond this relatively modest figure. Cable in the US reaches 65% of homes and exceeds this figure in many parts of Europe where cabling began in the early '80s, as it did in Britain.

It is no longer self-evident that the DTI build commitments that require the operator to pass every home will lead inexorably to aggressive marketing and a pricing structure that will introduce cable into large numbers of homes. High levels of take-up would have been more likely if build-costs had been cushioned by laying cable alongside other utilities and work had been well under way before the arrival of DTH satellite. In Northern Europe where cable *did* arrive before the present generation of satellite channels it went into the ground with other utilities and take-up of 70-90% in many cities is experienced. With subscriptions a third to half that to be found in Britain, customers choose to *opt-out* from this sensible way of receiving television rather than *opting-in* as they do here. Cable can be made to work as a genuine public or part-public utility and in that form can provide a public service by improving reception and clear the roof-lines of dishes and aerials at a reasonable cost.

3.   Telephone Services

Telephone services on cable have yet to make a major impact, but the marketing advantage of reduced telephone bills might suggest that it will be telephony that will help retain and expand subscribers. But telephone is only cheaper on cable because the telephone market is so highly regulated that it favours the cable companies and Mercury. [5] How long the market will remain distorted by the DTI and Oftel in order to restrict BT's ability to outpace competitors - in the name of open competition - is questionable. Will the DTI's loyalty towards cable persist if other technologies prove more adept at providing competition with BT? Should other ways of delivering telephony be kept out of the local market in order to support cable when its efforts to compete have so far been miserable compared with the sacrifice of regulation required to encourage them?

There are too many economic and technological factors as well as changing political priorities between today and the completion of the 135 franchises to predict cable's future with any certainty. For the immediate future BT's involvement in carrying television on its telephone networks has been excluded in order to encourage cabling. BT's ability to deliver television on existing twisted pair telecommunications lines will test both cable operators and regulators within the next couple of years.

While cheaper telephone services in the short term are a very positive inducement to the heavy telephone user to join cable these telephone subscribers are unlikely to be the heavy television viewers. Neither are these two types of customer – business and domestic – likely to share the same parts of town.

4.   Satellite Competition

At present cable does not represent a significant threat to BSkyB. But the cable companies are planning to launch their own cable-only channels to give themselves a distinct service. It would be no surprise to find BSkyB counter any threat that would marginalise or reduce income from its own channels by giving away free dishes to households making a two or three year commitment to subscribe to their premium services. Satellite dish installations outnumber cable connections in the UK by 5:1.

The expansion of both satellite and cable assumes a growing increase in the demand for multi-channel television. Yet recession or no recession that demand has been slow to emerge. Arguably while unemployment reduces disposable income it increases disposable hours. Cable and satellite are comparatively cheap ways of providing the family with something to do.

Out of subscription income cable has to support its build as well as its payments to BSkyB and the other satellite suppliers for programming. The cable experience in Britain is markedly different from that in the Benelux countries and Germany where it is the cable companies who receive carriage income from satellite channels seeking distribution.

The time when satellite can regard cable as an insignificant contribution to its overall operation grows ever nearer: a time may not be far away when the satellite companies will have the option to squeeze cable out of business. Cable lacks both take-up and a special portfolio of programmes to give it a unique edge. What cable does have is telephone and an artificially created price advantage.

5.   Turnover of Customers

The high levels of turnover – or churn – of existing subscribers experienced by cable companies eats away at the benefits to be gained from taking on new subscribers. The cost of making the connection to each home is not presented in full (or at all) as a charge to the customer and is not recovered when subscribers opt-out soon after subscribing. Cable companies are guarded about discussing churn. While it would be an exaggeration to say that cable television customers are actually an expense to a cable network, this is not entirely without foundation. A significant percentage of subscribers cost more than they are worth to the company.

It is evident that a loyal core of subscribers, perhaps 60-80% of the total number of households actually subscribing in each franchise, support any growth in the business. The high turnover among the other less committed 20-40% of the subscriber population is very expensive to maintain and very expensive to renew. Reliable customers need separating from the fickle. And cable companies have not been good at spotting the difference. The trick for the cable operator is to find a way of leaping beyond the relatively low numbers of subscribers without at the same time increasing the number of high turnover subscribers and thereby draining resources just to support the increased momentum. But are there loyal customers still to be found?

6.   Growth Follows Completion of Build?

Subscriber numbers should increase in the years following the build because every home interested can get access to the service. Only in the completed franchise can the number of subscribers be a true measure of the interest or resistance to the services. Yet take-up in the completed towns is no better than elsewhere. In fact, it is falling off.

Aberdeen increased its number of subscribers between October 1991 and October 1992 by 1553 and the level of penetration rose from 11.1% in January 1990 to 15.9% in October 1992. Yet the actual number of subscribers added for the year October 1991-October 1992 is only 57% of the total number added for the year January 1990-January 1991.

In Coventry there has been a net loss of 1478 subscribers for the year October 1991-October 1992. Coventry is not growing, it is actually declining.

Croydon and Swindon both show an increased level of penetration but this growth is not reflected in a comparison of annual subscriber numbers. Between October 1991 and

	% Franchise homes Passed	% Penetration Oct 1992	% Penetration Jan 1990	Start Year	Additional Subscribers for Oct 91-Oct 92	Jan 90-Jan 91
Aberdeen *	100	15.9	11.1	1985	1553	2720
Coventry	98.4	8.5	13.5	1985	-1478	1484
Croydon	97.8	22.8	21.4	1985	1144	3034
Swindon	92.8	29.7	21.3	1984	1585	6731

* Aberdeen completed build in 1989 new houses added from inside franchise area.
Statistics from *New Media Markets*, 3rd December 1992

TABLE 1: Cable growth among completed and near complete franchises.

October 1992 Swindon recruited 23.5% of the number of subscribers it had achieved between January 1990 and January 1991. Croydon recruited 38% of its January 1990 to January 1991 figures in the year October 1991 to October 1992. (See Table 1.)

7.   The Changing Cable Brief

There are at least two very different explanations for why cable companies that have completed their build are failing to make significant headway into the market their service can now supply.

> The public are unwilling to subscribe in these areas because of the price, programme service or quality factors or a combination of all three.

> The cable company is satisfied with a slow rate of growth or a standstill so long as the recruitment of new subscribers succeeds in replacing those lost but does not add to costs by increasing churn.

The second hypothesis suggests that beyond a certain level of penetration cable companies are fighting an increase in commercial loss if they go any further. More customers leads to a higher number of disconnections and a greater marketing burden reliant upon the income from the loyal subscribers.

A further factor in explaining the slow growth in subscriber numbers is that revenue from telephone services runs at a ratio of 10:1 compared with television income. This seems to be the growth point focused upon by the franchises nearing completion.

There is an incentive for the cable operator to secure as rapidly as possible a significant portion of the business telephone market. While the government can be relied upon to favour cable this telephone customer base will remain loyal because of pricing and for so long as service quality is high. Unlike the quality of a television programme, the quality of a telephone call is largely dependent upon the customer not the cable company: at least for content. This is one less factor to concern both the customer and the company. A further factor is that performance in telephony is not counted in subscriber connections but in the telephone demand of each subscriber. Therefore the interest of cable companies in telephony is subscriber quality and not subscriber quantity. Apparently low levels of subscriber connections in themselves provide no indication of the quality of the telephone subscribers – and the size of their bills – actually being connected.

Since cable companies can't be forced by regulation to recruit customers, only to pass a prescribed number of homes, the cable companies can justify a domestic standstill in commercial terms if successfully in pursuit of telephone customers. In this new, or rather amended, approach cable television services are extraneous baggage in the marketing of telephony and data services to small and medium businesses. Cable television also has a more down-market attraction than business telephony. There's a marketing conflict that has not yet been happily overcome.

The favourable incentives the government has introduced into regulation to encourage cable companies to 'cherry pick' the prosperous telephone communities will when taken to their commercial conclusion put pressure on the provision of telephone services for those users living in less bountiful areas. Cable is not so much a public service as it is a destroyer of such services.

8.   Conclusion

Chasing the rich-pickings of telephony provides one further reason why after almost a decade of activity cable is less and less likely to be the principle means through which to deliver the local television service the public and local organisations require. Lower take up of a higher quality subscriber is the telephone message that enables profitability to be secured without reaching high levels of subscribers.

Figure 1 shows the Cable Authority's estimated growth of households able to take a cable service following the late surge of franchising in 1989-1990. On top of the Cable Authority estimate are black columns showing actual growth provided by the ITC to *New Media Markets*. A further estimate of how cable may continue to develop in the coming two and a half years has been added in the shaded columns. It is based upon a projection of growth on past performance.

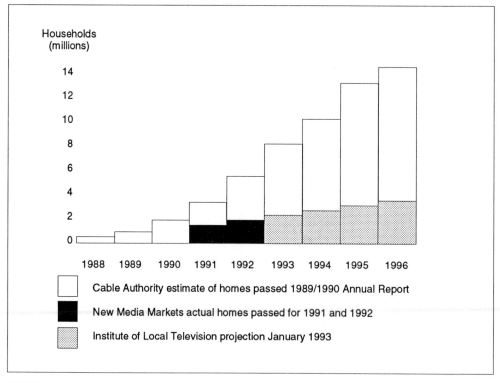

FIGURE 1: The Rate of Cable Growth

References

1. Edinburgh Television Ltd have invited Oftel to press United Artists to allow ETV's local service to be distributed on the local cable network. Oftel are currently negotiating with UA.

2. *New Media Markets*, Financial Times Newsletters, London, December 1992

3. For an indication of the level of compromise reached by the ITC with the cable industry it is worth comparing the remarks attributed to Director of Cable and Satellite, Jon Davey in *New Media Markets* in 1988 on cable build expectations with those attributed to him in January 1993 on the poor expected build for the year ahead:

New Media Markets, January 1988:

The authority:

> expects the award of a franchise to involve a presumption that the construction of the system will follow in a timely manner. Franchisees cannot expect to continue to hold rights to a franchise if they do not implement it within a reasonable time.

New Media Markets, January 1993:

> I was hoping that we would certainly exceed the million mark this year and I did not consider that to be over-ambitious. The Cable Television Association's's figure [of 800,000] isn't much more than last year and I find that hard to accept.

> When you consider the number of operators which are actively building, one really ought to be seeing significantly more cable being built in 1993.

PART TWO

Commentary & Critique
Local Public Service Television

8   Making Local Work

Dave Rushton, Institute of Local Television, reprinted from *Television*, the Royal Television Society Journal, December 1990

1.   Introduction

The debate on local television gathered momentum in 1990 with proposals that Channel 5 be run as a national channel with upwards of 50 city opt-out stations providing a few hours local television each day. How will so many local stations be financed? Will they provide the quality of programming we expect from the terrestrial television service?

Granada's Waddington Television Village wired the community for multi-channel TV and showed the villagers making and viewing their own television. This seemed to have an amazing psychological impact on broadcasters. [1]

Taken with this general interest, there is some evidence from research in Edinburgh that a local television service and participation in local television could be in demand. Over 90% of the people in Edinburgh would like a local news service while as many as 56% of the people surveyed would like to participate in local programmes. (See Kitchenman, Edinburgh Survey 1989, Chapter One).

A widespread demand for greater participation in local television raises some far reaching questions about the current limitations of public service broadcasting. If high levels of enthusiasm for local television were to be found in several towns and cities across the UK how might this service be introduced?

2.   Local television today

Local television so far in the UK takes the form of community channels delivered on broadband cable. These services have arisen mainly because cable operators believe they are obliged to provide a service in their franchise.

Section 7 of the 1984 Cable and Broadcasting Act encourages local voluntary and community involvement in local cable programming using facilities made available by the cable operator. The uneven quality and poor availability of this community programming, together with the low levels of cable take up and slow rate of build, have to date provided an inadequate base for advertising to support community channels.

Yet advertising is not the only source of revenue for local channels on cable. The findings of a recent survey (Bowditch, Edinburgh, 1990, Appendix Five) suggest that subscription will be the main source of revenue income for local cable channels. The apparent willingness of people to pay a subscription for local television is a further indication of real enthusiasm for this 'missing' element in television broadcasting.

3.　Local Authorities - the new regulators?

Cable companies characterise their primary function as programme delivery. Programme making is some way down their priority list. Many cable operators will take some convincing before providing sufficient capital investment to support even a limited amount of programming. Yet, local television is one valuable and unique contribution which cable can presently make. Local programming is an obvious way of creating local identification with the cable service.

If either BSB or Sky should collapse cable will be left with very little high-demand programming and an expensive network.

With 120 new cable franchises still to commence building [at the end of 1990] there are many bargains to be struck between local authorities and cable companies. Local authorities can do much to indicate to cable operators how important local services will be and help stimulate cable company investment in these services.

In Edinburgh two channels have been set aside by the cable franchise for use by a local company set up to provide a local television service. [2] Edinburgh Television Ltd will involve production companies, community and educational organisations as well as local investors in the development of these channels.

Guaranteed access to distribution is crucial for a long term broadcasting business, as the ITV companies know well enough. A contractual separation of the local channels will provide the programme provider and local commissioning organisation with some valuable long term security upon which to raise finance. Strong, well funded and independent local channels will provide a distinctive element in an otherwise almost exclusively US controlled operation. Local control of broadcasting is by no means an insignificant part of this debate. The US cable and telephone companies have a 90% stake in UK cable.

4.　Keeping the customer satisfied

Two surveys in Edinburgh found a very high level of interest in local television, especially in local news. (92% of people interviewed were interested in a local news service.) In a later questionnaire, 92% of people questioned about Channel 5 favoured programming from and about the local area While regional and national programming was also anticipated favourably from Channel 5 (85% and 91% interest respectively), European material (75%) was twice as attractive as North American material (37%) for screening on the new channel.

Cities and towns support local papers and local radio, it comes as no surprise to find a growing interest in local television emerging from the public. Still, this evidence of enthusiasm for local television only draws on the interests of the residents of one capital city in the UK. Meanwhile, there are some examples from Europe that add weight to the Institute's suggestion that studies on local programming demands should be undertaken in other UK towns and cities.

5.   Two Dutch examples

There are two types of local channel currently offered on Dutch cable that are worth introducing, one professional channel and the other comprising the work of community and voluntary programme makers. Cable in the Netherlands is widely available for the urban population, installed and operated by the public utility companies, usually telephone and gas/electricity, who provide upwards of twenty channels, including the Astra channels and BBC I, BBC2 and ITV. Public experience of cable in the Netherlands is at least four or five years ahead of our own. The take up is so high (over 90% in some cities) that multi-channel TV Is available to most of the urban population.

Rotterdam's STADS TV

STADS TV is a highly professional local news service provided by upwards of twenty journalists and crew. The nightly hour long show is currently broadcast live from the restaurant of the Rotterdam World Trade Centre and repeated from video throughout each evening.

Cable reaches 96% of Rotterdam's homes and the nightly news magazine is seen in its entirety by 13% of the city population, in part by 17% and viewed at least once a week by 38% of the residents. The station has been on air since April 1989, with an annual budget of more than a £1 m provided by the cable operator, city fathers and local industrialists. The channel regularly provides news and sports programming to the national Dutch TV service, so enhancing the city's profile across the country.

Advertising from a daytime teletext and radio service contributes to STADS TV's revenue, as do special programmes made for other European channels. The service is expected to be profitable within three years.

The SALTO Foundation

In Amsterdam a local foundation, SALTO brings together representatives of local voluntary and community organisations and other local interests, to administer Amsterdam's access channel.

SALTO's programme providers are usually minority, religious and cultural organisations who pay a varied hourly rate for their programmes to be broadcast. Technical resources are in short supply, but innovative and lively styles result in programming which is widely watched. Minority programming is viewed at some time each month by 30% of the Amsterdam population, or 200,000 people.

A professional local news service similar to that provided in Rotterdam is being considered for a second channel.

6.   Research on local TV

The following figures come from two Edinburgh studies undertaken for the Institute of Local Television by Peter Kitchenman in August 1989 and Lyndsey Bowditch in August 1990. In both studies, the interviewees were selected using the ACORN neighbourhood classification to identify the representative samples. [3]

Among the 56% of people interviewed in 1989 who expressed interest in taking a cable television service, 87% were interested in a local television channel. Interest in the local channel was only bettered by the film channel, (92%). All persons interviewed in the 1989 survey (100% of the sample) were asked questions on types of local programming they would favour (regardless of the delivery method):

> 92% were interested in a local news service
>
> 91% were interested in local special interest programmes
>
> 80% were interested in local current affairs programmes
>
> 75% were interested in programmes showing local entertainers and local neighbourhood and city festivals
>
> 56% were interested in programmes covering local amateur and professional sports events and meetings

As a delivery method for a local television service cable is attractive. The area covered by a cable franchise often, although by no means always, coincides with local political and administrative districts. This is the case in the franchises of (eg) Norwich, Edinburgh and Birmingham. It may be more difficult, however, for local organisations to establish a unique service where two or more operators share a well defined territory (eg) Glasgow or indeed one cable operator covers two or three distinct cultural or administrative districts (eg) West Lothian & Falkirk

7.   Financing local television

a. Local channels on cable

Bowditch's 1990 survey in Edinburgh sought an indication of the level of subscription people would be prepared to pay for the local service on cable.

83% of the Edinburgh sample were willing to pay a monthly subscription for a *'quality local television service with an emphasis on local news'*.

Of that 83%:

> 30% were willing to pay £5.00 per month
>
> 16% were willing to pay £4.00 per month
>
> 26% were willing to pay £3.00 per month
>
> 15% were willing to pay £2.00 per month
>
> 12% were willing to pay £1.00 per month
>
> 2% were willing to pay less than £1.00 per month

Therefore, 87% of these households were willing to pay £2.00 and over per month.

b. Channel 5 Local Stations

Channel 5 local stations offer a potentially greater audience for a local television service than cable channels, but dilute the local relevance in proportion to the area of delivery and the size of population. Yet Channel 5 local television should be free of the slow rate of cable installation and the constant marketing required to obtain profitable levels of cable take-up. But can advertising alone provide enough income to support a local terrestrial television service for individual towns and cities and their adjoining districts in the UK?

8.   The New Channel 5

Let's just wipe that old Channel 5 slate clean for one moment and imagine that the research has shown local television to be a service in great demand from several cities (perhaps, second only to a film channel). Should this necessarily be a commercial service? Isn't this local television the service which Channel 5 might be invented to provide?

9.   Public local stations

How could this service of 50 or so local stations be funded? There are two clear options that coincide with contrasting broadcasting philosophies:

> 1) *The commercial approach.* This faces the seemingly insurmountable difficulty of finding sufficient advertising from scratch to run a quality service that will attract the advertisers to pay for the service .... no better than a rat chasing its tail, or no real option at all!

> 2) *A public collection of local stations.* A percentage of the BBC licence fee could be provided to local television trusts to set up and run the local service. 'Would you like to see some of the licence fee support a local television service in your area' - could feature on each TV licence application in order to gauge public enthusiasm. (This is not so bizarre - West Germany's city open channels are funded from the licence fee.)

A public service comprising 50 or so local television stations could share channels 35 and 37 with a commercial operator providing a national service at different times of the day. This would have the merit of preserving the public/commercial split among the five terrestrial television channels on a more or less 50:50 basis.

Of the two options, instant commercial viability would be a heavy weight to place on local television. Of other new commercial television ventures, Sky has relied on long-term media investment and Channel 4 on the revenue of an existing national ITV advertising and marketing structure. Both forms of commercial operation have required a substantial cushion of cross-investment in anticipation of building longer term commercial success.

Can small-scale local television be expected to buck the need for initial economic support necessary for both Sky and Channel 4 and somehow create its own local advertising on the hoof?

An allocation from the licence fee would mean a part of the broadcasting service could become accountable to a public most benefiting from involvement in the service. Surely a widespread demand for local television is an oblique British way of saying that the broadcasting service is missing a visual ingredient?

There is a third option:

> 3) *A 'quality and diversity levy' from the Channel 3 bids to set up and establish the local stations element of Channel 5.*

This might make the form of Channel 3 bidders detailing their stake in independently managed local stations in their areas as one indicator of the quality of local service intended within their franchise. Perhaps a less ambiguous solution would be for start-up capital for local television to be provided direct from the ITC drawing on the Treasury windfall from the successful Channel 3 bids.

In practical terms, this commercial levy should provide a one off injection of start-up capital and at least five years of revenue support for each local commercial service for which medium term demand can be established. But, local television touches more fundamental issues than the organisation, manufacture and supply of local pro-grammes.

10.   Freedom of Expression

Local television unbridles broadcasting and provides an opportunity for developments consistent with technical opportunities as well as social demands. We cannot consider local television in the UK without comparing freedoms of speech and access to the means of expression in this country with those of our European neighbours with whom we expect to share much else in the next few years.

A federal system comprising national, regional and local centres of broadcasting could well be a genuinely popular alternative, without being populist and uncritical.

In the Netherlands local television is administered by foundations set up in each city and town who receive funding from the public cable companies and encourage radio and television programming from organisations representing a wide range of views. Since cable reaches a high percentage of homes and is a genuine public utility, local television on cable is tantamount to a public service in the Netherlands. In West Germany local open channels are supported by the national television licence and limit opportunities for a monopoly of views taking hold in the media. In Australia the concept of public television which is gaining momentum, comes from the public seeking control of local television for broadcasting over their own areas.

A local television service can identify with, be answerable to and involve the people in its area. The real choice in broadcasting in the UK is between more large scale and centralised television services and small scale and locally accountable television stations. Isn't the first choice just more of the same, and the second choice the only *really* new television for the '90s?

References

1. For a detailed account of the Waddington local TV experiment copies of *The Television Village* are available for £9.50 from TV Village, P O Box 4000, London W3 6XJ, 1990.

2. An agreement was reached between directors of Cablevision (Scotland) to provide two channels to Edinburgh Television for local use but the agreement was later denied by United Artists, the American company which took over the Edinburgh franchise.

3. The 1989 Edinburgh research was a face to face survey of a tightly controlled quota sample of 240 adults aged over 18 provided by market analysts CACI according to the ACORN neighbourhood classification. The 1990 telephone survey comprised a balanced sample of 60 adults drawn from the 1989 sample. This sample is far too small for the results to be offered without qualification and is included insofar as questions appearing in both surveys provided a similar pattern and distribution of results.

9. Amendments to the ITC's *Draft Invitation to Apply for Channel 5*

Amanda Gibbs & Dave Rushton, Institute of Local Television, 1991

The Fifth Channel Seminar was organised by the BFI, Northern Regional Arts Board, Manchester City Council, North West Arts Board, Northern Arts Board and Yorkshire & Humberside Arts Board in Manchester on the 11th December 1991. The Seminar was supported by National Transcommunications Ltd, Sony Broadcast, Panasonic Broadcast Europe, MacMillan UK Limited, KPMG Peat Marwick and Television Week. The purpose of The Fifth Channel Seminar was to debate the *Draft Invitation* and to identify common cause among parties interested in Channel 5.

The Seminar was attended by upwards of one hundred representatives of companies and organisations with an interest in the Channel 5 bid. The Institute of Local Television presented the accompanying *Amendments to the Draft Invitation* to the Seminar. The presentation followed a Channel 5 City meeting of representatives of production and broadcasting interests from five of the cities identified in the ITC's *ref: 28/91 July 30th Updates Plans for Channel 5* which made the prospect of *discrete local services* available for the *distinct localities* of Sheffield, Liverpool, Tyne & Wear, Edinburgh and Nottingham.

It is the Institute's view that the five cities of Sheffield, Liverpool, Nottingham, Tyne & Wear and Edinburgh – identified by the ITC as one of a pair with Leeds, Manchester, Birmingham Teesside or Glasgow have a more discrete local service potential than that available to the larger partner. In fact, the balance of the service area remaining to this larger neighbouring city is similar to that available to the regional Channel 3 output – minus, that is, the discrete population in the city to be served by the specific new frequency.

We are not convinced that the rump of a regional service offers a sufficient degree of distinctiveness for a local service to be able to sustain a commercial operation in such direct competition with Channel 3. The view upheld in the Channel 5 City discussions in advance of the 11th December presentation was that the five distinct local areas of Sheffield, Edinburgh, Nottingham, Liverpool and Tyne & Wear/Newcastle had been provided with sufficient integrity in relation to reach and signal footprint to enable a healthy and distinctive commercial local television service to be formed for these areas.

In addition, we all believe that there will be markets for services covering communities of interest within the regional and sub-regional conurbations surrounding the other Channel 5 transmitters, whether sharing cultural, religious or ethnic interests, and that such services should be encouraged.

Yet we have found the argument for a specific local utilisation of the other transmitters and frequencies difficult to uphold within the *Draft Invitation* and have failed to find the necessary support among other published documents on Channel 5 or within the ITC's duties under the *Broadcasting Act* to support a more substantial claim for local television in amending the *Draft Invitation*. What we have found is, however, overwhelmingly convincing for these five city frequencies and necessitates these amendments.

The Institute would add, that should there be no acceptable bid made for Channel 5 as a whole that these five city frequencies are of such importance, and local services in such public demand, that they should be made available for local use with an option to opt-in a satellite service to provide the national component.

1.   The ITC Draft

Our focus for the *Draft Invitation*, and that of the other participants in the Channel 5 City discussions so far, has been to consider the provisions for geographic local communities only. The changes to the *Draft Invitation* that we recommend to the ITC are on the face of it very minor indeed. They are intended to strengthen the small hand the ITC has revealed on behalf of potential local television services.

That said, we believe these changes will precipitate a general shift in thinking at the ITC – and the BBC – over the coming months and years that will align and affirm local television as a distinctive third tier service; a service not dependent upon one particular form of delivery; a service that is defined instead by the size of its audience and by its local qualities of accountability and accessibility. Here we focus our attention on making *Amendments to the Draft Invitation to Apply* and on providing a critical frame-work within which to assess a quality local television service.

We believe these *Amendments* are consistent with the duties placed upon the ITC by the Broadcasting Act 1990 and will ensure that the important potential offered in the ITC's *July Update* – of making *discrete local services* available for *distinct localities* – is fully and comprehensively realised with a quality local television service in each of these areas.

2.   A Quality Local Television Service

The distinguishing feature of the five discrete frequency allocations is that they have been provided *firstly* to enhance the potential for localised services and *secondly* to add (only) 2% extra audience to Channel 5. Some of these frequencies will not interfere with video recorders, enabling an early start-up date for services in those cities. Furthermore, for the cities of Edinburgh and Liverpool (at least) a strong cultural and commercial rivalry with their larger neighbours gives these local services an added edge.

For Edinburgh, this distinction was the starting point in examining the demand and potential for a local television service for the city. This led to the formation of Edinburgh Television Ltd and Edinburgh Television Trust in 1989 to run a local service in the city and to train non-professional programme makers for direct community involvement in programming.

While the Institute of Local Television emphasises the potential these frequencies offer for local services in these five areas we make this emphasis in a way that is entirely consistent with the ITC's duties under the Act and in terms which disturb as little as possible the opportunities for choice and commercial freedom of operation for the overall Channel 5 service.

Our seeming concern for only 2% of the service may appear disproportionate. Yet the ITC has itself devoted considerable man-hours, technical expertise and computer time already to identify these frequencies for these distinct localities – distinctive as communities for the long term commitment they have shown towards securing an independent television broadcasting or production base in their area. Small as it may be, this 2% represents a very important and commercially realisable beginning for a universal local television service in these cities.

In undertaking to amend the *Draft Invitation* we recognise that neither the Broadcasting Act nor the ITC make special allowance for local television. We must argue instead that an *effective* and an efficient use of these five city frequencies should be interpreted as being complied with if they are used for local and national use and not simply for national use. That is to say, so far as a local television service is both commercially feasible and socially desirable in any or all of these five distinct localities we believe that the local claims for transmission on these frequencies must not be ignored or overlooked within the terms of the Act, regardless of the priorities of a national television plan for Channel 5.

In other areas of the country, the lack of such great attention to the frequency reach as given to these five does not permit us to draw the strong conclusions that the *best* or *most effective use of frequency* would be ignored if they were not used for a local service. We believe that there are other areas in which a local service could thrive, but these lack the same precision of purpose and distinctiveness of localisation the ITC accorded these particular five in July 1991.

The Institute asks the ITC that in interpreting the efficiency and effectiveness of each Channel 5 bid that the best use of these five frequencies be taken into account. This is not a demand for a quota of hours in favour of each local service. Schedules will be a matter for negotiation between local and national interests and for due consideration among Channel 5 bidders and aspiring local operators.

We would not seek emphasis on particular programming strands, but rather stress the quality of the local service in terms of the independence of that service from the national service and the opportunities for local participation and cultural diversity in management, production and programming. For some cities a short and perhaps repeated burst of quality news programming may be the most competitive and demanded local service initially. Other services will find another priority more appropriate and consistent with advertising and public demand.

For local television the quality of the local service, and an equality of opportunity to broadcast, are equal priorities. The local service is distinguished from all other television services by the involvement of the community and the diversity of the service from one city to another. We argue that local television must be genuinely local – in programming and accountability – for it to pass any worthwhile quality threshold. For local television there is *no quality without equality – of access and accountability.*

In addition, the Institute asks the ITC to give consideration to the commercial implications of these local services in countering a Channel 3 regional monopoly and to enable and encourage fair competition with the regional Channel 3 services in these areas.

3.   Local Television Audience

We believe that 200-250,000 net adult viewers is the minimum audience for a viable commercial local television service funded by advertising (rather than subscription). In a well targeted and distinctive service this minimum reach will support profitably an hour or more of quality news based programming run near to peak time viewing. (Edinburgh Television figures.) We suggest that 400,000 viewers may prove to be the maximum size of a commercial local television service in the UK. [1]

This upper limit is equally as important as the lower advertising threshold. Commercial problems will arise for a local television service unable to differentiate itself clearly from the established Channel 3 regional provisions. This is a particular problem for the Channel 5 large reach transmitters that are available. These problems of distinction all increase as regional and local services approach the same coverage and scale. Unless each service can develop a unique cultural or social focus it will be difficult to dislodge the regional provider without very large sums of investment in exceptional programming and, perhaps, a lengthy battle of advertising attrition.

We would argue that at this critical point, programming targeted at communities of interest, rather than geographic communities, offers better commercial prospects for those areas served by large reach transmitters.

4.   The Local Technical Performance Code

It is most important to address the technical performance code for local television as a distinct and unified standard for a unified third tier of professional, commercial and public service television – local television. The Institute believes that future local cable channels and Channel 5 local channels may better be able to work together, in exchanging some programming, and in offering a coherent face to the viewer if the same technical standards apply for all forms of professional local television.

The Institute argues that in the medium and longer term it will be most appropriate to define and regulate local television services as a distinctive third tier of television with the service determined by audience size.

We would emphasise that a unified standard for local television services should be set at a different level than that applicable for Channels 3 and 4 and the balance of the national or regional Channel 5.

This local television standard should apply for programming determined by potential audience reach, that is to say programming for a maximum net audience of approximately 400,000 adults. [1] (This threshold coincides with the bottom end of regional Channel 3 distribution, with the exception of the Channel Islands service, and coincides with the largest of the individual cable areas.)

There should be a dispensation within the technical performance code governing Channel 3, 4 and 5 national and regional services in order to allow for a second-run of material originated for the local television services and for compilations or incorporation of material from this third tier into the second and first tiers. This second-run material might usefully be regulated through an annual hourly quota.

The technical performance code for local television should allow the use of industrial and professional acquisition technology – currently S-VHS or Hi-8 – editing to professional MII or SP Beta. We suggest a broadcastable tape may be a third generation MII or SP Beta copy. There may be a desire to differentiate between signals generated by single and three chip cameras, a differentiation comparable to ENG and Studio uses for equipment in current broadcasting. But we would argue that it is important to remain with the Hi-8 and S-VHS formats or their future equivalents.

A new technical performance code encompassing the signal details arising from such a configuration of equipment and tape use (above) would enable a local service with a comprehensive range of programming strands to be financially viable within the audience size described. In addition, the relative low cost of the acquisition technology will, we believe, encourage a wide range of programme making opportunities some of which will include the work of non-professional programme makers and enable the service to pursue a diverse approach in programming and to involve the local community in using their local service.

We would argue that the development of non-professional access is fundamental to the opportunities that *experience related* local television can provide and is a distinguishing feature of this service from both regional and national television. Access is more directly mediated and editorialised in regional services in virtue of a demand to sustain more generalised interests.

We believe that the improved quality in the overall television *service* as a result of introducing local television together with new opportunities for programme making and wider participation more than compensates for a small reduction in broadcast signal quality. We accept the need to ensure that such a reduction is defined in terms which ensure so far as it is possible that the new local technical performance code does not become a licence to reduce the technical standards of the overall television service. We would offer the suggestion that over time, say five years and/or as profitability reaches an acceptable level within each local operation, the application of the local technical performance code is reviewed and local television services obliged to migrate to the full performance code for all but their access or non-professional programming strands.

5. Local Television in Other Countries and UK Demand

Over the last three years the Institute of Local Television has worked to define and establish criteria for the introduction of local television services in the UK. Its research has extended to consideration of European, North American and Australian approaches to local TV services.

Three important factors have emerged which are common to many of these local TV operations:-

1. Local television services are independently organised for each distinct area they serve – there is no 'local' formula.

2. Participation and local involvement are an important and highly valued quality in a local television service – the viewer can also be a participant, and this is positively encouraged.

3. The local television service is distinctive in representing the cultural and (as appropriate) commercial identity of each area – the USP to both viewers and advertisers is that local is the locally controlled alternative which provides a service in which their place and their view has some priority. [2]

The common thread identified in viewer surveys by the ITC is an *attachment to their area* and in Institute surveys, *a high demand for local television services.* We would suggest that there are strong public feelings of identity and participation being expressed through these studies and that they are being frustrated by the scale of regional television distribution and the centralised nature of the regional and national television broadcasting services that the transmission system has encouraged.

Because of its highly localised form, local television presents a diverse and distinctive new television culture. A departure from what has been possible and from what has become established as a cultural and professional monopoly.

Elsewhere we have described the potential viewer relationship to a local service as *experience related* television rather than *vicarious* television. That is to say, the differences of a 'local' service from other television services follows directly from the services *being provided in a way that is sensitive and answerable to each local audience as well as the markets they serve.*

A quality local television service is therefore marked by programming that widely reflects the diversity and interests within its transmission or cable area and which is structurally responsive to local demands.

In our presentations over the last two years we have had opportunities to explore and to debate at public meetings and at producers' meetings throughout Europe the fundamental qualities and distinctions of local services and to consider the ways in which attachment to such services is secured for their particular viewing publics.

Local television offers a point of view to viewers within an area with a shared culture and economy. This vantage point also enables larger national or international concerns to be viewed and interpreted, relating them to experiences and concerns represented locally.

As well as distinctively local programming, local television offers a locally focused view of international issues and helps reinforce the value of the *local experience* by seeking *local value* and *local meaning* as the point from which to begin an understanding and interpretation of wider issues.

Local television provides a distinctive commercial and cultural television broadcasting alternative to the centre-to-periphery approach of national and regional television.

It is widely held among our European local television neighbours that local television provides a cultural safety-valve to alleviate the pressures and reduce the condescensions arising from an *increasingly* centralised and global broadcasting culture, a culture which strives to appeal to a widespread and often undifferentiated cultural market at the expense and to the neglect of idiosyncrasy, diversity and difference.

In the Institute's qualitative studies a sense of *local place* and *local space* has been requested from the new television services, to add a deliberate counter balance that favours where we live, and helps to maintain relevance for that area, for its ideas and its locally held views.

With transmitter frequencies (and cable channels) now being deliberately (rather than accidentally) configured for *discrete local services* for *distinct localities* (ITC's *July Update*) broadcasting can no longer claim to be distinguished exclusively by its centralised perspective and its transmitter configurations.

> Local means local to that area.
> Local *means* local control of the local service.

6.   Suggested Amendments to the ITC Draft

The Institute has drawn up amendments to the *Draft Invitation to Apply for Channel 5* in the light of comments presented by representatives of city television operations at The Fifth Channel Seminar in Manchester on the 11th December 1991.

Each city service will make its own individual representations to the ITC and our general view is not intended to detract from the detail of particular local needs.

Yet, these Amendments offer a consensus view shared by the Channel 5 City representatives who met on the 10th December 1991. [3]

7.   The Broadcasting Act 1990

The Institute's proposed *Amendments to the Draft Invitation* have been framed in terms of the following references from the Broadcasting Act 1990, Part 1, 2 (2) (our italics)

It shall be the duty of the Commission -

(a) to discharge their functions under this Part and Part II as respects the licensing of the services referred to in subsection (1) in the manner which they consider is best calculated -

(i) *to ensure that a wide range of services is available* throughout the United Kingdom, and

(ii) *to ensure fair and effective competition* in the provision of such services and services connected with them; and

(b) to discharge their functions under this Part as respects the licensing of television programme services in the manner which they consider best calculated to ensure the provision of such services which (taken as a whole) *are of high quality and offer a wide range of programmes calculated to appeal to a variety of tastes and interests.*

This reference supports the argument that Channel 5 should be distinctive from Channel's 3 and 4.

From the Broadcasting Act 1990 Part 1, 28 , page 29

(2) In determining the minimum area of the United Kingdom for which Channel 5 is to be provided the Commission shall have regard to the following consideration, namely that the service should, so far as it is reasonably practicable, *make the most effective use of the frequencies on which it is to be provided.*

This latter point is interpreted in the light of the more general duty of the ITC *to ensure a wide range of services is available* and in the light of the *discrete local services* and the *distinct localities* having been identified and configured for five local services (see ITC's *July Update*). It would not be an effective use of these frequencies, in particular, if they were not used for their primary intended purpose: viz to provide local television services.

Local television services are understood in the light of *programmes calculated to appeal to a variety of tastes and interests* – such tastes and interests, we argue include the *local interest to determine the nature of that service and to operate the service.*

References

1. A more detailed study carried out in Edinburgh in 1992 suggests that a potential audience of 750,000-1m will be required for a service based on advertising at the current Channel 3 average of seven minutes of advertisements per hour. Cable services can carry a higher average of nine minutes per hour.

2. The European experiences and local models have been the subject of seminars and conferences and have been documented and described in the Institute's publications. (For example: *Really New Television*, Institute of Local Television, Summer 1989; *2nd*

Really New Television, ditto, December 1990; *Channel 5, RTS Journal*, December 1990; *Local Hero, Televisual*, August 1991 and *No Local Yokels, RTS Journal*, December 1991).

The demands from the viewing public in the UK have been identified in surveys conducted by the Institute and by the ITC (among others) and point to a substantial and unfulfilled interest in localised television services. (See *Mapping Regional Views*, ITC 1990/91; *Reading the ITC's 'Mapping Regional Views'*, Institute of Local Television, April 1991).

3. The following amendments were proposed to the ITC and unless otherwise stated references are to changes to the *Draft Invitation to Apply*, ITC, 1991. These proposals were made for a *Revised Invitation*.

1) ITC Document *28/91 ITC Updates Plans for Channel 5* to be referenced in Annex B page 63 of the *Revised Invitation to Apply for Channel 5*.

2) Enter the following new strand 11 in para 79 page 25 of the *Revised Invitation*:

11 Local

The local television service is defined for those areas for which discrete local services have been identified (see *28/91 July ITC Updates Plans for Channel 5 Annex B*) - the five distinct localities of Sheffield, Tyne & Wear, Nottingham, Edinburgh and Liverpool. There may be other distinct localities where a discrete local service becomes feasible. A reasonable proportion of programming will be local and provided from among programme strands 1-10. These programmes will be widely representative of local interests and the cultural diversity found in each distinct locality.

3) Amend sentence at end of para 79 page 25 to read:

Strands 1-9 and 11 exclude children's programmes.

4) Addition to para 85 page 26 to include:

Distinctive elements within a quality local television service are cultural diversity and community participation. These elements are secured through the independence of each local service and the service's support by a representative local advisory panel.

5) Paragraph 80 to now read 7 non-mandatory strands.

6) Amend obligations to carry the full terrestrial service on satellite to enable local opt-outs to function.

7) Make provision for local television research and training from Channel 5 licence fees consistent with increased demand for local television services.

10   Channel 5 and Local Television

Dave Rushton, as background paper for Scottish Enterprise Tayside, March 1992.

> This is the time for towns and cities to grasp the policy issues raised by new media and exploit the opportunities for access and information, for consultation and therefore greater integration, via a genuinely local media network. [1]

In most of its publications, the Institute of Local Television has restricted its use of 'local television' to mean a service for a relatively specific and distinguishable community. In most cases the Channel 5 transmitters do not provide a sufficiently discrete signal to warrant the 'local' tag. (see Figure 1, overleaf)

Smaller cities and larger towns that will be in reach of Channel 5 transmitters would get a more realistically local service from a properly regulated cable service fulfilling its utility bargain by offering a channel for independently run local services. For cable companies to offer such a service there may need to be some incentive that favours cable over DTH as the preferred form of delivery. This would require government intervention.

Many of the Channel 5 transmitters offer a signal that will reach virtually the same population as regional Channel 3. This is just not attractive to advertisers.

> What advertisers want, more than anything else, from TV is a variety and a richness in the programmes shown - which, in turn, will deliver all types of audiences, not just the predominantly old and down-market bias delivered us by ITV. [2]

Even where the transmitter signal does not stretch right across the Channel 3 region, it will still be largely insensitive to local interests. The Sutton Coldfield Channel 5 signal will reach the major cities of Birmingham, Coventry and Wolverhampton – each with its own distinct economic and cultural characteristics. The signal from Winter Hill near Manchester will also reach most of Liverpool.

> At the moment, if I wish to promote a low alcohol beer or lager in Manchester or Liverpool, using specific retailers, I have to advertise on Granada TV (forgetting, for just a moment, local media). This limits my opportunities. And yet consumption of low alcohol beer and lager varies between Manchester and Liverpool. [3]

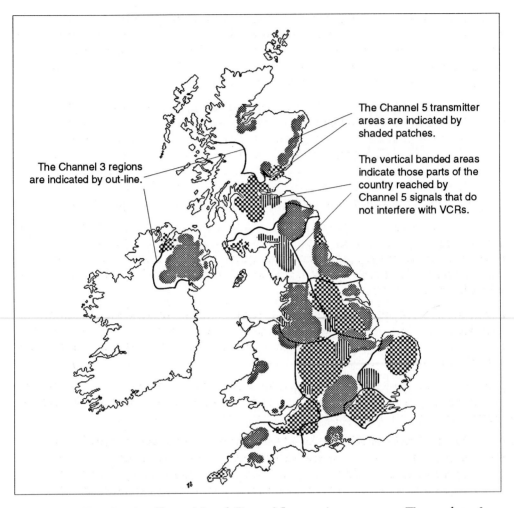

The Channel 5 transmitter areas are indicated by shaded patches.

The vertical banded areas indicate those parts of the country reached by Channel 5 signals that do not interfere with VCRs.

The Channel 3 regions are indicated by out-line.

FIGURE 1: Map showing Channel 3 and Channel 5 transmitter coverage. The number of people within reach of many Channel 5 transmitters is equal to or exceeds the population in reach of a regional Channel 3 signal.

The Institute of Practitioners in Advertising believes that local airtime would sell at a 20% premium relative to ITV airtime as it provides a unique opportunity for local advertisers to advertise on television at a low capital cost. [4]

There is no doubt from Institute of Local Television studies and the ITC's research for *Mapping Regional Views* what the viewer wants – a local television news service. 'Local news' is news from an area with which the viewer closely identifies. Most of the Channel 5 transmitters made available cannot be reconciled to achieve the viewers' demands, nor the advertiser's requirements.

According to *Mapping Regional Views* [5] viewers are not particularly interested in what happens news-wise in neighbouring counties or districts, they are mostly seeking news of local, national or international relevance. [6] Regional television is too small to be national and yet too big to be local. The regional offering is inadequate and poorly targeted. Local news interests the viewers in terms of their experience. Does the advertisers' interest coincide with that of the viewers?

> For Channel 5 to survive in the more competitive commercial television landscape of 1994 and beyond it will need to provide programming that is new and different to that available from other terrestrial and satellite channels. For this reason the IPA believes the best format for the channel is for it to provide a local, town/city based element ... Evidence from the USA shows that local programming, especially news, delivers very high ratings – in many cases higher than for successful network programmes. [7]

Certainly local television would add to the variety and specificity of audiences. The interest of advertisers and audiences in local television services, especially news so far as viewers are concerned, seems ahead of a political willingness to encourage an equality of broadcasting in which the small scale, locally owned, publicly accountable television service can be started.

If opt-outs are to offer a unique cultural as well as commercial contribution to broadcasting on Channel 5, then each opt-out must envisage providing a service appropriate to its scale and market(s) – a service for all possible viewers or a service for specific communities within its reach?

A simple Tesco supermarket formulae for local or city TV that could be opened up across the country as Channel 5 is rolled out would be inadequate for both viewers and advertisers. Variety and local definition are important.

> National brands will be able to construct media plans comprising a national core, using, perhaps BSkyB and Channel Four, with regional upweights, using Channel 3 and local upweights, using Channel 5. Furthermore, local opportunities for national advertisers will emerge. [8]

The ITC in reply to expressions of interest in Channel 5, noted the potential for local services but responded to the dangers of delays that adding new transmitters would involve:

> It was recognised that replanning of the currently proposed transmitter arrangements for Channel 5 to provide maximum opportunity for local services would present two significant complications. Such replanning would be likely to result in a reduction of the overall coverage of Channel 5 from the maximum level of approximately 70% and could delay the possible starting date for a new channel by at least a year or eighteen months. [9]

What is local television?

By local television then, the Institute means a television service related to an area that is the focus of administrative, cultural, economic and/or social interest for the viewers. In other words, local television covers a social and geographical territory which is broadly familiar to the viewer, an area within which news is generated, where broader national and international news stories are likely to have a specific interpretation and is an area comprising a social and economic culture with which the viewer identifies.

Is there a sufficiently shared sense of what is local so far as transmitter reach is concerned? There seems to be a general agreement between the ILT's city-based local studies of what viewers' demand and the ITC study based upon the viewers' response to regional television drawn from viewers across the UK.

The viewers' demand for a local television news service should be framed by the potential for an effective relationship with those institutions which include: work; education; transport; politics and cultural as well as other social and commercial centres with which people identify. Furthermore, while local is assessed in geographical terms as a matter of coincidence between the distribution of signal from a transmitter and a particular population within reach of a signal, for the service to be 'local' there must be a further coincidence of shared interest among issues and concerns affecting the lives of those people within reach of the signal. It is this latter element which distinguishes the 'local' transmitters allocated to Channel 5 from the rest. Only in a few other cases are the transmitters already allocated to Channel 5 able to fulfil the criteria of localness as understood by the viewers.

The common issues shared among a particular population are the staple diet of local newspapers, and include decision making and events that either affect or are likely to affect the people linked in that local area. These particular events distinguish themselves from those in a larger arena insofar as the individual is most likely to be affected by or have a political or social contribution to make to them. Larger scale national or international issues can percolate down to a more local level. Local television's public service role will be to help stimulate participation in democratic and social processes which are currently regarded with some apathy.

We have suggested in *Reading the ITC's 'Mapping Regional Views'* that the difference between local and other forms of television news is an emphasis favouring the *experiential* over the *vicarious*. Local news affects our lives in an immediate sense, national or international news in a general way (sometimes) but only ultimately connects with us as individuals through its local ramifications.

While the health service as a whole is the subject of national policy, the service at the local hospital is of importance to those who may need to use it. Education is a national priority, but the local school is where our children are educated, and it is the local education authority who currently organise that service. The implementation of policy regarding health and education is important in a specific way to all requiring hospital services and to all having children of school age, but in a *particular* area. Regional news is too big to be local, and too small to be national. Nothing much happens at the organisational or cultural level that coincides with the region as circumscribed by the regional television service.

The regional approach, by persistently missing the focus that is real in our lives and by passing off its product as more local than it can possibly be, is mystificatory rather than enlightening. Regional news denies us the local news we need and we appear to want since it occupies the space in the television schedule where local news ought to be and denies local news substance by its appropriation of this name.

Conclusion

'Local news' is more valued than 'regional news' because what happens locally affects our lives; what happens regionally (in television terms) does not. Regional news is a bundle of local news stories trimmed to suit the lack of focus each can have at any one time for the majority of viewers. Obviously, what happens nationally affects our lives too but most directly through its local manifestation.

Only in those transmitter areas served by the less powerful and more local Channel 5 transmitters will the public demand for local services coincide with the means to distribute a signal via available transmitters capable of satisfying that demand. (Figure 1)

As the population in a Channel 5 transmitter area climbs above the 500,000 mark (or thereabouts) so the local-ness of each service will in most cases diminish. As more than one centre of population – or more than one cultural, administrative, economic and political centre – becomes covered by its signal, so the significance and reference is diluted or becomes largely irrelevant for many viewers. It follows that the larger the scale of the local service, the more abstracted the focus upon any particular viewer for the programme makers and for the advertisers.

What is clear from the ample evidence in the ITC's *Mapping Regional Views* is that people are not looking for more programming with a regional bias. What they get from the regions is about right. What the viewer wants is local news.

From an advertising point of view the more diffuse and region-like a Channel 5 opt-out service becomes, inevitably the closer and more direct will be its competition with the regional Channel 3 service for existing advertisers. If the regional Channel 3 and 'local' Channel 5 services are forced to compete directly for the same audience because of similarity in scale and reach then ultimately the less distinctive the local service will appear in the public imagination.

Clearly, a regional or sub-regional service on Channel 5 has more flexibility than its Channel 3 rival since it can run more hours of regionally biased programming and put more attention on its regional rather than national characteristics. But whatever a quasi-regional service from Channel 5 might be, it will not be a local service. It should not be passed off as such.

A local service will only be viable *commercially* if it can provide an audience of interest to potential advertisers.

But a large population in itself is not needed to make a local service commercially successful. A higher percentage of available viewers watching local TV than regional

TV would compensate for a lower potential audience and through that local loyalty attract advertisers at a premium. In addition, the viewers for a local service might themselves be particularly attractive to advertisers, otherwise served by a less discriminating Channel 3 region which fails to engage a particular segment of the audience with programming with which they identity.

> Channel 5 won't only attract local advertising, in the same way that the many local US stations don't only attract local advertising. National and regional money will flow to the station in pursuit of the audience attracted to it by its unique programming mix. [10]

Two factors are important here, sufficient local-ness to meet the news needs with which the particular viewing public closely associates and sufficient distinctiveness in the local service from its larger more abstracted regional Channel 3 competitor to attract a commercial level of advertising revenue. From studies for Edinburgh Television a commercial service of editorial and technical quality comparable to regional television suggests an audience base approaching 1m people For a smaller audience the service will need to rely on higher levels of audience interest than the regional service obtains.

The trick for local television on Channel 5 will be to find communities with sufficient identity to provide 'localness' yet of a size necessary for advertising. The overall population available to the broadcaster might be of less importance than the quite realistic expectation that there is a higher than regional average of viewers waiting for local news.

References

1. Steven Barnett, *Fifth Channel Seminar*, Manchester, December 1991.

2. *Advertising Revenue Prospects for Channel 5*, Institute of Practitioners in Advertising, October 1990.

3. Brian Jacobs, *Funding Local Television*, Executive Media Director, Leo Burnett Advertising, *2nd Really New Television Conference*, December 1990 (unpublished mimeograph).

4. *Advertising Revenue Prospects for Channel 5*, Institute of Practitioners in Advertising, October 1990.

5. *Mapping Regional Views*, ITC, London, 1990.

6. *Reading the ITC's 'Mapping Regional Views'*, ILT, 1990.

7. Ibid, 4.

8. Ibid, 3.

9. *Proposals for Advertising the Service*, ITC, December 1990.

10. Ibid, 3.

11 'Star Rating' Channel 5 Transmitters

Dave Rushton, Institute of Local Television, April 1992

The ITC's *Invitation to Apply for Channel 5* (April 1992, ITC) focused attention for *local* opt-outs upon transmitters which were added to the list for Channel 5 as recently as July 1991 – these were Craigkelly serving Edinburgh, Storeton serving Liverpool, Fenham serving the Newcastle area and the transmitters serving Sheffield and Nottingham. Details of these and the other Channel 5 transmitters have been presented in Table 1.

With the exception of Fenham (serving Newcastle) the frequencies allocated to these new transmitters do not interfere with VCRs because they avoid using channels 35 and 37. With single large city populations able to receive a signal from one of these non-interfering transmitters a local city opt-out service is now feasible Aside from their non-interfering signals, what is most unusual about these particular transmitters is that they are local transmitters introduced at the last minute into an otherwise nationally oriented transmitter pattern.

The ITC has prepared the way for a local television service in Edinburgh that offers something more local than the regional programming from STV; a service for Liverpool which distinguishes itself from Granada; one for Sheffield different from Yorkshire; for Nottingham separate from Central and for Tyneside apart from Tyne-Tees.

These handful of transmitters have a very special role to play in a Channel 5 service. But are they the only transmitters from which local city opt-out services could be provided?

Several cities and competing centres of population lie within reach of the signal from the larger Channel 5 transmitters. Almost all of these have a coverage of well over 1m viewers. The opt-out contribution at this scale will primarily be regionally focused rather than local – a direct competition with Channel 3 whose viewers they will share identically. It is the transmitter reaching up to 1m viewers that present us with the most interesting and truly local potential. A 3-Star Rating has been offered to transmitters from which we feel a city-sized local news opt-out should be viable (Table 1).

Our thinking has been framed in terms of opt-outs capable of providing a local news service, largely because research over the last few years has shown convincingly to ourselves, the ITC and to many Channel 3 bidders, that local news is the unprovided service the public would most like to see on their screens. The Star Rating takes account of the number of viewers we think necessary to support a commercial service through advertising.

While some of the Channel 5 transmitters make a local service possible in some parts of the country it will eventually make no difference to the viewer whether they receive their local TV channel on cable, over the air or down the phone line. What does matter though is that the local option is made available soon and that the small advances that the Channel 5 transmitters offer in this direction are not ducked or disregarded.

Because the number of viewers is crucial to an advertising led service it might be possible to increase the coverage from some of the smaller Channel 5 transmitters . We think that by moving some of the transmitters a few kilometres, especially those not viewed in the original plan as having a local opt-out capability, the available audience might be increased. Alternatively, the signal strength could be increased, especially for the non-interfering transmitters. (An increased audience in reach of these transmitters offers a bonus in minimising video re-tuning. We come to this later.)

The engineering and demographic principles upon which the transmitter plan for Channel 5 has been based are not consistent, either with a single national vision or a collection of local city options. It is possible that the barely whispered Channel 6 (it was thought it might cover 30% of the country in the White Paper) might well be represented by the late and very singular additions to Channel 5. But in another way, these local add-ons are merely a reflection of an important shift of emphasis that Channel 5 has already contributing to terrestrial broadcasting in the UK. This has been to break away from a long standing policy to doing nothing with potential television spectrum unless a service could be fashioned that would ultimately be universally available. For local public service television the important criteria is universality within the local area.

With spectrum for local television in some parts of the country quite evidently available, tying it late in the day to Channel 5 bears a mixed message. Might this spectrum not be swallowed up as part of a national service or indeed go down with a sinking Channel 5? Either way, spectrum once found and located inside Channel 5 might be misused, resulting in Channel 3 remaining in splendid commercial isolation when in fact competition and public choice is possible.

If there is a will to see local television begin with Channel 5, and to use spectrum appropriately, which we suggest there is, then the ITC would probably welcome suggestions for enhancing the coverage of those more marginal transmitters in order to further advance additional local television opportunities.

For the Channel 5 transmitters to play a part in providing a better more comprehensive service, it may not be Channel 5 in its entirety that is the agency that is able to deliver the breadth, quality and originality of service that's required. One interesting candidate for fine tuning the local coverage would be the Churchdown Hill transmitter. Churchdown Hill's C5 transmitter does not cause VCR interference and its signal covers a distinctive audience in Cheltenham and Gloucester, an area on the edge of two Channel 3 regional services. Yet as presently configured, the signal will only serve 220,000 people. Can this coverage be usefully extended by increasing the strength of the signal or by relocating the transmitter or by doing both?

Transmitter	Major City	C5 Channel	Net Coverage 1000s +	Gross Cov'ge 1000s +	Channel 3 Area	Channel 3 Population 1000s	C5 Gross Pop as % of C3 Pop	C5 Net Pop as % of C3 Pop	No. <100,000 Towns/Cities Reached	Local Opt-out Star Rating 0-3
Belmont	Doncaster	35	1,210	n/a	Yorkshire	4,553	27%	n/a	4	0
Black Hill	Glasgow	37	2,820	n/a	C. Scotland	2,831	100%	n/a	2	0
Black Mountain	Belfast	35	1,090	n/a	N Ireland	1,067	102%	n/a	1	0
Blaen Plwf	Aberystwyth	35	41	n/a	Wales & West	3,597	0.3%	n/a	0	0.5*
Burnhope	Newcastle	35	2,465	n/a	N. East	2,266	109%	n/a	2	0
Caldbeck	Carlisle	56	159	n/a	Borders	501	32%	n/a	1	0.5
Cambret Hill	Newton Stewart	37	13	n/a	Borders	501	3%	n/a	0	0
Chelmsford	Chelmsford	35	164	n/a	London	8,975	2%	n/a	0	0.5
Churchdown Hill	Gloucester	48	220	n/a	Wales & West	3,597	6%	n/a	1	2
Craigkelly	**Edinburgh**	48	263	583	C.Scotland	2,831	21%	9%	1	3
Croydon	London	37	10,447	n/a	London	8,975	116%	n/a	-	0
Durris	Aberdeen	35	313	n/a	N. Scotland	920	34%	n/a	1	2
Emley Moor	Leeds	37	3,966	n/a	Yorkshire	4,553	87%	n/a	4	0
Fawley	Southampton	35	679	n/a	South & S East	4,234	19%	n/a	2	3
Fenham	**Newcastle**	37	50	999	N. East	2,266	44%	2%	2	2
Huntshaw Cross	Barnstaple	35	95	n/a	South West	1,292	8%	n/a	0	0
Londonderry	Londondery	37	101	n/a	N. Ireland	1,067	9%	n/a	0	0.5
Mendip	Bristol	37	2,045	n/a	Wales & West	3,597	60%	n/a	3	0.5
Mounteagle	Inverness	35	111	n/a	N. Scotland	920	12%	n/a	0	0.5
Nottingham	**Nottingham**	34	234	684	Midlands	7,266	9%	3%	1	2-3
Oxford	Oxford	35	750	n/a	Midlands	7,266	10%	n/a	1	2
Perth	Perth	35	59	n/a	N. Scotland	920	6%	n/a	0	2**
Plympton	Plymouth	35	195	n/a	S. West	1,292	16%	n/a	1	2
Presely	Pembroke	37	165	n/a	Wales & West	3,597	5%	n/a	0	0.5*
Redruth	Redruth	37	147	n/a	S. West	1,292	12%	n/a	0	1
Sandy Heath	Bedford	39	352	n/a	East of England	3,262	13%	n/a	0	2
Selkirk	Galashiels	35	52	n/a	Borders	501	10%	n/a	0	0
Sheffield	**Sheffield**	67	179	663	Yorkshire	4,553	15%	7%	1	3
Storeton	**Liverpool**	39	80	600	North West	5,126	12%	2%	1	2-3
Sutton Coldfield	Birmingham	37	6,095	n/a	Midlands	7,266	84%	n/a	6	0
Tacolneston	Norwich	37	477	n/a	East of England	3,262	17%	n/a	1	1
Tay Bridge	Dundee	37	184	n/a	N. Scotland	920	20%	n/a	1	2**
Winter Hill	Manchester	35	6,882	n/a	N. West	5,126	134%	n/a	6	0

Notes:

Transmitters and cities in bold identified by ITC in *Invitation to Apply for Channel 5* as having local opt-out potential

Channel 5 figures derived from the ITC's *Channel 5 Map* and July 1991 ITC *Updates Plans for Channel 5*

Channel 3 figures from BARB, Television Universes: individuals 1992.

+ Net coverage indicates the size of audience able to receive the best signal from this transmitter. Gross coverage indicates the size of audience able to receive a good signal from this transmitter.

The difference in populations between the net and the gross coverage are those viewers with a choice of transmitter

* Blaen Plwf and Presely might be linked to form a South West Wales opt-out

** Perth and Tay Bridge might be linked to form a Tayside opt-out

Compiled by the Institute of Local Television, April 1992 for the Royal Television Society.

TABLE 1: Star Rating local opt-outs for Channel 5.

As Table 1 shows, some of the original 25 Channel 5 transmitters are already of the right size and location to provide a local shot in the broadcasting arm. The Fawley transmitter, (reaching Southampton and Portsmouth) should provide a highly competitive and probably very profitable local opt-out service, especially since this will be the only Channel 5 service available (without a satellite dish or cable hook-up) in the South. A consortium of local interests recently formed Solent City TV to provide this service in what is the most important local opportunity to be found among the channel 35/37 transmitter options.

It is no surprise to find that the four non-interfering transmitters offer the greatest local opt-out potential, since these were added to Channel 5 in support of the principle of local services. But despite being free of retuning implications these transmitters are not totally free of other difficulties.

The majority of the potential audience from the Craigkelly transmitter (serving Edinburgh), the potential audience from the Storeton transmitter (for Liverpool) and the audiences for Sheffield and Nottingham, are viewers who will be able to receive as good a signal from a neighbouring transmitter. (See Table 1, for a comparison between the net and gross coverage.) That neighbouring signal will, however, interfere with VCRs. In fact, unless other steps are taken, for many viewers VCR interference will occur regardless of whether they tune to a non-interfering transmitter.

There is no doubt at all that the opt-outs using the non-interfering transmitters will have to reach a very high proportion of the viewers they 'share' with the neighbouring transmitter in order to be commercially viable. Their own 'net' audience cannot support a sufficient advertising market to finance a local opt-out service. The 'gross' audience is vital.

Another unique point about the late transmitters added to Channel 5 is the fact that their net audiences contribute very little to the overall Channel 5 audience total. The net contribution nationally is very small indeed in some cases.

The Storeton transmitter adds a mere 0.2% extra viewers to the total Channel 5 audience because 520,000 potential viewers of the Storeton signal are equally or better able to receive a Channel 5 signal from Winter Hill broadcasting from nearer Manchester but with a more powerful signal. These 520,000 viewers could ignore the Storeton signal altogether. To a greater extent viewer redundancy applies with the Fenham transmitter (serving the Newcastle area) in comparison with Burnhope as an alternative source for the Channel 5 signal. For Fenham, the figures are 50,000 net coverage set against 999,000 gross coverage – or as many as 949,000 people who have the choice between the signal from Burnhope or Fenham, should both broadcast together. The timing of roll-out here will be crucial. The Broadcasting Act calls for the effective use of transmitters, and for these non-interfering transmitters their effective role is first and foremost 'local' not 'national'. If Burnhope goes on air much before Fenham, there will be no audience for a local service on Tyneside. Unless these transmitters are broadcasting local programming at their potential audiences they might as well not be there at all. Yet there is a useful synergy here to get 'local' underway early.

With the exception of Fawley, all the potential 3-Star stations must go on air before their neighbour or risk losing valuable viewers. If Storeton is not on air first, it will have at worst just 80,000 viewers to broadcast to. If Craigkelly is not on-air first it will lose some of its potential audience of 583,000 viewers and fall back instead towards the 263,000 net viewers. Only the non-interfering transmitters at Churchdown Hill, Sandy Heath and Caldbeck do not have this problem.

Because there is no re-tuning to hinder the early start-up of the non-interfering transmitters, groups interested in providing a service for Edinburgh, Sheffield, Liverpool and Nottingham must be ready to re-transmit the national Channel 5 channel from a satellite signal and to go on-air ahead of the terrestrial roll-out in the neighbouring area. If they can do this, their unique local news service will help attract audiences where Channel 5 will otherwise be non-existent. For Channel 5, the local services will add national viewers ahead of the planned roll-out .

The ITC indicated in their July 1991 paper introducing these transmitters that they are capable of providing a discrete service for distinct areas. Their additional significance is that they give a national Channel 5 operator a reason to respond to local programming demands and likewise for local operators to construct a suitable arrangement with Channel 5 which increases the viewing public ahead of schedule.

In conclusion, there are two important considerations that will affect how local television develops on Channel 5:-

> Firstly, the non-interfering transmitters need to be on air in advance of their video interfering neighbours so that the large number of potential viewers represented in the overlapping signal can be recruited to the opt-out service before the neighbouring transmitter steals the audience away.

> Secondly, while installing their aerials the local operator can introduce a signal combiner with a filter to block channel 35 or 37 which will reduce the number of VCRs that will be affected by Channel 5 when channel 35 or 37 goes on air from the neighbouring transmitter.

In order to be effectively used, as the legislation requires, these local opt-out transmitters must actually *be used*. Their engineering and demographic emphasis suggests they ought to be providing a local service. The public has declared that this is what it wants. Subject to a commercial case being made local television is what these transmitters should be providing.

These transmitters are so important, and so unique in comparison with the national characteristic of the Channel 5 pattern and the rest of terrestrial broadcasting, that if Channel 5 does not go ahead, these transmitters should be allocated to city services. These services might then decide to opt-in a national channel should this be necessary.

12 The European Meeting of Local Television

Dave Rushton, re-printed from *Television*, Royal Television Society Journal, December 1991

The European Meeting of Local Television held at the Palais de l'Europe in Strasbourg on the 30th and 31st October 1991 brought together some 400 delegates from both Eastern and Western Europe to explore the different circumstances and varying support for local television services in their countries. A special effort had been made to involve local and regional broadcasters from Eastern Europe.

So what is local television? There is no simple answer, though several shared principles emerged among the 1400 or so diverse local TV stations across Europe.

With minimal local television on cable in the UK and immediate prospects pinned on local opt-outs for Channel 5, the British found themselves sharing concerns for the future of local public service television with colleagues in the newly pluralistic Eastern European countries.

The comparison between the UK and Romania or Poland is not merely ironic: in both East and West there is a growing concern that deregulation of broadcasting or a more commercially favoured broadcasting market will replace the centralised state broadcasting bureaucracies and push aside the public demands and support for locally accountable television (and radio) services.

By contrast, for two decades in the Benelux countries and in Sweden and Germany, successful open broadcasting systems have been operating within a legal framework that supports local broadcasting in the form of terrestrial and cable channels. This service is supported by subscription or licence fees and guarantees either a community organisation or an individual with access to make programmes and to broadcast locally.

This is quality public service television with the emphasis on equality, and each local station makes an important social contribution amidst the larger scale and often commercial and state run programming. For the new advertising supported local news channels in the Netherlands, audiences of 20% are claimed; these are high figures in competition with twenty or more other channels.

For the Italians, the thousand blooms of commercial local television that blossomed in the seventies and eighties are in many cases choking to death because there has been no regulation on frequencies. In Italy pirate broadcasters occupied the airwaves, sometimes with just a single picture – and then sold these frequencies to the highest bidder. Despite recent efforts by the Italian government to bring to order the prevailing Babel this chaos seems to have been commercially manipulated in the interests of the larger networks.

The Belgian, Dutch and German experience is probably the most instructive so far as cable goes. In these countries a public utility water, gas, electricity or telecoms has been given the task of laying cable, these companies often use their existing trunking and combine installation of plant and work schedules. The benefits of reduced costs in a shared infrastructure are reflected in low subscriptions and this has helped cable reach towards 100% of homes in towns and cities where cabling is taking place.

Yet in those cable countries where the subscription is above £10.00 per month – cable subscription is only £100.00 per year in Belgium – and where the infrastructure is mostly reliant on private financing and separate trunking – notably in France and the UK, the number of subscribers is too low for a local public broadcasting service to function, or at least to function with confidence. A France and the UK a community channel will teeter on the brink of regular broadcasting, France having lost six local channels from a total of twenty in the last few months because – without subscribers and without advertising – revenue has not been available to maintain the services.

In the UK the cable companies are expected to spend some £4bn on just digging the ditches and trenches in which to lay their cable – an expensive hole in the ground that differentiates the UK from the more successful cabling parts of Europe and is a burden that the subscriber will have to pay for. In the UK, cabling is virtually at a standstill with targets being missed and expectations being renegotiated.

The Strasbourg conference formed a European Organisation of Local Television in which each national and regional association could be represented. The sheer diversity of local television cultures that has sprung up throughout Europe is the strength of local television and any definition of each country's local television services will be left to national or regional associations to work out – the only proviso being that a public service remit be part of the objective of each local service.

Enthusiasm for a European network of programme exchange gained the support of delegates and the Human Rights Committee of the Council of Europe as well as the Standing Committee of Regional Authorities – especially keen to preserve and promote regional identity and culture in the expanding Europe.

With the support of the Council of Europe, the new European Organisation of Local Television will provide a European voice for local television alongside the European Cable Federation and the European Broadcasting Union. It will argue for appropriate standards, for international training, for financial support and encourage opportunities for local programming to cross frontiers. Perhaps most importantly for the UK – and for Eastern Europe – it will help us resolve anomalies on theatrical rights. It has already shown us how unequal our access is to television broadcasting in Britain.

APPENDICES

1　Section 7, Cable and Broadcasting Act 1984

7. (1) In deciding whether or to whom to grant a licence, the (Cable) Authority shall take into account all matters appearing to them to be relevant.

(2) Without prejudice to the generality of subsection (1) above, in deciding whether or to whom to grant a licence for the provision of a prescribed diffusion service in any area, the Authority shall take into account the extent to which the applicant or each applicant proposes to do the following things, namely:-

(a) to include a range and diversity of programmes;

(b) to include in the programmes matter which originates within the European Economic Community and is performed by nationals of member states;

(c) to include in the programmes an increasing proportion of such matter;

(d) to include programmes of an educational nature, programmes calculated to appeal specially to the taste and outlook of persons living in the area and programmes in which such persons are given an opportunity to participate;

(e) to include programmes provided otherwise than by himself or by associates of his;

(f) to include programmes provided by local voluntary associations and to assist such organisations in the preparation and production of programmes;

(g) to include in the programmes matter which is calculated to promote the understanding or enjoyment of programmes by persons who are deaf;

(h) to provide, or secure the provision of, related services.

(3) In this section "local voluntary organisation" includes a local branch of a national voluntary organisation.

Cable & Broadcasting Act 1984, pp 45-46, HMSO, 1994

2   Local Channel Survey, 1989

In April 1989, aggregated across all 11 broadband cable franchises there are 470,203 homes passed by cable in the UK (*Annual Report*, Cable Authority, 1989).

There are 11 operating cable companies serving 11 franchise areas. 5 of the 11 cable companies provide locally made programming.

Those operating are Croydon (United Cable), Swindon, Coventry, Clyde and Aberdeen. Most of the other 6 companies provide a local text service. Westminster has ambitious plans for local services.

Local & Access Channels

Swindon, Coventry, Clyde and Aberdeen have either a dedicated local channel or access channel depending on the extent of local programming produced by the cable station.

Some stations provide both local and access channels. Swindon, Coventry, Clyde and Aberdeen transmit between 6 and 10 hours of local material per week, including repeats. In all cases the local programming is carried on a separate channel.

Aberdeen Cable currently runs as an access channel with all the programming being produced by local non-profit organisations.

Programme Sources

With the exception of Aberdeen (4% station, 96% outside sources) and Westminster Cable (planning 100% outside sources) most of the local programming from the other stations was sourced from within the station. Clyde Cable, Swindon, Coventry and Croydon (United Cable) produced between 95 and 100% of their own local programming.

Programme Production

Local programme production per week by Croydon, Swindon, Coventry, Clyde and Aberdeen is so little that it can't be reasonably subdivided into the 9 categories listed in our questionnaire. Most of the programming is local news and current affairs. Only five companies were able to indicate the breakdown of local programming on offer.

Discounting the optimistic Westminster Cable, (who were planning extensive programming) Swindon, Clyde, and Croydon produced between 15 minutes and 1.5 hours news per week, with Croydon producing an additional half hour weekly documentary and Aberdeen, Swindon and Clyde screening between 2 and 5 hours of local leisure, sport and educational programming.

Programme Budgets

Again Westminster appeared optimistic when anticipating an hourly budget of £1000-2500 on local programming, set against up to £250 an hour at Swindon and Croydon.

Coventry, Clyde and Aberdeen did not separate local programming expenditure per broadcasting hour from their total station budget.

Virtually 100% of all programming was "subsidised by the station". While 90% of Westminster's programming costs were to be supported by sponsorship.

Sponsorship

With the exception of Croydon and Coventry the other stations carried locally sponsored programmes. Locally sponsored programme making is currently such a small percentage of programming as to be of little significance. What little sponsorship there is tends to come from banks and local authorities.

Start-up Dates

All existing broadband cable networks started up between 1984 and 1986 and had extensive production studios, control rooms and editing facilities integrated into the cable station from the start. For the most part, these have all been financially written off and so the only significant overheads are personnel and maintenance of equipment.

Production Equipment

Cable stations generally possessed hi-band or Betacam equipment for local programming.

Community Participation

Most of the cable stations visited agreed that local programming would be improved by community involvement in programme planning and making. However, most disagreed with the statement that "local programming is improved by community involvement in editorial policy making".

Training

Training in programme making was offered by three of the nine respondents producing local programmes, Aberdeen, Docklands and Coventry. Both Aberdeen and Coventry conduct comprehensive training courses in camera work, editing, script writing and programme planning. Swindon, Coventry, Clyde and Aberdeen all provided training facilities and specially prepared courses for local would-be programme makers or contributors.

Clyde and Swindon provide ad-hoc training to community groups. Clyde is also currently providing production training courses to corporate organisations who want to produce in-house videos.

Churn

Churn, which is defined as turnover of subscribers or rate of cancellation of subscriptions, is usually quoted as a percentage. For these stations churn currently ranges from 15 to 30%.

Employment

The developing UK cable company employs up to 120 personnel. This includes cable installation teams as most companies are still in the build phase. The cable installation is undertaken by direct or contract labour.

Aberdeen Cable, which is the only company to have finished their build, employ approximately 90 people. This includes 60 staff in customer services and sales. Staff involved in marketing stood at between 20-35%. With the exception of Coventry, local programme production and coordination staff did not exceed 10%, and was as low as 2% at Croydon.

Local Programming Staff

Croydon, Swindon, Coventry, Clyde and Aberdeen have respectively 2.5, 1, 6, 5 and 1 staff dedicated to local programme production, training or administration.

Swindon, Coventry and Clyde cable stations produce most of their local programming in-house. However, local organisations will occasionally provide material for screening on the local channel.

Aberdeen started off in 1985 with a complement of 18 production staff dedicated to local programming. Within 18 months, 16 production staff were made redundant as local programming costs could not be sustained by the company.

Local Advertising

Few of the cable stations visited showed local advertisements. However, advertisements were often an integral part of the channels brought in from others. Many made the comment that local advertising would not be considered until penetration had reached 12,000 homes connected. Only one or two slotted in locally made advertisements into ready purchased channels.

All advertisements shown on local channels were designed for the cable company franchise area. There was no advertising sourced nationally or regionally for local screening.

All advertisements targeted specifically to a franchise area were locally produced.

Peak advertising rates for those few cable stations that did provide advertising were of the order of £140.00 for a 30 second slot.

Advertising package rates were generally not provided. However, Swindon and Clyde did have a comprehensive menu of packages to offer to advertisers. Clyde are currently promoting "infomercials" — these are 30 minute programmes focussing on how to use products purchased from retailers such as DIY stores.

Where carried, local advertising covered products, services and retailing. Most cable stations said that local companies and organisations were interested in using cable television as an advertising media.

All companies felt there was a lot of potential for growth in local advertising on cable.

Microwave

Companies were evenly divided as to whether or not they would use Microwave Video Distribution Systems to increase their market share.

3   Tables 9-14, 16, 19 & 21

In paid full-time employment (over 30 hours per week)	37%
In paid part-time employment (between 10 and 30 hours per week)	16%
In paid part-time employment (less than 10 hours per week)	3%
Unemployed	6%
Sick or disabled and unable to work	4%
Retired	16%
Full-time education (mature student)	2%
Full-time education (young person)	4%
Housewife/househusband	12%

TABLE 9: Employment Categories in Survey (n = 240)

i	Households with person living alone age under 24	1%
ii	Households with person living alone aged 25-34	3%
iii	Households with person living alone aged 35-65	2%
iv	Households with retired person living alone	6%
v	Young married couple (or living as married) with no children - principal wage-earner aged under 25	1%
vi	Small households with an infant: households containing one or two adults with one or two children at least one of whom is under 5	8%
vii	Other households with children: households containing one or two adults with three or more children, or households containing more than two adults and one or more children	12%
viii	Larger households with children: households containing one or two adults with three or more children, or households containing more than two adults and one or more childen	14%
ix	Other large adult grouping: households of three or more adults	23%
x	Elderly couples: two person households with principal wage-earner retired	9%
xi	Small adult only households not included in v or x above	21%

TABLE 10: Household type (n = 240)

212

Are you (or were you, if retired) the principal wage-earner in this household?	
Yes	42%
No	50%
Not applicable	8%
Don't know	0%

TABLE 11: Principal Wage-earner (n = 240)

Under £2,500	5%
£2,500 - £4,999	10%
£5,000 - £9,999	15%
£10,000 - £14,999	20%
£15,000 - 19,999	15%
£20,000 - £29,999	13%
£30,000 or more	11%
Don't know	7%
Refused	4%

TABLE 12: Household Income Groups (n = 240)

Go out and buy it after reading about it	13%
Wait till you have heard something good about it from a friend	24%
Wait until a number of friends have tried it	16%
Buy it only after it has been on the market quite a long time	25%
None of these/don't know	22%

TABLE 13: Innovators to Laggards in Survey (Refer Q 13) (n = 240)

0	66%
1	9%
2	16%
3	8%
4 or more 1%	

TABLE 14: Number of Children in Household (n = 240)

	£10	£8	£6	Sample Size n
Age Group				
16-24	46%	39%	57%	35
25-34	55%	58%	71%	55
35-54	49%	51%	50%	90
55+	17%	18%	22%	60
Social Grade				
A	46%	54%	54%	13
B	35%	35%	44%	55
C1	37%	41%	51%	76
C2	60%	62%	67%	55
D	41%	41%	44%	27
E	21%	29%	36%	14
ACORN Group				
B	54%	58%	75%	24
C	50%	50%	50%	8
D	13%	13%	25%	8
E	50%	50%	56%	32
F	50%	54%	54%.	24
G	56%	59%	66%	32
H	0%	0%	0%	8
I	29%	33%	42%	24
J	40%	43%	50%	40
K	33%	35%	45%	40

Note:
Those results where the sample size is small will be highly unstable.

TABLE 16: Cumulative percentage likely to subscribe to a basic package priced at various levels in relation to the discriminators age, social grade and ACORN group. (n = 240)

	£10	£8	£6	Sample Size
				n
Age Group				
16-24	34%	40%	57%	35
25-34	27%	36%	49%	55
35-54	18%	29%	52%	90
55+	5%	8%	17%	60
Social Grade				
A	8%	23%	39%	13
B	16%	20%	40%	55
C1	16%	24%	45%	76
C2	29%	36%	60%	55
D	26%	37%	48%	27
E	7%	29%	36%	14
ACORN Group				
B	21%	29%	58%	24
C	13%	25%	38%	8
D	0%	0%	13%	8
E	25%	31%	56%	32
F	21%	33%	50%	24
G	32%	44%	59%	32
H	13%	13%	13%	8
I	8%	21%	38%	24
J	23%	25%	50%	40
K	13%	20%	38%	40

Note:
Those results where the sample size is small will be highly unstable.

TABLE 19: Cumulative percentage likely to subscribe to an all-in package priced at various levels in relation to the discriminators age, social grade and ACORN group (n = 240).

	Very Interested	Fairly Interested	Response % Neither Interested nor Uninterested	Fairly Uninterested	Very Uninterested
Age Group					
(sub sample size)					
16-24 (35)	9	45	11	14	20
25-34 (55)	15	58	4	5	18
35-54 (90)	11	46	6	2	35
55+ (60)	7	18	3	7	65
Social Grade					
A (13)	8	30	23	0	39
B (55)	9	29	9	11	42
C1 (76)	4	49	4	8	35
C2 (55)	18	56	0	4	22
D (27)	19	30	4	0	57
ACORN Group					
B (24)	8	71	0	8	13
C (8)	0	38	12	0	50
D (8)	12	25	0	25	38
E (32)	19	44	3	6	28
F (24)	13	46	0	4	37
G (32)	16	50	3	0	31
H (8)	0	0	12	13	75
I (24)	13	25	8	8	46
J (40)	8	38	12	2	40
K (40)	5	40	5	8	42

TABLE 21: Interest in subscribing to cable TV if it is affordable according to the discriminators age, social grade and ACORN group (n = 240).

4   Cable Growth,1983-1992

	Town	Homes in Franchise	No. Apply	Date Awarded	Cable TV started	Homes connected	% of franchise receiving Cable TV
1	Swindon	75,000	n/a	Nov 1983	Sept 1984	5,378	7.2
2	Aberdeen	91,000	n/a	Nov 1983	May 1985	14,897	16.4
3	Coventry	119,000	n/a	Nov 1983	Sept 1985		
4	Croydon	120,000	n/a	Nov 1983	Sept 1985	25,546	21.3
5	Northwest Glasgow & Clydebank	112,000	n/a	Nov 1983	Oct 1985	5,147	4.5
6	Westminster	107,000	n/a	Nov 1983	Oct 1985	11,138	10.4
7	Windsor, Slough, Maidenhead, Ashford, Staines, Stanwell, Heathrow	110,000	n/a	Nov 1983	Dec 1985	15,839	14.4
8	Ealing	105,000	n/a	Nov 1983	Nov 1986	13,288	12.7
9	Guildford (now combined with Aldershot below)	22.000	n/a	Nov 1983	July 1987	Build suspended	
9a.	Aldershot, Farnham, Fleet. Camberley, Woking, Farnborough, Godalming	115,000	1	Aug 1985	July 1987	Build suspended	
10	Belfast	136.000	n/a	Nov 1983	Withdrawn		
11	South Liverpool	125,000	n/a	Nov 1983	June 1990	13,953	11.2
12	Bolton	135,000	1	Aug 1985	July 1990	4,565	3.4
13	Cheltenham and Gloucester	90,000	1	Aug 1985	Not Started	-	-
14	Newham and Tower Hamlets	127,000	1	Aug 1985	April 1987	9,385	7.4
15	Wandsworth	100,000	1	Aug 1985	Not Started	-	-
16	Cardiff and Penarth	103,000	1	Feb 1986	Not Started		
17	Camden	70,000	1	Feb 1986	Dec 1989	8,470	12.1
18	Edinburgh	183,000	1	Feb 1986	May 1992	> 2,500	> 1.4
19	Preston, Chorley and Leyland	114,000	2	Feb 1986	May 1990	9,827	8.6
20	Southampton and Eastleigh	97,000	2	Feb 1986	Oct 1989	14,125	14.6
21	Luton, Dunstable and Leighton Buzzard	97,000	1	Feb 1986	April 1990	> 2,500	> 2.6
22	Kensington and Chelsea	68,000	2	Feb 1988	Sept 1989	7,823	11.3
23	Andover	12.000	1	April 1988	March 1990	> 2500	> 20.8
24	Blackburn.,Accrington, Nelson, Colne and Rossendale Valley	168.000	1	May 1988	Nov 1989	4,513	2.7
25	Birmingham and Solihull	465,000	2	Oct 1988	Nov 1989	27,804	6.0
26	Southend, Basildon, Brentwood, Chelmsford, etc	300,000	2	Nov 1988	Not Started	-	-
27	Gravesend, Chatham, Rochester, Gillingham, Maidstone and Sittingbourne	145,000	1	Nov 1988	Not Started	-	-
28	Hammersmith and Fulham, Brent, Barnet	280,000	2	Jan 1989	Dec 1990	5,405	1.9

29	Bristol, Bath, Weston Super Mare etc	350,000	1	Jan 1988	June 1990	13,321	3.8
30	Redbridge, Barking and Dagenham, Bexley	229,000	3	Jan 1988	Dec 1992	> 2,500	> 1.1
31	Reading, Bracknell, Basingstoke, Newbury, Newbury etc	215,000	2	Jan 1988	Dec 1991	> 2,500	> 1.2
32	Northampton	72.000	1	Jan 1989	up-graded system		
33	Greenwich and Lewisham	175,000	3	April 1989	Jan 1991	5,405	3.1
34	Crawley, Horley and Gatwick Airport	40,000	2	April 1989	Feb 1993	-	-
35	Greater Glasgow, Paisley, Renfrew	357.000	1	Not awarded	-	-	-
36	Motherwell, Hamilton, East Kilbride, Wishaw and Larkhall	120,000	2	April 1989	Mar 1992	> 2,500	> 2.1
37	Cumbernauld, Kilsyth, Airdrie and Coatbridge	55,000	2	April 1989	TBA	-	-
38	Dumbarton and the Vale of Leven	18,000	2	April 1989	TBA	-	-
39	Merton and Sutton	135.000	1	May 1989	Mar 1990	14,139	10.5
40	Kingston and Richmond Upon Thames	124,000	1	May 1989	Mar 1991	> 2,500	> 2.0
41	Cambridge, Newmarket, Ely. Saffron Walden, Huntingdon, St Ives, etc	134.000	1	June 1989	July 1991	6,266	4.7
42	Dudley, Sandwell, Wolverhampton, Cannock, Kidderminster and Bromsgrove	470,000	2	July 1989	Aug 1991	5,378	1.1
43	Lambeth and Southwark	191,000	2	July 1989	Jan 1991	5,405	2.8
44	Peterborough	58.000	1	July 1989	June1990	4,175	7.2
45	Norwich	83,000	1	July 1989	May1990	> 2,500	> 3.0
46	Colchester, Ipswich, Felixstowe, Harwich and Woodbridge	126,000	2	July 1989	Build suspended		
47	Haringey	80.000	2	Sept 1989	Dec 1990	3,022	3.8
48	Waltham Forest	83.000	2	Sept 1989	1993	-	-
49	Leicester	147,000	1	Sept 1989	April 1991	5,867	4.0
50	Nottingham	230.000	1	Sept 1989	Sept 1990	> 2,500	> 1.1
51	Brighton, Hove and Worthing	110,000	4	Oct 1989	Mar 1992	3,246	3.0
52	Exeter, Plymouth and Torbay	236,000	1	Dec 1989	TBA	-	-
53	Harpenden, Hemel Hempstead, St Albans etc	100,000	3	Nov 1989	Mar 1991	> 2,500	> 2.5
54	Watford, Richmansworth, Bushey, Borehamwood. Potters Bar etc	95,000	2	Nov 1989	Jan 1992	> 2,500	> 2.6
55	Stevenage, Welwyn, Hatfield, Hitchin etc	100,000	4	Nov 1989	TBA	-	-
56	Stoke on Trent, Newcastle under Lyme	140,000	2	Dec 1989	TBA	-	-
57	Swansea, Neath. Port Talbot	110,000	1	Nov 1989	Jan 1991	> 2,500	> 2.3
58	Newcastle, Gateshead. Nth & Sth Tyneside	325.000	3	Dec 1989	Sept 1990	> 2,500	> 7.1
59	Warrington. Widnes, Runcorn	121.000	1	Jan 1990	TBA	-	-
60	Chester and Ellesmere Port	61,000	1	Jan 1990	TBA	-	-
61	Stafford and Stone	24,000	3	Dec 1989	TBA	-	-
62	Dorchester, Weymouth and Portland	33,000	1	Feb 1990	Franchise revoked		
63	Dundee, Monifieth and Carnoustie	81,000	2	Jan 1990	Nov 1990	8,993	11.1
64	Perth and Scone	18,000	1	Jan 1990	TBA	-	-

65	Portsmouth, Fareham, Gosport, Havant	150,000	5	Feb 1990	Sept 1991	9,504	6.3
66	Derby and Spondon	89.000	2	Feb 1990	Oct 1990	> 2,500	> 2.8
67	Leeds	289,000	5	Mar 1990	1993	-	-
68	Wakefield, Pontefract, Castleford	94,000	5	Mar 1990	TBA	-	-
69	Margate, Ramsgate and Broadstairs	52,000	1	Feb 1990	Franchise revoked		
70	Bromley	117,000	3	Mar 1990	1993	-	-
71	Loughborough and Shepshed	24,000	2	Mar 1990	Combined with Leicester		
72	Mansfield, Sutton & Kirby-in-Ashfield	58.000	1	Mar 1990	1993	-	-
73	Havering	90,000	2	April 1990	1993	-	-
74	Dartford and Swanley	35,000	1	Mar 1990	June 1993	-	-
75	Harlow, Bishops Stortford, Stansted	43.000	3	Mar 1990	TBA	-	-
76	Stratford, Warwick. Leamington, Kenilworth	44,000	3	Mar 1990	TBA	-	-
77	York and Harrogate,	78.000	2	Mar 1990	TBA	-	-
78	Bournemouth, Poole, Christchurch	110,000	3	April 1990	TBA	-	-
79	Salisbury	15.000	1	April 1990	TBA	-	-
80	Winchester	33,000	3	April 1990	1993	-	-
81	Telford	50,000	4	April 1990	May 1992	> 2,500	> 5
82	Hackney & Islington	150,000	2	April 1990	Dec 1989	8,470	5.6
83	Doncaster and Rotherham	192,000	7	May 1990	TBA	-	-
84	Rugby	24,000	2	April 1990	TBA	-	-
85	Nuneaton and Bedworth	43,000	2	April 1990	TBA	-	-
86	Hinckley	20,000	2	April 1990	Franchise revoked		
87	Tamworth	25,000	2	April 1990	Franchise revoked		
88	Grantham	30,000	1	April 1990	1993	-	-
89	Newark	18,000	1	April 1990	1993	-	-
90	Melton Mowbray	30,000	1	April 1990	1993	-	-
91	Manchester, Salford and Trafford	363,000	5	May 1990	System for sale		
92	Bury and Rochdale	143,000	4	May 1990	TBA	-	-
93	Oldham and Tameside	170,000	6	May 1990	TBA	-	-
94	Stockport	113,000	6	May 1990	Franchise for sale		-
95	Wigan	110,000	2	May 1990	June 1992	3,545	3.2
96	Epping, Loughton, Chigwell,	45,000	1	May 1990	1993	-	-
97	Dover, Deal, Folkestone and Ashford	77, 000	3	May 1990	TBA	-	-
98	Aylesbury, Amersham, Chesham	62,000	4	May 1990	TBA	-	-
99	Harrow	79,000	5	May 1990	Dec 1991	> 2,500	> 3.2
100	Hillingdon	92,000	5	May 1990	Aug 1991	> 2,500	> 2.7
101	Hounslow	79,000	4	May 1990	Dec 1991	> 2,500	> 3.2
102	Enfield	105,000	3	May 1990	Sept 1991	5,154	4.9
103	Hertford, Cheshunt, Ware	60,000	3	May 1990	TBA	-	-
104	Sheffield	210.000	8	May 1990	TBA	-	-
105	Thamesmead	11,000	1	May 1990	Jan 1991	5,405	49
106	Greater Glasgow	274,000	1	June 1990	TBA	-	-
107	Paisley and Renfrew	67,000	2	June 1990	TBA	-	-
108	Bearsden and Milngavie	16,000	1	June 1990	TBA	-	-
109	Worcester, Redditch	70.000	3	June 1990	TBA	-	-
110.	Sunderland, Durham,	200,000	2	June 1990	TBA	-	-
111	Oxford, Abingdon	55,000	3	June 1990	TBA	-	-
112.	Barnsley	82,000	3	June 1990	TBA	-	-
113	Bedford	55.000	2	June 1990	TBA	-	-
114	Bradford	175,000	6	June 1990	Oct 1992	> 2,500	> 1.4

219

115	Halifax and Brighouse	75.000	5	June 1990		Franchise for sale	
116	Huddersfield and Dewsbury	148,000	5	June 1990	TBA	-	-
117	Burton-On-Trent, Swadlincote, Ashby	40,000	2			Franchise revoked	
118	Carlisle	30,000	2			Franchises handed back	
119	Corby, Kettering, Mkt Harboro	90,000	3	June 1990	TBA	-	-
120	Darlington	34,000	3	June 1990	TBA	-	-
121	Middlesbrough, Stockton, Hartlepool	170,000	2	-	-	-	-
122	North Surrey (Elmbridge, Runnymede)	71,000	3	June 1990	1893	-	-
123	Epsom, Mole Valley, Reigate,	98,000	3	June 1993	1993	-	-
124.	Falkirk West Lothian	30,000	1	June 1990		Franchise for sale	
125	Glenrothes, Kirkcaldy, Leven	60,000	1	June 1990	Sept 1991	2,510	4.2
126	Greenock, Port Glasgow, Gourock	32,000	2	July 1990	TBA	-	-
127	Great Yarmouth, Lowestoft,	64,000	1	July 1990		Franchise for sale	
128	Wisbech, March, Whittlesey	21,000	1	July 1990		Franchise for sale	
129	Grimsby, Cleethorpes	63,000	1	July 1990	1993	-	-
130	Haywards Heath, Burgess Hill	25,000	2	-	-	-	-
131	Lancaster, Morecambe	40,000	0	-	-	-	-
132	Lincoln	30,000	1	July 1990	1993	-	-
133	Liverpool North, Bootle, Crosby	100.000	2	July 1989	May 1990	4,519	4.5
134	St Helens & Knowsley	100.000	4	July 1990	TBA	-	-
135	The Wirral	120.000	4	July 1990	TBA	-	-
136	Macclesfield, Wilmslow	45,000	2	May 1990		Franchise for sale	
137	Newport, Cwmbran, Pontypool	85.000	2	July 1990	TBA	-	-

The only unfranchised towns with upwards of about 20,000 homes – are the following:

Blackpool	Chesterfield	Crewe	Dunfermline
Eastbourne	Hastings	Hull	Lisburn
Londonderry	Scunthorpe	Shrewsbury	Southport
Tunbridge Wells			

Other towns of significant size not covered by franchises are:

Ashington	Ayr	Banbury	Bangor, Co. Down
Barrow	Barry	Bexhill	Bognor
Boston	Braintree	Bridgewater	Bridlington
Bury St Edmunds	Camborne	Canterbury	Chichester
Clacton	Colwyn Bay	Dumfries	Fleetwood
Hereford	Herne Bay	Horsham	Inverness
Kilmarnock	Lancaster	Llanelli	Lytham St Annes
Malvern	MerthyrTydfil	Morecambe	Northwich
Stirling	Taunton	Tonbridge	Whitehaven
Whitstable	Workington	Worksop	Wrexham
Yeovil			

It is these towns - and many even smaller - for which the Independent Television Commission can expect in the future to consider local delivery franchises under the provisions of the Broadcasting Bill.

Notes:
Franchise population from 1989/1990 Cable Authority Annual Report
Figures for subscribers and the start of service from *Who's Who in Cable & Satellite*, WOAC, Dunstable, January 1993 and *New Media Markets*, Financial Times, various issues 1990-1992

5   Pilot Local C5 Survey Edinburgh, 1990

Lyndsey Bowditch, Edinburgh Survey of local television subscription interest and Channel 5 programme origin and content, August 1990

We conducted our survey among an initial sample of 60 people, drawn according to the ACORN neighbourhood classification. This sample is obviously too small for reliable forecasting and too small to be broken down significantly to reveal interest among social grades, age ranges, men and women. It is proposed to increase the sample to 240 people. In the interim to establish some indication of accuracy we have compared our findings with a comprehensive survey of the same ACORN neighbourhood groups, conducted in August 1989, and have bracketed the corresponding the earlier figures from key questions that appear in both surveys. The 1990 survey has been conducted by phone, the 1989 survey door-to-door.

In both questionnaires we asked:

On how many days a week would you say you watch television? (See Figure 1.)

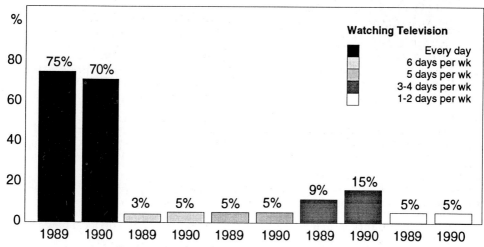

FIGURE 1: On how many days a week would you say you watch television?

On a day when you watch television, for how many hours do you view? (See Figure 2.)

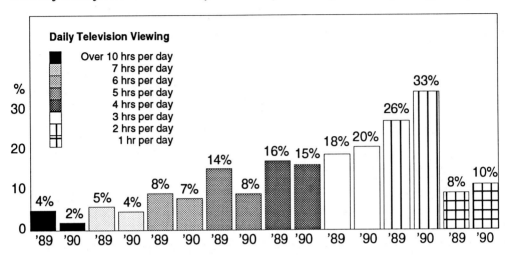

FIGURE 2: On a day when you watch television, for how many hours do you view television on average?

We asked:

How often do you buy the Edinburgh Evening News? [local evening paper] (See Figure 3.)

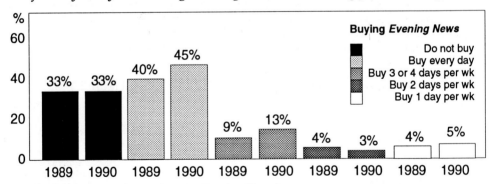

FIGURE 3: How often do you buy the Evening News?

Edinburgh Television intends to provide a quality local television service with an emphasis on local news comparable to national and regional television. This will be supported by subscription and advertising.

Assuming that there is a way of delivering this service to you, I should like to ask you some questions about subscriptions ......

> For a high quality local television service with an emphasis on local news would you be willing to pay?

17% of people would only subscribe to local television if the service is free.
83% of people would be willing to pay subscription for local television services.

Figure 4 indicates the monthly subscription this 83% would be willing to pay.

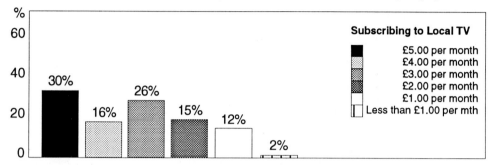

FIGURE 4: Amount people willing to pay among the 83% willing to pay for local television.

Of the total sample, 71% of people would be willing to pay £2.00 and over per month for local television. Of those willing to pay a subscription for local television, 87% would be willing to pay £2.00 and over per month.

What is the value placed on programme origin and content for Channel 5?

We asked:

> A new television service, Channel 5, is expected to begin broadcasting in Britain in the next few years. Please indicate on the range from 'very important' to 'very unimportant' the value you place on the origin and content of programmes for the new channel. How important are?
>
> Programmes about/from N America?
> Programmes about/from Europe?
> Programmes about/from Britain?
> Programmes about/from the Region/Country?
> Programmes about/from the local Area/City? (See Table 1.)

	Very Important	Fairly Important	Neither Important nor Unimportant	Fairly Unimportant	Very Unimportant
North America	10%	27%	25%	22%	17%
Europe	22%	53%	13%	10%	2%
Britain	53%	38%	5%	3%	-
Region/Country	38%	47%	5%	10%	-
Local	65%	27%	5%	3%	-

TABLE 1: Importance of programme origin and content.

6 Channel 3 Regional Populations and Channel 5 Transmitter Populations

	1000s
North Scotland	
Channel 3 adult population	920
Channel 5 transmitter populations as % of North Scotland C3 population:-	
Mounteagle (111)	12%
Durris (313)	34%
Perth (59)	6%
Tay Bridge (184)	20%
The combined Perth & Tay Bridge C5 transmitter populations expressed	as
a % of neighbouring Durris C5 transmitter population	77%
Opt-out candidates?	
Mounteagle (111) Perth/Tay (243) combined & Durris (313)	
Central Scotland	
Channel 3 adult population	2,831
Channel 5 transmitter populations as % of Central Scotland C3 population:-	
Black Hill (2,820)	100%
Craigkelly (263 net)	9%
The Craigkelly C5 transmitter population expressed	
as a % of Black Hill C5 transmitter population	9%
Opt-out candidates?	
Craigkelly (263 - 583 gross[+])	
Borders	
Channel 3 adult population	501
Channel 5 transmitter population as % of Borders C3 population:-	
Cambret Hill (13)	3%
Selkirk (52)	10%
Caldbeck (159)	32%
Opt-out candidates?	
Selkirk (52)	

Northern Ireland

Channel 3 adult population	1,067
Channel 5 transmitter population as % of Northern Ireland C3 population:-	
Black Mountain (1,090)	102%
Londonderry (101)	9%
The Londonderry C5 transmitter population expressed as a % of Black Mountain C5 transmitter population	9%

Opt-out candidates?
Londonderry (101)

North East

Channel 3 adult population	2,266
Channel 5 transmitter population as % of North East C3 population:-	
Burnhope (2.465)	109%
Fenham (50 - net)	2%
The Fenham C5 transmitter population expressed as a % of Burnhope C5 transmitter population	2%

Opt-out candidates?
Fenham (50 - 999 gross[+])

North West

Channel 3 adult population	5,126
Channel 5 transmitter population as % of North West C3 population:-	
Winter Hill (6,882)	134%
Storeton (80 - net)	2%
The Storeton C5 transmitter population expressed as a % of Winter Hill C5 transmitter population	1%

Opt-out candidates?
Storeton (80 - 600 gross[+])

Yorkshire

Channel 3 adult population	4,553
Channel 5 transmitter population as % of Yorkshire C3 population:-	
Emley Moor (3,996)	87%
Sheffield (179 - net)	7%
The Sheffield C5 transmitter population expressed as a % of Emley Moor C5 transmitter population	5%

Opt-out candidates?
Sheffield (179 - 663 gross[+])

Wales & West

Channel 3 adult population	3,597

Channel 5 transmitter population as % of Wales & West C3 population:-

Blaen Plwf (41)	0.3%
Presely (165)	5%
Mendip (2,045)	60%
Churchdown Hill* (220)	6%

The Churchdown Hill C5 transmitter population expressed as a % of neighbouring Mendip C5 transmitter population	10%

Opt-out candidates?

> Mendip (2,045) & Churchdown Hill (220) & Presely (165) possibly combined with Blaen Plwf (41)

East, West and South Midlands

Channel 3 adult population	7,266

Channel 5 transmitter population as % of Midlands C3 population:-

Sutton Coldfield (6,095)	84%
Sandy Heath (352)	5%
Churchdown Hill* (220)	3%
Nottingham (234 - net)	3%

The Churchdown Hill C5 transmitter population expressed as a % of neighbouring Sutton Coldfield C5 transmitter population	4%
The Sandy Heath C5 transmitter population expressed as a % of neighbouring Sutton Coldfield C5 transmitter population	6%
The Nottingham C5 transmitter population expressed as a % of neighbouring Sutton Coldfield C5 transmitter population	4%

Opt-out candidates?

> Churchdown Hill (220) & Sandy Heath (352) & Nottingham (234 - 684 - gross[+])

East of England

Channel 3 adult population	3,262

Channel 5 transmitter population as % of East of England C3 population:-

Tacolneston (477)	17%
Sandy Heath (352)	13%
Chelmsford (164)	6%

The Sandy Heath C5 transmitter population expressed as a % of neighbouring Tacolneston C5 transmitter population	73%
The Chelmsford C5 transmitter population expressed as a % of neighbouring Tacolneston C5 transmitter population	34%

Opt-out candidates?

> Sandy Heath (352) & Chelmsford (164)

London

Channel 3 adult population	8,975
Channel 5 transmitter reach as % of C3 London population:-	
Croydon (10,447	116%
Chelmsford (164)	2%
The Chelmsford C5 transmitter population expressed as a % of Croydon	
C5 transmitter population	2%
Opt-out candidates?	
Chelmsford (164)	

South & South East

Channel 3 adult population	4,234
Channel 5 transmitter reach as % of C3 South & South East population:-	
Fawley (679)	19%
Opt-out candidates?	
Fawley (679)	

South West

Channel 3 adult population	1,292
Channel 5 transmitter population as % of South West C3 population:-	
Huntshaw Cross (95)	8%
Plympton (195)	16%
Redruth (147)	12%
Opt-out candidates?	
Plympton (195) & Redruth (147)	

Notes:

* Figures expressed in 1000s

** Discrepencies in transmitter reach eg C5 transmitters reaching over 100% of available population due to differences in forecasting transmitter power . Channel 3 regional figures may include viewers living in regional overlap areas, ie. viewers drawn from both viewing options. Opt-out candidates include small populations that could join with neighbouring local services; Selkirk - Craigkelly, or Plesely - Blaen Plwf or form a service on a combined basis viz; Perth - Tay Bridge in juxtapostion to the more dominant Durris transmitter serving the Aberdeen area.

+The gross reach of Nottingham, Craigkelly, Storeton, Sheffield and Fenham transmitters include households able to receive signals from an adjacent Channel 5 transmitter. The gross figures are *minimum* populations for commercial opt-out proposals.

For Channel 5 the net estimate of available adult population is based on computer projectionspublishd by the ITC.

Channel 3 population data supplied by BARB, January 1992.

Glossary of Terms

A/B switch

A simple switch given to a viewer for selection between two input sources, such as an aerial and the cable system. Not necessary with broadband systems.

Access channel

A channel that the cable operator makes available for use by anyone with something to say or present (community groups, individuals, etc.) usually - though not necessarily - with facilities made available free of charge by the operator.

Addressability

The facility by which the subscriber's home equipment may be controlled remotely by the cable operator, in order to allow disconnection, the provision of pay-per-view, or changes in the level of service.

ALTO

Association of Local Television Operators. Trade association and lobby for local television services.

AML

Amplitude Modulated Link. A type of microwave transmission for multichannel point-to-point television links.

Bandwidth

Part of the frequency spectrum: that part of the spectrum required for a specific purpose; e.g. a television channel occupies a bandwidth of 8 Megahertz, whereas a telephone conversation utilises only 4 Kilohertz.

Basic service

The service obtained by a cable subscriber paying the minimum charge. It will normally comprise the broadcast services plus a range of other 'free' channels. A 'basic channel' is one included in the basic service.

Bird

Colloquial description of a satellite.

Bit

Unit of measurement of data transmitted in digital form. Hence the measurement of CC the capacity of a cable system to carry information will be in terms of Kilobits or Megabits per second (Kbits/s Mbits/s).

Broadband

Cable with the capacity to carry a large number (eg 25 or more) television channels. Interchangeable with wideband.

CATV

Community antenna television. A cable system covering a whole community, eg a town.

Churn

Turnover of subscribers/cancellation of subscriptions. Usually quoted as a percentage rate.

Closed user group

Cable channel available only to a specific group of subscribers.

Coaxial cable

Cable consisting of a central conductor (usually copper) surrounded by, and insulated from, another conductor. It is the standard material used in present-day cable systems. Signals are transmitted through it at different frequencies, giving greater channel capacity than is possible with twisted pair cable but less than is allowed by optical fibre.

CTA

Cable Television Association. The United Kingdom trade association.

DBS

Direct broadcasting by satellite The use of a satellite to transmit high-power television signals for reception direct by individual viewers, though such services will also be carried on cable systems.

Double Illumination

Transmission of a television channel from two separate satellites, particularly for a transitional period when a change from one satellite to another is being undertaken.

Downlink

The transmission from a satellite to an earth station.

Downstream

The direction of signals transmitted from the cable head end to the subscriber.

Drop

The cable connection from the street in to the subscribers' premises. The term is sometimes (but not always) confined to those subscriber connections from overhead rather than underground cable.

DTH

Direct to home. Used to denote satellite signals received by an individual viewer via a dish aerial, as distinct from via a cable system.

Earth station

Transmitting or receiving point for satellite transmissions.

ECS

European Communications Satellite. A series of satellites operated by Eutelsat. The first of the series, ECS I, carries nine European television channels distributed to cable systems, at one time including two British channels (Sky Channel and Super Channel since moved to the Astra satellite).

Footprint

The earth coverage area of a transmission from a satellite. Like a torch beam, the strength of the signal will weaken the further one moves from the centre, but this can be compensated for by using a larger receiver.

Franchise

The right to install and operate a cable system in an area of more than 10,000 homes, bestowed by the licences granted by the Cable Authority (now the ITC) and by the Department of Trade and Industry.

FSS

Fixed service satellite. A term used for a satellite in a fixed orbital position providing telecommunications services. Also called low powered satellites or telecommunications satellites. In contradistinction to DBS.

Gigahertz (GHz)

Frequency of one billion cycles per second. These higher frequencies have not so far been used for broadcasting purposes but they can be utilised for satellite television transmissions. The 12 GHz band to be used for DBS has previously been allocated to outside broadcast microwave links.

HDTV

High definition television. A clearer sharper picture using considerably more lines than the present 625. Cable systems already have capacity to carry such services when they are introduced.

Head end

The control centre of a cable system.

Hertz

The unit of frequency of electromagnetic waves (cycles per second) (see also Gigahertz and Megahertz). 'Hertzian' is sometimes used as a description of over-the-air terrestrial transmission, as distinct from cable.

Homes passed

The expression in common usage as the measurement of the size of a cabled area, meaning the total number of premises which have the potential to be connected to the cable system.

Hubsite

An intermediate control point in a switched cable system between the head end and the local switching point. In systems provided by BT, it was planned to locate hubs within each local telephone exchange.

Infomercial

A long-form advertisement designed to give information about products or services.

Interactivity

The facility for two-way communication, though the sophistication of the interactive capability may vary depending on the technology used in the cable system.

ISDN

Integrated Services Digital Network, together with Broadcast-ISDN, the agreed European standard for telecommunications and broadcast cabling respectively.

ITC

Independent Television Commission. The new regulatory body which absorbed the functions of the Cable Authority together with most of those of the IBA.

Institute of Local Television

UK's independent consultancy, research and development agency for local television services and publications.

Leased access channels

A category of cable channel (particularly in USA) made available by the local operator on a commercial basis rather than as a free community service, as will normally be the case with access channels.

Local avail

The availability within a national channel of slots for the insertion at cable systems of local advertising.

MATV

Master antenna television. A cable system confined within a block of flats, small housing development etc, served by a common aerial. In contradistinction to CATV.

MVDS (or MDS or MMDS)

Microwave or multipoint video distribution service. A television distribution system to subscribers using omnidirectional microwave transmissions. It depends on line of sight between transmitter and aerial and has a range of about 10-20 miles. It has grown in the USA as a new medium for pay-television. It has not so far been authorised by the UK government.

Megahertz (MHz)

Frequency of one million cycles per second.

Microwave

Wireless transmissions at very high frequency as a means of providing telecommunications links (including television distribution) between two places. Depends on line of sight Operated in the UK by British Telecom and Mercury. See also MVDS.

MSO

Multiple systems operator. A cable operator running a number of different cable systems.

Must-carry

The obligation on cable systems to carry certain channels, usually the broadcast services.

Narrowband

Sometimes used to distinguish cable from broadcasting. More particularly, the function of distributing a range of television channels or programmes designed to meet various minority interests rather than to offer mass appeal.

NCTA

National Cable Television Association. The representative industry body of the USA.

New build

Cable system installed in area not previously cabled. A term used to distinguish new systems, or parts of systems, from upgrades.

OFTEL

Office of Telecommunications. The licensing and monitoring body established by the Telecommunications Act 1984.

Off-air

Normal broadcast television signals. A term often used to distinguish aerial reception from cable reception, or broadcast channels (BBC, ITV etc.) from cable channels.

Optical fibre

Cable made of glass fibres through which signals are transmitted as pulses of light. Capacity for a very large number of channels can easily be provided. Becoming more widely used in cable systems.

Penetration

The measurement of the take-up of cable services. The number of subscribers is expressed as a percentage of the homes passed.

PPV (Pay-Per-View)

Payment made for individual cable programmes as opposed to a monthly subscription for a whole channel or group of channels. Envisaged as a means of providing certain popular sporting events or blockbuster movies for which subscribers may be prepared to make a special payment. Cannot very effectively be done on an old-fashioned cable system but is straightforward with a system providing control of each subscriber's services from the head end (addressability).

Premium channel

Channel available only for additional subscription over and above the basic service.

Programme provider

Company assembling programmes into a service to be provided to cable systems.

Return path

The means by which messages are transmitted back through the cable system from the subscriber to the head end.

SMATV

Satellite master antenna television. An MATV system with a receiving dish for picking up and distributing satellite television signals. Any system of up to 10,000 homes may be licensed without the competitive franchising procedure.

Switched Star system

New generation of cable system in which full bandwidth is provided from the headend to local switching points which are programmed to supply each subscriber with whichever channels are being paid for through an individual line of lower bandwidth.

Channel selection then takes place at the switch, rather than in the TV set or set-top box, but in response to the subscribers use of his remote control. Such systems have greater interactive capability.

Strand mapping

Preparation of preliminary maps prior to the detailed system design showing the likely route of cable ducting. So called from USA usage, where the strand is the wire support for overhead cable swung between poles.

Subscription channel

A channel for which the subscriber pays a specific subscription over and above the charge for the basic service.

Take-up

Rate or number of subscribers taking the cable service (see also Penetratlon)

Tap

The feed off a main cable (usually in tree and branch system) to the subscriber's 'drop'.

Tier

A level of cable service depending on the amount of the subscriber's payment. It reflects the packaging of channels at different prices.

Transponder

A transmitter on a satellite.

Tree and branch

Topology of one type of cable system, of traditional design. It comprises a trunk cable from which each subscriber link is tapped off. Because all parts of the system carry the totality of the services provided, it is difficult to build much interactive capability into such systems.

TVRO

Television receive only. The dish for receiving satellite television signals.

Twisted pair

Type of cable used extensively in British cable systems in the past, comprising twisted pairs of wires each carrying one channel. Most systems of this kind have capacity for four television channels; some have six, none have more.

Upgrade

An old cable system installed for broadcast relay purposes but now utilised for the provision of new programme services.

Uplink

The transmission from an earth station to satellite.

Upstream

The direction of signals transmitted from a cable subscriber to the operator's head end.

Wideband

Cable system with the capacity to carry a large number (eg 25 or more) television channels. Interchangeable with broadband.

Media titles available from John Libbey

ACAMEDIA RESEARCH MONOGRAPHS

Satellite Television in Western Europe (revised edition 1992)
Richard Collins
Hardback ISBN 0 86196 203 6

Beyond the Berne Convention
Copyright, Broadcasting and the Single European Market
Vincent Porter
Hardback ISBN 0 86196 267 2

Nuclear Reactions: A Study in Public Issue Television
John Corner, Kay Richardson and Natalie Fenton
Hardback ISBN 0 86196 251 6

Transnationalization of Television in Western Europe
Preben Sepstrup
Hardback ISBN 0 86196 280 X

The People's Voice: Local Radio and Television in Europe
Nick Jankowski, Ole Prehn and James Stappers
Hardback ISBN 0 86196 322 9

Television and the Gulf War
David E. Morrison
Hardback ISBN 0 86196 341 5

Contra-Flow in Global News
Oliver Boyd Barrett and Daya Kishan Thussu
Hardback ISBN 0 86196 344 X

CNN World Report: Ted Turner's International News Coup
Don M. Flournoy
Hardback ISBN 0 86196 359 8

Small Nations: Big Neighbour
Roger de la Garde, William Gilsdorf and Ilja Wechselmann
Hardback ISBN 0 86196 343 1

BBC ANNUAL REVIEWS

Annual Review of BBC Broadcasting Research: No XV - 1989
Paperback ISBN 0 86196 209 5

Annual Review of BBC Broadcasting Research: No XVI - 1990
Paperback ISBN 0 86196 265 6

Annual Review of BBC Broadcasting Research: No XVII - 1991
Paperback ISBN 0 86196 319 9

Annual Review of BBC Broadcasting Research: No XVIII - 1992
Paperback ISBN 0 86196 368 7
Peter Menneer (ed)

BBC WORLD SERVICE

Global Audiences: Research for Worldwide Broadcasting 1993
Edited by Graham Mytton
Paperback ISBN 0 86196 400 4

Media titles available from John Libbey

EUROPEAN MEDIA RESEARCH SERIES

The New Television in Europe
Edited by Alessandro Silj
Hardback ISBN 0 86196 361 X

Aid for Cinematographic and Audio-visual Production In Europe
Jean-Noël Dibie
Hardback ISBN 0 86196 397 0

Media Industry in Europe
Antonio Pilati (ed.)
Hardback ISBN 0 86196 398 9

Broadcasting and Audio-visual Policy in the European Single Market
Richard Collins
Hardback ISBN 0 86196 405 5

BROADCASTING STANDARDS COUNCIL PUBLICATIONS

**Violence in Television Fiction: Public Opinion and Broadcasting
Standards**
David Docherty
Paperback ISBN 0 86196 284 2

Survivors and the Media
Ann Shearer
Paperback ISBN 0 86196 332 6

Taste and Decency in Broadcasting
Andrea Millwood Hargrave
Paperback ISBN 0 86196 331 8

A Matter of Manners? – The Limits of Broadcast Language
Edited by Andrea Millwood Hargrave
Paperback ISBN 0 86196 337 7

Sex and Sexuality in Broadcasting
Andrea Millwood Hargrave
Paperback ISBN 0 86196 393 8

BROADCASTING RESEARCH UNIT MONOGRAPHS

**Invisible Citizens:
British Public Opinion and the Future of Broadcasting**
David E. Morrison
Paperback ISBN 0 86196 111 0

Keeping Faith? Channel Four and its Audience
David Docherty, David E. Morrison and Michael Tracey
Paperback ISBN 0 86196 158 7

**Quality in Television –
Programmes, Programme-makers, Systems**
Richard Hoggart (ed)
Paperback ISBN 0 86196 237 0

School Television in Use
Diana Moses and Paul Croll
Paperback ISBN 0 86196 308 3

INSTITUTE OF LOCAL TELEVISION

Citizen Television: A local dimension to public service broadcasting
Dave Rushton (ed.)
Hardback ISBN 0 86196 433 0

Published in association with UNESCO

Video World-Wide: An International Study
Manuel Alvarado (ed)
Paperback ISBN 0 86196 143 9

UNIVERSITY OF MANCHESTER BROADCASTING SYMPOSIUM

And Now for the BBC ...
Proceedings of the 22nd Symposium 1991
Nod Miller and Rod Allen (eds)
Paperback ISBN 0 86196 318 0

It's Live – But Is It Real?
Proceedings of the 23rd Symposium 1992
Nod Miller and Rod Allen (eds)
Paperback ISBN 0 86196 370 9

Published in association with THE ARTS COUNCIL

Picture This: Media Representations of Visual Art and Artists
Philip Hayward (ed)
Paperback ISBN 0 86196 126 9

Culture, Technology and Creativity
Philip Hayward (ed)
Paperback ISBN 0 86196 266 4

Parallel Lines: Media Representations of Dance
Stephanie Jordan & Dave Allen (eds)
Paperback ISBN 0 86196 371 7

Arts TV: A History of British Arts Television
John A. Walker
Paperback ISBN 0 86196 435 7

ITC TELEVISION RESEARCH MONOGRAPHS

Television in Schools
Robin Moss, Christopher Jones and Barrie Gunter
Hardback ISBN 0 86196 314 8

Television: The Public's View
Barrie Gunter and Carmel McLaughlin
Hardback ISBN 0 86196 348 2

The Reactive Viewer
Barrie Gunter and Mallory Wober
Hardback ISBN 0 86196 358 X

Television: The Public's View 1992
Barrie Gunter and Paul Winstone
Hardback ISBN 0 86196 399 7

Media titles available from John Libbey

REPORTERS SANS FRONTIÈRES

1992 Report
Freedom of the Press Throughout the World
Paperback ISBN 0 86196 369 5

1993 Report
Paperback ISBN 0 86196 403 9

IBA TELEVISION RESEARCH MONOGRAPHS

Teachers and Television:
A History of the IBA's Educational Fellowship Scheme
Josephine Langham
Hardback ISBN 0 86196 264 8

Godwatching: Viewers, Religion and Television
Michael Svennevig, Ian Haldane, Sharon Spiers and Barrie Gunter
Hardback ISBN 0 86196 198 6
Paperback ISBN 0 86196 199 4

Violence on Television: What the Viewers Think
Barrie Gunter and Mallory Wober
Hardback ISBN 0 86196 171 4
Paperback ISBN 0 86196 172 2

Home Video and the Changing Nature of Television Audience
Mark Levy and Barrie Gunter
Hardback ISBN 0 86196 175 7
Paperback ISBN 0 86196 188 9

Patterns of Teletext Use in the UK
Bradley S. Greenberg and Carolyn A. Lin
Hardback ISBN 0 86196 174 9
Paperback ISBN 0 86196 187 0

Attitudes to Broadcasting Over the Years
Barrie Gunter and Michael Svennevig
Hardback ISBN 0 86196 173 0
Paperback ISBN 0 86196 184 6

Television and Sex Role Stereotyping
Barrie Gunter
Hardback ISBN 0 86196 095 5
Paperback ISBN 0 86196 098 X

Television and the Fear of Crime
Barrie Gunter
Hardback ISBN 0 86196 118 8
Paperback ISBN 0 86196 119 6

Behind and in Front of the Screen – Television's Involvement
with Family Life
Barrie Gunter and Michael Svennevig
Hardback ISBN 0 86196 123 4
Paperback ISBN 0 86196 124 2